AROUND VANCOUVER ISLAND ON MY KAYAK

FELIPE BEHRENS

Author - Felipe Behrens, 1984

Title - Around Vancouver Island on my Kayak

Cover Photograph by Felipe Behrens

Editor - Richard Dionne

Copyeditor - Richard Dionne & Britt Collins

Interior Design by Felipe Behrens

Publisher - Around on my Kayak, 1st ed. Miami Florida

Photographs by Felipe Behrens unless noted otherwise

Map Illustrations by Rafael Bromberg

ISBN: 979-8-3481-9791- 9

ACKNOWLEDGMENTS

My journey around Vancouver Island could not have been done without the support of innumerable people and friends. My mother gave me steadfast support and encouragement in the endeavor. Jay Rose from Paddle Sports of Naples was my go to person for kayak related questions; David Slepak received my kayak in Seattle and saved me from having to portage several miles to the launch point of the expedition; a waitress at the cafe in Lund, provided me with the combination for the lock at the marina bathroom where I got a free shower and a clean place to sleep the night; JF Marleau and Justine Curgenven were the best guides anyone could ask for when paddling around Brooks Peninsula and spoiled me with the best meals I have ever eaten in a kayaking expedition (they even chopped the onions nice and small the way I like it); a lady from Tahsis offered me a bed for a night and cooked fantastic fish and chips; my friend Lee Richardson from Best Coast Outfitters shared his insightful local knowledge of many incredible places I visited along the way; and last but not least, Rockpool Kayaks and Falcon Sails whose equipment took me through the one thousand mile journey without ever once having even a minor issue.

This book is the result of the combined effort of many people, whose support, time, and encouragement were essential. I want to give special thanks to my editors Richard Dionne and Britt Collins. As a first time writer, they were instrumental in guiding me through the book writing process, and bringing the story to life; and Rafael Bromberg who created the map illustrations in the present volume.

"I love to live vicariously through reading about the adventures of a fellow kayaker. This is one of those trips we all dream about. Vancouver Island is a great wilderness with constant exposed settings and great points of interest. All this through the viewpoint of an experienced kayak sailor makes it even better." - Patrick Forrester, President of Falcon Sails, https://www.falconsails.com/

"I was sent a copy of Felipe's book to proofread a small section and the next thing I knew I was a third of the way through the book! A well written adventure that puts you in the kayak seat of an expedition from the original idea to the return to life after a grand adventure. I thoroughly enjoyed the read!" - Jay Rose,Paddle Sports of Naples, https://www.paddlesportsofnaples.com/

"This is a book filled with adventure and how to be open minded in the face of unforeseen circumstances and packed with information for anyone planning a kayak trip, even if not as demanding as this one, to understand how decisions relative to the weather and coastal environment are made to the best of one's ability. The journey is filled with unique insights into the local wildlife, geology, history and personal growth in overcoming challenges as they come up, and sprinkled with humorous anecdotes, colorful characters, and Canadianisms discovered along the way. Felipe embarked on a loft sea kayaking adventure, and through his book, he takes us along with him." - Tom Nickels, RiverWind Kayak, www.riverwindkayak.com/

"Felipe's eloquent storytelling skillfully navigates the challenges and triumphs of circumnavigating Vancouver Island's breathtaking coastline. The book vividly describes the challenges of circling the island while capturing its stunning landscapes and the adventurous vibe.It's a story that celebrates the island's natural beauty and the bold, adventurous mindset required for such an expedition. His words and carefully chosen visuals make the entire experience come alive in a captivating read for anyone drawn to the allure of exploration. The book is an ode to exploration, and a must-read for both seasoned kayakers and armchair adventurers alike." - Lee Richardson, Best Coast Outfitters, https://www.bestcoastoutfitters.com/

"The Rockpool Taran has become the choice for paddlers who want a fast kayak but that can also handle conditions in the open seas and currents. Felipe's 1000 mile journey is not only a testament to his determination, but also an example of the incredible versatility of this great kayak that will continue to be the vessel of exploration for adventurers seeking to go to the most remote and wild coastlines around the world." - Mike Webb, Rockpool Kayaks. http://www.rockpoolkayaks.com/

"This is a story that takes you from the comfort of your home, and jolts you into an adventure through some of the wildest coastlines in Canada. Felipe's colorful narrative about his struggles and triumphs during the journey are a relatable yet unique insight into the world of expedition paddling, normally only experienced by kayakers lucky enough to undertake such an endeavor. Anyone planning a long kayak expedition should read this book." - Freya Hoffmeister, www.freyahoffmeister.com/

"Around Vancouver Island on my Kayak' chronicles an exhilarating journey along the rugged coastline, blending adventure and nature in a compelling narrative. Author Felipe Behrens skillfully captures the challenges and triumphs of circumnavigating Vancouver Island, providing vivid descriptions of the diverse landscapes and encounters with wildlife. The personal reflections add depth, fostering a connection between the reader and the author's transformative experience. The book seamlessly combines travelog and outdoor exploration, making it a captivating read for kayaking enthusiasts and armchair adventurers. With its engaging storytelling and immersive details, 'Around Vancouver Island on my Kayak' invites readers to embark on a vicarious expedition through the pristine waters of the Pacific Northwest." - Paddler Magazine, www.paddlermagazine.com/

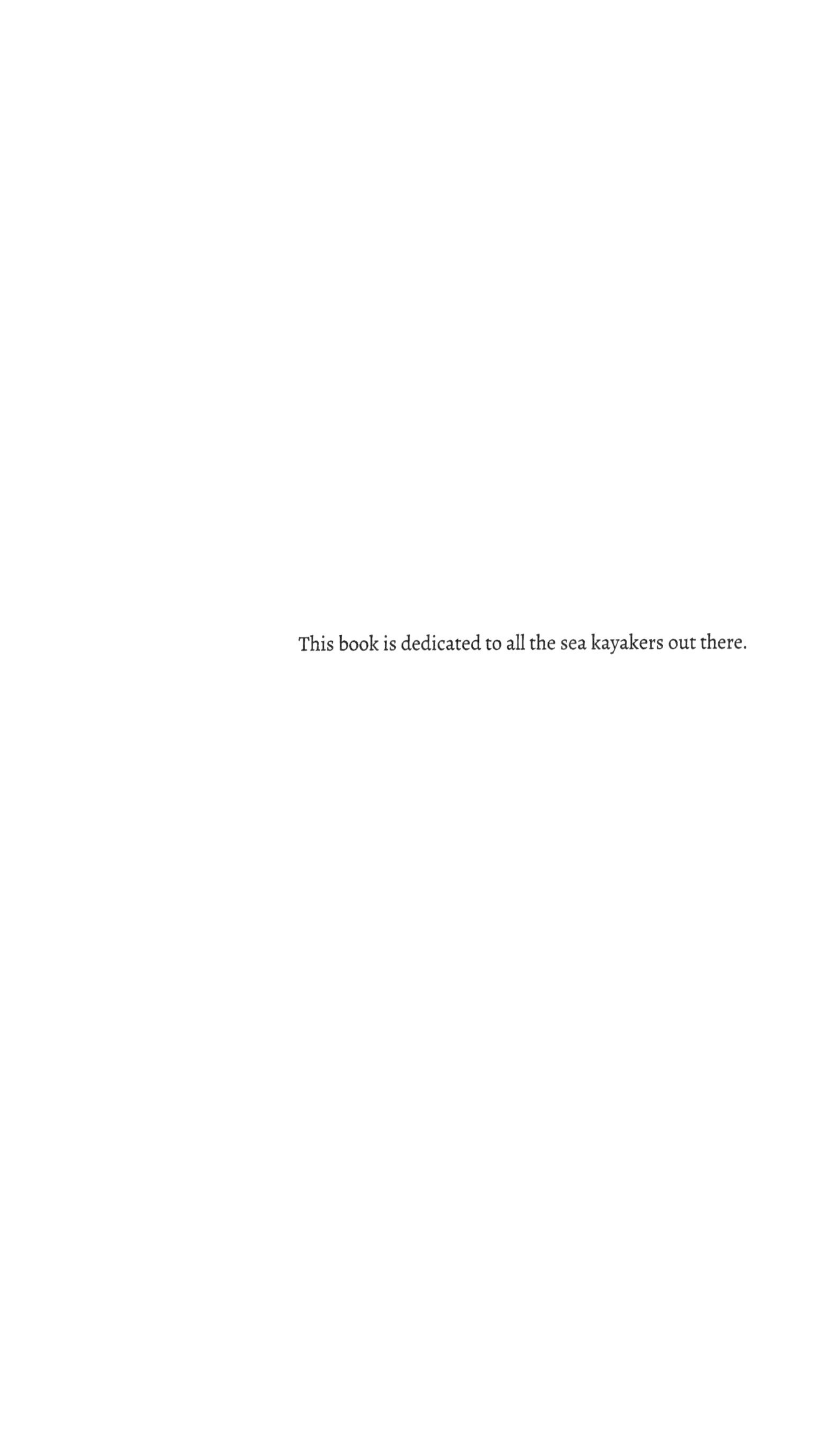

This book is dedicated to all the sea kayakers out there.

The chief task in life is simply this: to identify and separate matters so that I can say clearly to myself which are external, not under my control, and which have to do with the choices I actually control.

- Epictetus

TABLE OF CONTENTS

A calm day on Vancouver Island's West Coast

INTRODUCTION

Vancouver Island in British Columbia has some of the wildest and most beautiful stretches of wilderness and pristine waters that hide bears, whales, colonies of seals and otters, and so many fascinating creatures. Few places offer such diversity in climate, culture, and geography packed in one island that has long attracted people from all walks of life chasing adventure.

In the summer of 2022, I shipped my kayak from my home in Miami, Florida to Seattle, Washington, to circumnavigate this incredible place. Having previously paddled around Florida and Puerto Rico, this would be my most ambitious journey yet: a 1,000-mile adventure around the largest island in Canada's Pacific coast.

"Why do you always want to go on these crazy trips?" my friends often asked me.

"For the same reason I like chocolate ice cream. Because I like it, it's who I am," I'd answer, or something along those lines whenever the question came up.

If there is one thing I have learned over the years paddling my kayak it's that the horizon is never infinitely far away. You start to see glimpses of what lies above the waterline sooner than you want or expect. And before you know it, you'll be at the destination. When your feet touch the boat ramp, all you have from your journey are the memories. Hopefully, they are memories worth remembering.

My two months paddling around Vancouver Island were exciting, challenging, and memorable times. If you are supposed to make lemonade when life gives you lemons, then when life gives you the opportunity to embark on an epic journey, you must make it a great adventure worth telling.

This book is the story of how this adventure unfolded.

CANADA
UNITED STATES
WASHINGTON STATE
MT BAKER
SEATTLE
EVERETT
VANCOUVER
SAN JUAN ISLANDS
STRAIT OF GEORGIA
VICTORIA
PORT ANGELES
PORT SIDNEY
RACE ROCKS
SOOKE
MT OLYMPUS
NANAIMO
OLYMPIC PENINSULA
BRITISH COLUMBIA
POWELL RIVER
PORT RENFREW
JUAN DE FUCA STRAIT
CAPE FLATTERY
COURTENAY
BAMFIELD
PACIFIC RIM NATIONAL PARK
QUADRA IS.
CAMPBELL RIVER
VANCOUVER ISLAND
UCLUELET
TOFINO
FLORES ISLAND
TAHSIS
HESQUIAT PENINSULA
NOOTKA ISLAND
PORT MCNEILL
QUEEN CHARLOTTE SOUND
PORT HARDY
BROOKS PENINSULA
QUATSINO SOUND
PACIFIC OCEAN
CAPE SCOTT
N

PART 1 - A NEW JOURNEY BEGINS

It was just before midday when the nose of my kayak touched the sand on Condado Beach in front of the Sandy Beach Hotel in San Juan, Puerto Rico. The last few minutes of the journey around the island were the most challenging, a kind of parting gift from the ocean as if the sea were saying, "Consider yourself lucky I didn't give you too hard a time. I could have done a lot worse."

Coming in for the final landing I had to squeeze through a narrow gap in the shoals where the swells crumbled with foam and the submerged boulders would have easily given me a new set of hull scratches like a paw slap from a cougar. On the final approach I had to contend with a steep beach and dumping waves. I rode the crest of the swell to the very last moment as though I were holding a lit firecracker between my teeth, and with two reverse strokes, let the wave crash in front before quickly jumping out of the boat and dragging it up the sand.

I'm done, I thought. *Three and a half weeks and I paddled around the world's eighty-first largest island.* The phone started ringing. Mom and Dad were eager to talk to me. They had been following along with the GPS tracker and no doubt now saw that I had closed the circle and stopped moving.

It's a big deal. You should be thrilled. You saved up the vacation time, shipped the kayak, planned the route, marked the landings, and judged the weather. What am I ... what are you missing? asked the voice in my head.

"I don't know," I said aloud. The end of the journey is always awkward.

This last day of the adventure had been the best. Departing from Seven Seas Beach, a crescent shaped sliver of coastline rimmed with mangroves and palm trees on the northeast corner of the island, I pointed my kayak westward, let the trade wind fill my sail, and swept over the ocean swells in the shadow of the El Yunque rainforest where the mountains were rimmed with low-hanging clouds. And then, 30 miles and five hours later, it was over.

Being on an adventure over the open ocean is like being sequestered into a world where you can afford to only focus on what's in front of you, or below. Sometimes it's a barreling swell forcing you into a brace; other times it's the shallow rock you have to swerve to avoid. In calm weather, it might be the curious nurse shark swimming under the boat, the shy sea turtle that dove abruptly after it caught sight of you, or an elusive pod of bottlenose dolphins taking a breath on the surface before disappearing into the deep. Or even the flying fish suddenly jumping onto your lap. Anything, hours or days into the future, has to wait its turn; your head doesn't have to worry about it. You are absolved of all responsibilities.

Until you set foot on the beach and start responding to that nagging voice in your head. *Isn't this the part in the hero's journey where you're supposed to feel elated, fulfilled, and wiser? The challenge has been overcome; the road of trials is complete. Share the boons and the elixirs of your newly acquired wisdom. What was the phrase Joseph Campbell used, "You're now the master of Two Worlds."*

Two Worlds? I answered surprised. *As soon as I'm back home I'm not even going to be the master of my own work desk.*

The beach was packed with tourists. Two kids were making a sandcastle on the flat shelf above the break zone. One of them had just brought over a bucket with wet sand and they were now decorating their creation with drip spires. Above them were dozens of blue parasols and beach chairs from the hotel where a few guests lounged lazily with margaritas in one hand and cellphones in the other. One weird looking dude with ultra dark sunglasses sat on his chair with his legs spread wide and was bobbing his head up and down to a beat he was listening to with comically large headphones. I walked right in front of him carrying the front third of my sectional kayak over my head – but he didn't even flinch. Everyone was going about their pedestrian lives, and now, so was I.

Even though it was still early in the day, I was already pressed for time. By 5 p.m., I had to have the kayak and all the gear delivered at the Port of San Juan ready and packed for shipment by sea (you can make a kayak fly, but it takes a few thousand dollars to perform that kind of miracle). My flight home to Miami was early the next day.

I ran around San Juan buying packing supplies and fetching the kayak travel bags I had left in a long-term self-storage depot. Then I had to find some unfortunate taxi driver whom I was going to, one way or another, convince that I could fit my kayak inside their minivan, and we would drive together to the port. "Trust me, it can be done. I've done it with my car, and I have a Toyota Prius."

There wasn't enough time to dry the gear. The damp spray skirt, life jacket, wetsuit, and everything else was all tossed haphazardly into the kayak hatches with the dirty laundry that wouldn't be washed for at least a week. I sprinkled in a generous amount of borax powder, but the sealed, dark, and moist environment proved to be the perfect petri dish conditions to grow an exuberant mossy jungle of mold and fungi.

On Monday I was back at work, and the journey around Puerto Rico was now just a memory. A few weeks later, the nights camped on the beaches, the challenging surf landings, the inquisitive shark that came to nibble my rudder, the time I nearly hit a coral head, and my battles with the headwinds - all of it was hazy and faded. Even the nasty mofongo plantains served in clam broth with red bell peppers I had to chicken scratch out didn't taste so bad in my memory anymore.

I could do with another adventure sometime soon, I thought to myself.

I've worked as a professional wastewater engineer for the past 15 years. I design and plan the processes and treatment systems for municipal wastewater plants. I size treatment tanks, select pumps, specify pipes, valves mixers, aerators, membrane filters, and evaluate the biology and chemistry of the treatment processes. It is an interdisciplinary endeavor. I work with civil engineers who plan the site layouts and the distribution of the utilities; structural engineers responsible for the concrete columns and foundations of the buildings; electrical engineers who wire all the equipment and instruments; architects (who I am sure never thought they'd ever work in a wastewater plant) that lay out the floor plans; and a multitude of suppliers and contractors.

Is it an interesting job? It can be. The most fulfilling project I worked on in my career was a new treatment plant for the wastewater from a microchip factory in Portland, Oregon. Fundamentally, the work itself was not too different from any other treatment plant design I had worked on before. It had many of the same process elements, though the chemicals used in the microchip production that had to be removed from the water were more exotic and we had a specialized chemical engineer in the project to work on that. What was unique for me was the client's explicit demand that all team discipline leads be solely dedicated to this one project and be present onsite.

For six months, the other team members and I were flown in from across the globe, housed in the same condominium, and given four vehicles to share. We commuted together every day to and from the worksite, three or four in a car. We had breakfast, lunch, and dinner in the same cafeteria, worked in the same open-floor office, set up rows of folding tables, and held morning progress meetings nearly every day in the same conference room. It was a tough job. Deadlines and budgets were tight, the hours were long, the afforded personal workspace was minimal. It certainly wasn't worth the bump in pay.

Nonetheless, I was happy to be there. The shared toil bred a shared sense of purpose and camaraderie. After spending nearly every day together, my coworkers became my mates and we came to know each other's backgrounds. Sanjay, the electrical engineer from Bengaluru spoke every day with his wife at 6 a.m. and 6 p.m., given the twelve-hour time difference. John, our HVAC engineer from Chicago, had a daughter who was heading off to medical school. Cindy, the Autodesk coordinator, lived with her mother and brother in New Orleans. David Angus, our process engineer, spoke with an accent that clearly gave away that he hailed from New South Wales in Australia. And of course, there was me, the guy from Florida who liked to kayak. It was during the course of this project that someone, I've long forgotten who, mentioned that I should one day check out the kayak scene in the Pacific Northwest.

When the pandemic came, however, we all switched to the new work-from-home routine. The group camaraderie evaporated and the social bonds with work friends frayed. For me, a bachelor with no kids and living on my own, work from home meant work alone. I had one work buddy I kept in close contact with. We met about eight years prior at a different company and worked together on several projects at the three wastewater treatment plants in Miami and we grew professionally together. Everything from new oxygenation tanks, pump stations, collection systems, power stations, and oxygen production plants we did together, and were always bouncing ideas off each other to work through the designs. When the company we worked at was acquired, we jumped ship almost together. She left a few months earlier, and I soon followed and applied for a position at the same firm where she had just been hired. Although I cannot say for certain, I'm sure I got the new job in no small part because of her recommendation.

I was very sad when she decided to jump ship again. "I'm going to miss you," I told her. "If things weren't lonely until now, they definitely will be from here on."

"Oh, I'm only going a few blocks down the road to the Miami-Dade Water and Sewer Department. I get to be your client," she said with a laugh.

"That'll be kind of weird. Until now, you worked with me. Now I will be the one working for you."

"Haha. Maybe someday you'll come to work for the County too. Miami-Dade's hiring. And if you go on another kayaking trip do post the logs and pictures on Facebook. I loved the Puerto Rico trip. The shark that bit the back of your kayak was really scary though. Don't get eaten ..."

I've noticed a strange thing about the kayak journeys I've done. When I paddled around Puerto Rico and around Florida, I don't remember once feeling lonely, even though I sometimes didn't see anyone for days. Whereas back at work, I have several conference calls a day with my coworkers, but everything feels very impersonal and distant. The moment I hang up the phone, the only sound I hear is the humming of my AC unit. I suppose that is because kayaking alone is something I choose to do while being alone at work is a predicament of the situation. Perhaps it is the constantly evolving scenery on the kayak, versus the sameness of the computer monitors with open spreadsheets. Perhaps it is because on the kayak I have the freedom to let my mind choose where it wants to take me, and on my desk I tell my thoughts which tasks they must focus on. Or perhaps it's simpler than that: kayaking I do because I like it, work I do because I have to. But do I have to? Who's making me do it?

My head needs another long break, I thought. *Maybe when I come back I'll feel more alert and motivated.*

For a few weeks I marinated some thoughts on how best to approach my supervisor and request some extended time off. I then shot off an email hoping for the best.

Dear Mr. Anderson,

Over the course of the pandemic many of us have, I am sure, begun to feel considerable burnout, both from the isolation and the blending of our personal and professional lives. I had never thought that I would ever succumb to such hardship, but after a year and a half I must admit that it has begun to wear on me as well. To avoid falling victim to burnout like so many, I would like to ask if the company can allow me to take unpaid leave in the coming summer. I have reviewed my current workload and concluded that after an early June deliverable I will be relatively light on work, and any remaining project responsibilities can be passed on to others. We have sufficient time to prepare the transition. I will have about a month of accumulated vacation time by the summer and was hoping that I could take an additional month off. The tentative dates would be from Monday, May 31, returning Monday, August 8.

Please let me know if this is an arrangement that can work.

Felipe

For so many years after the Great Recession, employees had little to no leverage to make asks from their employers. Unemployment was high, no one was hiring, and salary raises and benefits were scant. For my first kayak journey around Florida, I had to save up two years of vacation time, and string the Christmas and New Year's holidays together with Martin Luther King Day to have enough time for the journey, as well as promising that I would be available to quickly drop everything and return to the office (or even a nearby company office) should the need arise. On one occasion I took a whole afternoon phone call on my kayak in the middle of the Gulf of Mexico to discuss the modeling results for the oxygen distribution system in one of the wastewater plants.

"We're getting an error message in the results that say the model is having to artificially add pressure to node N45 at the discharge of oxygenation tank 4," my colleague in the office told me over the speakers on my phone tied to my life jacket, while I visualized the pipe network in my mind and at the same time threw in a stern brace with the paddle to surf down a few small swells.

"That might be because the split that goes to tanks 5 to 7 is closer to the production plant than tanks 1 to 4," I responded after some thought. "Try throttling the butterfly valves on tanks 5 to 7 to see if the flow rebalances and call me back."

"Okay. It's a little better, but now the model says there will be too much back pressure at the production plant."

"Try to upsize pipe segment P56 on the common manifold to tanks 1 to 4 from 6 to 8 inches."

"Now the model is not converging."

"Then try changing the relaxation step for the modeling iterations in the settings menu from 0.1 to 0.05 and double the number of iterations. The model runs may be bouncing around the answer. That's why it's not converging." And on and on we went with the sun drifting closer to the horizon until all the issues were resolved.

However, the pandemic completely inverted the power dynamic between workers and employers. The media kept babbling story after story about a "great resignation." People were quitting their jobs for greener pastures and sometimes even ghosting their employers the moment a better opportunity came along. At my company, we even received a 5 percent cost-of-living adjustment across the board mid-year and accumulated sick leave could now be used for vacation. Employers were desperate to hold on to staff, while also poaching talent from their competitors.

My supervisor called me that same week.

"Hi Felipe, got your email. Yup. I am all for a little work-life balance once in a while. Can't let people burn out. We can work something out. What adventure are you planning this time around?"

"Another kayaking adventure for sure. Don't know where yet. I'm open to suggestions."

"How about the Pacific Northwest? Last time I was there I saw a lot of paddlers. Tim, our valve and pipe guy, lives in Tacoma. I know he's gone paddling in the San Juan Islands."

"That's an interesting idea. I have a friend who lives in Victoria on Vancouver Island who is a kayak guide; I'll see what kind of advice he can give me."

Two years before the pandemic lockdown, I had attended a kayaking symposium in Oregon. There I struck up a conversation with a Canadian who mentioned he'd paddled around Vancouver Island by himself the previous summer. "I did it for my sixty-fifth birthday. At sixty-five you're closer to the grave than you are to the cradle. Today can be the day I'll leave life behind; I had put off doing the journey for too many years already. It's a wonderful place, challenging and dangerous, but definitely wonderful."

"Really, and how so?" I asked, intrigued.

"Well, the weather can be miserable on the west coast. I waited five days before I had a window safe enough to paddle past the Brooks Peninsula, and even then, the swells were over ten feet. But the scenery is inspiring, and you will hardly find a place more beautiful. It's a bitter irony for me that I have lived nearly all my life in Vancouver and only really got to discover it so late in life. I started kayaking at sixty. Some things you learn late in life, and then you must rush to catch up on what you missed."

I felt captivated by his enthusiasm. *If he has the strength to do a journey like that at sixty-five, what excuse do I have to not do it before I'm forty?*

A strange coincidence happened a few days after my conversation with my supervisor. On a Friday night I was scanning through my Facebook feed when I came across a video from Lee Richardson, the same friend from Victoria who was the kayak guide I mentioned in passing to my supervisor. I first met Lee in Nova Scotia during a kayaking trip to the Bay of Fundy he was organizing. On our first two days we paddled the Shubenacadie River (aka the Shubie), a milky brown stream laden with clay and silt deposits from ice age sediments that empties into the Minas Basin arm of the Bay of Fundy. This river hosts a powerful tidal bore. I had never paddled on a tidal bore, and I had been handed a Delphin 16, a wide-beamed kayak I had never used before. When the first bore wave rolled in I was broached, walloped upside down, and could not roll back up. Fortunately, Lee had his eye on me and fetched me out of the water.

The video I was now looking at showed Lee kayak surfing a long gentle green wave all the way onto a white sand beach. The caption read, "A little break from the winter on the Matanzas Inlet."

I immediately knew the place. Matanzas Inlet was in north Florida. The inlet is a narrow estuary on the Atlantic coast, south of St. Augustine, sheltered from the ocean by a large white sand spit crossed by an overpass of the A1A Highway. It's a fantastic location for kayaks to surf as the beach is wide and flat, and the falling tide on the estuary forms several gentle standing waves. I had been there to hone my kayak surfing skills a few times before, and even camped on the spit during my Florida circumnavigation.

"Hey man! You're doing a paddle vacation in Florida and didn't tell me? I'm heartbroken!" I joked over the phone.

"Yeah! Landed in Jacksonville yesterday. I'm leading a course with two other guides for a week. Want to join us for the weekend?"

"I'll get the kayak in the car and head over tomorrow morning!"

An opportunity to paddle outside of South Florida is tough to pass up. The winter weather in Miami is mild, but the ocean is hardly a place to build up your sea kayaking skills. The waves are barely bigger than ripples and it takes a serious storm to whip up the water enough to get the surfers out.

I got on the road at 4 a.m., drove through the night and dusk, and parked next to the bridge across the inlet a little after sunrise. The sea was choppy and the north wind had chilled the air to a hair-raising 50°F.

"Don't make fun of my shivering; fifty degrees is really cold when you're from Miami. It was seventy-eight when I left home five hours ago before sunrise," I said to Lee, poking fun at myself. "When am I ever going to be able to try on a dry suit in Florida?"

I had just bought a new Kokatat dry suit the week before for the princely sum of $1,300. Normally I would never spend a ransom amount of money for something I will get so little use of, but I had already been thinking that I would be paddling somewhere cold this summer. The Canadian waters, whether it's up in Vancouver or Nova Scotia, are cold enough to numb you in less than a minute (at least that's how it feels when you're a Floridian, like me), and even the dry suit won't keep you alive for much longer than the time you need to get back inside your boat. A few years prior in late fall when I kayaked in Oregon and tried a few rolls in a dry suit, the cold seeping through the arms and legs would quickly muddle their usefulness and my head experienced a brain chill like I had swallowed a half pint of ice-cream.

The dry suit is an amazing piece of craftsmanship. Its layers of Gore-Tex fabric have microscopic pores, thousands of times too small for water to pass through, but thousands of times larger than the water vapor from your sweat which allows it to escape. Your body stays dry, even if chilled like meat in the freezer. The openings for the head and hands have latex gaskets tight enough to choke you and take a little getting used to, but their grip is flush to the skin and water has no way to slip through. Most impressive are the suit's zippers; I don't know what kind of craftsmanship goes into making a zipper's teeth seal together so perfectly that not a drop of water is able to slip through, but to me they are indistinguishable from magic.

"Make sure you pull the chest zipper closed all the way to the end; you don't want to leave a small gap and feel like the sea is taking a cold piss on you," Lee warned as I shoved my legs into the dry suit pants. "Also, try not to walk on the booty socks; they're tough but they do rip if you're shoddy with them. You'll also need to buy two things to have with you. Zipper wax and silicone spray. The zipper wax is to make sure that sand and salt don't get in between the zipper teeth, especially if you don't have a chance to wash the suit with fresh water, and the spray is so the gaskets don't become brittle over time. If they break, then the suit won't be watertight."

I surfed the waves in the inlet with Lee and his students for the next two days, practiced the paddle stern rudder while running down the face of a wave toward the beach, and duck-rolled under the breakers while paddling out from shore. In the afternoon on the last day, Lee got into some trouble. As he paddled in from the ocean under the inlet overpass, he got tangled on a fishing lure which immediately jabbed into his hand as he was carried by the current.

"Cut the line!" he shouted at the fisherman who was thankfully quick to respond.

Once on dry land we looked at his hand to see the damage. The two-inch hook went through the base of his index finger with the barb sticking out the other side, and it was definitely not coming out the way it went in.

"Looks like you'll need to make a visit to the nearest Urgent Care to get that removed," I said, "I hope you made a travel insurance plan to come to the States."

"Yep, you can't risk coming here without one. At least it wasn't in my good hand, so I can drive. I'll see you later."

That evening he showed up to meet us for dinner with a thickly bandaged finger but with a much happier face than the one he'd sported at the beach. We chatted about the surf conditions and waves we caught that day. I felt confident with how I handled the barreling swells breaking onshore, especially with rolling the kayak in the midst of the soup zone and keeping calm upside down, waiting for the thrashing waves to sweep by over me. Lee, however, gave me some stern advice.

"These waves are barely bigger than folds on a rug. They will be much bigger off Vancouver Island if you go out there ... and you have to be fit."

I had already spent some time studying the layout of the coastlines of Washington State and British Columbia and the predominant weather during the summer months. Vancouver Island sits in a nook cut into the continent on the border between the United States and Canada like a bread loaf sticking out of a basket, and stretches 275 miles from the capital of Victoria in the south on the Juan de Fuca Strait to Cape Scott in the northwest. That distance, however, is as the crow flies; it's more than twice that length if traveling by boat. The east coast of the island butts up against the continent forming a multitude of fjords, passages, tidal streams, and small islands but is otherwise generally well protected from storms and swells.

The west coast of the island, however, is exposed to everything the temperament of the Pacific Ocean wants to throw at it. Far away storms stir up swells as tall as buildings that run unimpeded for thousands of miles before thundering onshore, and near-gathering storms quickly transform a calm gentle sea into a giant foaming washing machine. Winds can also be ferocious. Even in fair conditions, they often reach hurricane force. You only need to scroll through a weather app with an extended forecast to see the map getting regularly doused with hues of blood red and royal purple to imagine the struggles any ships out at sea must be experiencing. To kayak along this rugged coast you need to plan your forays into the open ocean with the same caution a gazelle approaches a river for a drink. The weather may look calm and inviting in the early morning, but it won't give complacency a second chance, and knowing where the nearest sheltered bay or cove for an unexpected change of plans is essential.

"Well, hopefully if I go there, I can start by paddling north up the east coast of the island. I could paddle for enough days and miles in calm weather to build up enough fitness for the rough part." I jabbed at Lee, "Not all of us can exercise for a living."

"The east coast can be tricky too. Remember when you paddled with me on the tidal stream in the Surge Narrows on Quadra Island? You will almost certainly pass through there. If you arrive with the flow against you, the current will feel like a thundering mountain stream filled with overfalls and eddies. You'll be waiting half a day until the current slacks to go through, and then, who knows, maybe the wind changes direction and you'll be served a dose of wind against the current, and some very confused seas. And the currents in Johnstone Strait on the northeast coast of the island are no cake walk either. Don't expect any section anywhere to be easy. It's better to be pleasantly surprised, than bitterly disappointed."

Sectional Rockpool Taran. The kayak has its own dedicated space in the living room sofa, Key Biscayne Florida.

[TOP LEFT] *Arrival of kayak shipment in San Juan, Puerto Rico Circumnavigation.* [TOP RIGHT] *The Author, paddling his Wilderness Tempest kayak near Fowey Rocks, Key Biscayne Florida.* [MIDDLE] *City beach in San Juan, Puerto Rico Circumnavigation.* [BOTTOM] *A brief rest stop on Isla Piñeros, Puerto Rico Circumnavigation*

Miami Skyline, Florida Circumnavigation.

[ABOVE] Early morning sunrise near Cedar Key, Florida Circumnavigation
[BELOW] Campsite on Marco Island, Florida Circumnavigation.

[TOP LEFT] The Author, cold night camping, Florida. [TOP RIGHT] The Author, paddling near Key Biscayne, Florida. [BOTTOM] Atlantic Swells near San Juan, Puerto Rico Circumnavigation.

[ABOVE] The Author's Kayak, packed into a midsized car trunk, Puerto Rico Circumnavigation.
[BELOW] Campsite on Seven Seas Beach. Last day of the Puerto Rico Circumnavigation.

After getting locked assurances from work that I had the free time I'd need for the journey, I began to give due consideration about where I would go. The more I thought about it, the more Vancouver Island made sense. I traced a path on Google Earth and the distance came to about a thousand miles. If I managed to average 25 miles per day which was about what I had done around Florida, that would mean about 40 paddle days and some 20 rest days, an incredible luxury that would allow me to sit out any tumultuous weather, and maybe perhaps even take a side trip or two.

Additionally, Lee had given me a contact for a Canadian kayak company he'd worked with called the Skils, which would be organizing a two-week trip along part of the west coast of Vancouver Island.

"The owner's name is JF. I worked for him as a guide. He's a good guy. When you talk to him, tell him that you know me."

Their west coast island trip would be leaving from San Josef Bay just south of Cape Scott on June 26, and would head south for about 110 miles past Quatsino Sound, and around the Brooks Peninsula before finishing near a small settlement called Zeballos. Given my planned late May start, that would give me enough time to catch up with them at their starting point and tag along for that section of the journey. I felt particularly comforted by the thought of tackling some of the most challenging and isolated sections of my journey in the safety of a group of more experienced paddlers who no doubt would know more about the place than someone like me who had only seen it on maps and Google.

"You are welcome to join us," said JF, "Just be sure to be at San Josef Bay when we leave. We can't wait around for you, and it's not always easy to meet up on the water; the weather decides whether that happens."

I decided there and then that Vancouver Island would be the place for my adventure. Everything seemed to point toward it. I had enough time away from work to cover the distance, safety in numbers for the most dangerous section (hopefully), and even though Lee cautioned me against too much optimism, I was feeling confident that a month of practice paddling in relatively sheltered waters would prepare me physically and mentally for when the tough parts came around.

My next task was to figure out how to get the kayak across the country.

Every kayak owner knows that if you're not paddling your kayak, then it is a cumbrous piece of clutter. It's tough to find a place to store it when you're not using it, and it's tough to transport, especially if you want to travel with it.

For that reason, I knew that when I made the decision to sink a few thousand dollars into a brand-new kayak, I wanted to make sure I wasn't getting a big white elephant. I wanted a seaworthy kayak that was fast but also maneuverable; and it had to have lots of storage space for a multiday expedition, but not feel like a barge. Most importantly, it had to fit inside my Toyota Prius.

I found that the British Rockpool Taran 18 managed a reasonable compromise on all three categories. The boat is 18 feet long, but has a beam of only 20.5 inches, which makes it one of the thinnest one-person kayaks that is not a surf ski. "How does it not tip?" the random walker on the beach sometimes asks me, to which I respond, "It does. You just need to roll back up." The narrow beam and low back deck make that easy to do on either side.

The amount of storage space is huge (383 liters according to Rockpool), especially in the bow hatch which is humped like a sperm whale. At first I thought it was rather ugly and unsightly, but the uniqueness of the shape eventually grew on me, like a partner whom at first you are put off by their looks, but eventually like them because of their personality.

For an 18-foot kayak, it's incredibly versatile in all kinds of sea conditions. In calm weather, it tracks like an arrow but turns quickly on edge and brace. In crosswinds, it does have a tendency to weathercock which is when the kayak tries to turn towards the wind , but the rudder can compensate for that. Its ideal habitat is the open ocean where it catches the green swells like a dolphin, sliding down the face of one wave with enough speed to latch on the back of the one in front of it. In the surf zone it's a very capable kayak; the hull under the cockpit is flat and chined with sharp edges on the sides, so the paddler can bite into the wave without too much slipping and control their direction.

How does an 18-foot boat fit in a small mid-sized car? You cut it into three pieces. Rockpool is one of the few manufacturers I found that offers that custom option, at least they used to. To do it, the kayak is sliced into thirds at the bulkheads which are then sealed with reinforced fiberglass; the sections are held together with six marine-grade stainless steel hinges on each joint. There are, of course, some disadvantages to cutting up your boat; one of those is the increased weight from extra material which adds about 15 pounds, and the steering and rudder lines need to be fitted with disassembly blocks. For those inconveniences, I'm rewarded with the ability to carry my kayak through the front door of my house, lay it on my sofa, or squeeze it into my car (though at the additional inconvenience of limited rear view visibility), and have it transported to faraway destinations via a shipping company.

I made two additional customizations to my kayak. The first was getting a comfortable foam seat. Most British boats are fitted with a hard fiberglass pan seat with a rudimentary backband for lumbar support. After paddling for 10 to 12 hours, those sadist instruments make for uncomfortable chafed lesions around the waist and piercing lower backaches (I don't know why the Brits do this to themselves). That would not do for me. I carefully measured the cockpit cross section and ordered a custom-built foam seat from a company in Washington that specializes in making kayak seats.

The second customization was the addition of a kayak sail. Purists will squeam at the thought of adding sail to a kayak. "If you want to sail, get a sailboat," they'd say. However, I've found that a kayak sail is a valuable addition in a kayaking expedition. They extend the distance you can travel before needing to resupply, and lighten the physical effort needed when paddling with considerable weight of gear and supplies. It's a different kayaking style, but a pleasant one, nonetheless. A large sail isn't required to get a significant boost in speed; the power to weight ratio is considerably greater for a kayak than a sailboat, and an area of one square meter is usually enough to reach hull speed in a moderate breeze.

There are many types of kayak sails; the most convenient for expedition sea kayaks have a pivot mast which allows the sail to be stowed on the deck when not in use, and quickly deployed with a drawcord and fastened upright.

The biggest inconvenience of a kayak sail is the installation which requires several attachment padeyes for guidelines, mast stays, and bungee cords. There is only one way to install the padeyes; you have to drill holes in your kayak and secure them in place with Hex nuts and bolts. It takes confidence and the cold nerve of an open-heart surgeon to push a drill bit into the boat you just spent a boat load of money on. You don't get a chance to get it wrong.

I called up a contact at Crowley Marine Shipping to inquire about shipping my kayak to either Seattle or directly to Canada. Previously, I had used them to send the kayak from Miami to Puerto Rico and things had worked out much more easily than I had thought. I drove the kayak in the car along with all the expedition gear already stored inside the hatches to their facility where, after some paperwork, they had me place the three bubble-wrapped kayak sections on a wooden pallet and then carried it away with a forklift. I picked up the boat three weeks later at the port in San Juan. Their price had been unbeatable; only $256 total versus $300 for each piece if sent by air.

"Kayak Guy! Yeah, we remember you! We don't ship to the West Coast except to the Port of Los Angeles. Maybe instead of Vancouver, you could head down to Mexico. I hear the Baja Peninsula is beautiful, maybe even go as far as Panama! We can pick you up there and send your boat back to Miami no problem! Or wherever else you want to go. Unfortunately, for anywhere else you're going to need to find a land carrier, and I can't recommend you one."

"I'll keep you guys in mind for the future when I have a year or two to spare," I said.

I began to search for a land carrier. I immediately ruled out international shipping directly to Victoria on Vancouver Island as the prices were astronomical. For $5,000 one way I would be better off buying a new kayak there and giving it away at the end of the journey. The most economical option was to send it somewhere in the Seattle area, and then paddle into Canada. That would add some distance, but with two months allocated for the journey, that would not be a problem.

I contacted UPS and FedEx but both said that my package was much too large for them to take on. I began to feel a bit exasperated. What's the hassle of a three-piece kayak worth if you can't get it to where you need it at a reasonable price? I decided to appeal to the wisdom of the crowds and posted my conundrum on the Strictly Sea Kayaking Facebook group. Promptly, one of the members mentioned he had used a company called MoveIt. "When you call, ask for a guy called Joey. He'll know how to handle it. He's the kayak whisperer if you need to ship a kayak on the cheap."

"Even if it's a three-piece kayak?"

"Yeah, a little out of the ordinary, but he should manage it. Probably even easier 'cause it's not so long."

I called MoveIt the next day, inquired about Joey, and was promptly transferred. Joey was an avid kayaker living in Virginia Beach and owned a Sterling Reflection. "Kayak surfing here is really good on a windy day. The beach is flat and the waves break gently. No dumping rollers. Yeah, we can ship your kayak to Seattle. We'll pick it up and send it to whichever address you want."

"Great to hear! I don't have a destination address yet. I need to look for that next."

"Don't wait too long. Fuel prices are going through the roof with the war in Ukraine on top of all the inflation, and I can't lock you a price until I have a pickup date and destination. Right now to Seattle, based on the dimensions you told me, it would be $750."

"Sure, I'll call you again as soon as possible," I said, though feeling a little disappointed that "shipping a kayak on the cheap" wasn't so cheap.

Finding a shipping address in Seattle, however, would prove to be more difficult than I thought. The ideal location would be somewhere close to a boat ramp for an easy launch so I wouldn't need to rent a van or call a taxi.

I turned to Google Earth and scoured the shores of downtown Seattle for a suitable launch site. I thought I had a lucky find when I located the paddleboard shop on the harbor bay across from the Space Needle. I immediately gave the place a call but was disappointed. "Sorry, but this is not a good neighborhood. It's full of homeless people and we have break-ins all the time. If you can't put a cable and a lock through your equipment, it will grow legs in the night and you'll never see it again."

I turned to the Strictly Sea Kayaking crowd once again for some wisdom and posted: "Folks in the Seattle area, this summer I'm planning to paddle around Vancouver Island. Who among you would be kind enough to receive and hold on to a three-piece kayak for about a month? I'm from Florida. Will reward your inconvenience with great tales from the sea and some bourbon and rum. If you're close to a boat ramp that would be even more fantastic!"

I had several responses soon after. One was from the owner of a kayak shop called Tides and Currents. "Hey Felipe! Yes! I can handle it no problem! Send it over whenever you're ready! I'm forty-five minutes north of Seattle. The boat ramp is a little far, but we can figure that out when you're here."

"Sounds good then! Thank you!"

I called MoveIt to set the pickup date. Joey wasn't kidding about prices going up. After two weeks the shipping cost was now $950. I scheduled the pickup before the price ran out of my financial reach.

In these inflationary times, the only thing you could get on the cheap was what you should have bought a week ago

With two months to go before heading to Seattle, I still had an avalanche of things to do. In particular, this being a cold-water and potentially cold-weather journey, there were many items I wasn't normally accustomed to carrying. I made a list of everything I thought I'd need and determined if I already had it, or still needed to procure it before shipping the kayak to Seattle. These items would form my "expedition in a box" as I like to call it, packaged all together so I could start the same day I'd be landing.

CATEGORY	ITEMS	QUANTITY
	Bilge Pump - 12 in	2
	Paddle Float	1
	Antii-Chafe Cream 235 ml	1
	Medical Kit	1
Safety Gear	Reflective Rope	1
	Stohlquist Life Jacket	1
	Sinscreen 100 SPF	1
	Whistle	1
	WRSI Helmet	1

CATEGORY	ITEMS	QUANTITY
Kayak Gear	3M Paint Protection tape, 12 in wide Rolls	3
	Ball Bungees	10
	Bilge Sponges	3
	Deck Compass	1
	Spray Skirt	1
	Mesh Bags	2
	Nemo Kayak Cart	1
	Neoprene Booties	1
	Neoprene Paddle Gloves	2
	Nose & Ear Plugs	2
	Small-Mid Epic Wing Paddle	1
	Water Bottles	6
	Waterproof Velcro, 15 ft	1
	Werner Ikelos Euro Paddle	1
Camping Gear	32°F Sleeping Bag	1
	Bear Bangers	3
	Bear Spray	2
	Camping Knife	1
	Cliq Portable Folding Chair	1
	Compression Dry Bags 15 L	3
	Inflatable Pillow & Mattress	1,1
	MSR Zoic Tent (2-person)	1
	PVC Dru Bags (5 L, 10 L, 20 L)	10,2,2
	Shammy Woe Absorbent Towel	1
Clothing	Hiking Shoes	1
	Long Sleeve Polyester Shirts	3
	Long Sleeve Polyester Underwear	3
	Prescription Goggles & Sun Goggles	2
	Rain Jacket	1
	Rain Pants	1
	Shorts	1
	Short Sleeve Polyester Shirts	3
	Wide-Brim Hat	1
	Wool Jacket	1
	Wool Socks	5
Food	Cereal/Energy Bars	15
	Can Opener	1
	Canned Pasta	5
	Canned Salmon/Tuna	10
	He-Man Jelly Bean Packs	25
	He-Man Potion	3
	Nutella Jar 2 L	1
	Powedered Cheese Bag	1
	Titanium Spork	1
Dry Suit & Accessories	Kokatat Meridian	1
	Aquaseal Repair Gel	1
	Silicone Spray (for gaskets)	1
	Zipper Wax Sticks	1

CATEGORY	ITEMS	QUANTITY
Electronics	72,000 mAh Power Bank	1
	1,500 Lumen LED Head Lamp	1
	Cell Phone & Waterproof Case	1
	in Reach Explorer Mini Satellite Communicator	1
	Phone Charger	1
	Solar Lights	1
	VHF Radio	1
	Wall Tap Outlet Splitter	1
Kayak Repair	Ding All Epoxy Kayak Repair Kit	1
	Epoxy Putty Stick	1
	Extra Rudder Blade	1
	Fiberglass Cloth Roll, 60 ft	1
	Rubberized Waterproof Tape, 15 ft	1
	Serrated Scissors	1
	Smart Track Rudder Repair Kit	1
Misc Items	Guidebook: Sea Kayak Around Vancouver Island - by Doug Alderson	1
	Vancouver Island Book of Everything - by Peter Grant	1
	Hand Warmers	5
	Lighter	1
	Passport & Wallet	2
	Toilet Kit	1
	Toilet Paper Rolls	2
	WD-40 3 oz	1
	Ziplock Bags	10

Most of the gear I already had with me was from previous warm-weather expeditions, and I wasn't sure what I would need in a cold climate, in particular, what underlayers I should take as I didn't want dead weight taking up space. The weather in the Pacific Northwest is notorious for its cloudiness and persistent drizzle ("liquid sunshine" as it's called by some locals) that can last for days. The temperature is somewhat consistent at 50°F to 65°F year-round which is the dilemma range for anyone engaged in vigorous outdoor exercise. If you are overdressed, you will be overheating and sweating, and if underdressed, you will be shivering, especially on a sea kayak if you happen to take an involuntary swim. In recent years, however, the Seattle area experienced record summer heatwaves with temperatures sometimes reaching 100°F that persisted for days. Whether this summer would be another such year was anyone's guess. I decided to hedge my bets and bought a single wool jacket to go with the three long sleeve shirts I was planning to bring. If the weather skewed more to the cold, then I would just put on more layers.

The sleeping bag proved to be a pickle. It was one of the last items to arrive in the mail and was incredibly voluminous, even after crushing it in the compression bag. Two days before MoveIt was due to pick up the kayak for shipment, I did a dry run on packing all the gear into the kayak. Much to my chagrin, I discovered that the sleeping bag would not fit through the bow hatch opening and would need to go in the stern, in the same space I had designated for the kayak cart. I tried several different arrangements with the gear by moving things around between the bow, stern, and day hatches. I eventually settled with transferring the medical and kayak repair kits to the very front of the bow compartment as these would be seldom if ever used, thereby making room in the stern for the sleeping bag and the cart (which given how bulky it is, can only fit through the oval hatch in the back). When I closed all the hatch lids, I wiped the sweat from my brow and paused for a moment to admire my invisible work. From the outside there was nothing to see, but under the surface, it was a complex puzzle packed more tightly than the circuitry of a smartphone.

At that moment I received a text from Mom. "Did you know there are bears on Vancouver Island?"

As the son of a very protective Brazilian mother, I am, even as a 38 year old man with gray hair and a silvery beard, still a mama's boy. As far back as I can remember, she'd always checked up on me and kept me under her wing. At work, my colleagues sometimes joked that if my phone was ringing during a meeting, it was because my mother was calling me; it was true. When I was a kid, she mostly steered me away from the more combative sports like soccer in favor of more passive activities like sailing and tennis. Even today she will call to remind me to take a jacket if the weather will be cold, or an extra water bottle in the kayak when it's a hot summer day. Now that we live relatively close to each other, she is the most frequent guest at my house; my fridge is always stocked with healthy groceries, my bed sometimes makes itself, and my dirty laundry at times magically reappears in my dresser all washed and neatly folded.

"You know Mom, the reason I don't have a girlfriend is because you do everything," I sometimes say to her.

"I can't do every single thing a girlfriend is supposed to do," she would say.

Her perpetual preoccupation with me wasn't wholly unfounded. When I was three or four years old, my parents lost me on Copacabana Beach in Rio de Janeiro. I think my father had taken my younger sister to look at little fish swimming in the tidal pools down by the water while I was left with my toys under the beach umbrella. I don't know where my mom was at the time; perhaps she had been buying a snack or a fresh coconut from one of the many street vendors pushing their food carts up and down the beach, but for a few moments I was left on my own, and for some reason decided to go for a walk.

"Where's Felipe?" Mom asked Dad.

"I thought he was with you," Dad responded.

That whole afternoon Mom was inconsolable, thinking I had been washed away by a wave in the sea while Dad ran the whole length of Copacabana several times over. I was eventually found by the beach police near the Copacabana Fort two miles away. A beach vendor noticed me walking around aimlessly, gave me a tangerine popsicle, and contacted the authorities. "It was dripping down your little hands when we found you," my Mom told me.

On a different occasion when I was a little older, I was in a swimming pool in Sao Paulo, maybe playing with friends, when for some unknown reason I decided to walk out of the premises and must have gotten lost. A random lady noticed a kid wearing Speedos walking barefoot and alone some 10 street blocks from the pool. She grabbed me tightly by the arm and walked me back where the receptionist announced over loudspeakers that the parent of a boy named Felipe should immediately turn up at the club manager's office to pick him up. "They gave me a scolding for not taking better care of you, but at least I taught you how to use the crosswalk," Mom said. "You've definitely always been a walker and a wanderer..."

Those were just two instances. There are many more.

"Yes Mom, I know," I texted back. "It will be fine as long as I don't keep the food in the tent. In fact, what people do is they hang the food in a bag from a tree limb with a rope, and then the bear won't get to it."

"Okay, but what if your food is not what the bear is interested in? What if they think you're the food? The bears up there aren't the timid black bears you saw cycling in Colorado. They're big mean grizzly bears, and they won't be scared of you. Maybe you should take a gun with you."

"What? I'm not taking a gun with me. I don 't even know how to use one, and what do I tell the Mounties at the border when I cross into Canada and he sees I'm packing a nine-millimeter? That it's for the bears? That will go over as well as it sounds."

"What can you take with you then?"

"I'll buy some bear spray."

"Does it work?"

"It's bear spray, it's in the name."

"Okay then, take like ten with you."

"Mom, I'm not going to a bear disco party. Two will do. One for a bear, and one for a mountain lion if I come across one."

"There are lions there too!? Oh God. Take at least three then."

Later that day she sent me a YouTube video of a bear stealing a box of bird seed that had been hanging from a rope high up on a tree.

It doesn't matter what age you are, if your parents are present in your life, they will always volunteer their wisdom and advice on whatever it is you want to do, even a 1,000-mile kayak trip.

Mom wasn't wrong about the bears. There are several thousand black bears living on Vancouver Island year-round, though mostly in the north. In the summer months they are a common sight, snacking on berries and grasses on coastal trails or looking for shellfish at low tide on a beach. They are, however, usually shy, keep to themselves, and if you make enough noise while out on a hike, they will scupper away without you even knowing they were there. Brown bears (also known as grizzlies) on the other hand, would laugh at your shouts and foot-thumping gestures to intimidate them. They go wherever they please, but fortunately, tend to prefer to stay on the mainland where food is more plentiful given their big appetites.

Cougars, or mountain lions, are also present in all the dense forests of the island. They are ambush predators that can break into a sprint faster than a sports car and will easily clear a 30-foot gap across a stream with a pounce. They are, however, elusive, extremely quiet, and you would be lucky to even find a big cat pawprint. Stories about encounters with cougars usually feature a family hiking in the woods with small children. My thought is that the big cat must think the toddlers look like defenseless black-tailed deer fawns.

There are also rumors from locals that another type of cougar prowls the wealthy suburbs of major towns in British Columbia. The animal reaches maturity around the age of 45 and its preferred prey are rich single nerdy inexperienced men, usually tech entrepreneurs, who can afford cash purchases of property in the comically overvalued real estate market of Victoria.

The sea wolf, though, may be the most fascinating predator on Vancouver Island. This shy, tawny, silver-flecked animal is a bit smaller than its cousin on the mainland, the gray wolf, and lives only along the most isolated stretches of the Pacific coast. Almost like the polar bear, it lives nearly exclusively off a marine diet. It dives for fish in shallow waters and tidal pools, cracks open oysters and mussels, and scavenges for whales and sea lions that wash up onshore. They even have webbed paws and swim for miles from one island to the next. Perhaps in a few million years, like whales and sea lions, evolution will transform the sea wolf into another lineage of mammal that returns to inhabit the sea.

MoveIt came early one morning to pick up the kayak and gear. The whole process was easy enough. A midsize truck drove into my apartment parking lot, the driver gave me some paperwork to sign, and dropped down the backloading ramp with a pallet. We placed the three sections on top of it and then wrapped everything together with plastic film. I planned to have as little as possible with me on the plane, save for essentials like toiletries and the jacket Mom insisted I take in case it was chilly when I landed.

"Please get it there safely," I said to the delivery driver.

"It won't be a problem. If we can take that without any wrapping," he said pointing to a motorcycle strapped to a wooden base-frame, "we can take the three cotton balls of a kayak you have there."

The driver pressed a red button to lift the loading ramp, then dragged the pallet to the back of the truck, closed the hatch, and drove off. My hopes and worries were now on their way to Seattle. I tried not to think about it too much. Yet I still felt like a parent sending their kid off to school for the first time. From then until whenever I might see it again, my prized kayak was now on its own.

That same afternoon I got an unexpected message on my Facebook messenger. "Hey, is the red kayak still for sale?"

"Yes it is!" I replied.

The message referred to my other kayak which I had put up for sale about a month earlier.

Several years back I purchased my first expedition kayak. A red polyethylene Wilderness Systems Tempest 170. I had arrived home from a rolling class in Key Largo where I trained on the same boat model. The Tempest 170 hull is rounded and narrow and the back deck is very low and comfortable to lean on, both features that made learning to roll more effortless and forgiving than a hard chinned boat. I immediately began searching for a used Tempest near home. I found one in Melbourne, Florida, on Craigslist and drove up the next day to see it. The address was located in a mobile home park, and the person selling it was an elderly man with a diamond-white beard, silvery hair, and a face wrinkled like a pug weathered by a life spent outdoors, but his story didn't seem to be headed for a happy ending. Although he looked long in the tooth, he was slim, fit with a flat stomach, and had a wide frame like a refrigerator that gave him an imposing presence as he stood by the door.

After some small talk, he led me into the backyard of his mobile home where he kept the kayak. On the way through the living room I noticed that the TV was propped up on a pile of old books and magazines. It was tuned to Fox News. His sofa was a futon that hadn't been dusted in years, and the carpet was marked with sticky stains that I assumed were either wine or fruit juice. The room also reeked of cigarettes which were being inhaled by the man's wife who had the look of a hillbilly – discolored teeth, mangled hair, and goose-bumped skin.

"You gonna buy it, right?" she said excitedly after taking a long drag.

I looked at the old man. He didn't seem happy to be selling his kayak, and I speculated that it was his wife's idea. It's possible they were short on money and I doubt he would ever purchase another kayak again. I told him I'd pay his asking price and would give him some gas money as well if he drove the kayak to Miami for me. His wife grinned with happiness, but he showed no emotion and simply said he'd do it.

I think that when I bought the man's kayak I took a little piece of his soul too and the life he would no longer get to live.

"Okay, I'll be there this afternoon to take a look at it," came the immediate reply. After a couple hours, a white SUV pulled into my driveway. I had the kayak on a dolly with its red sail unfurled. The buyer was a short chubby man who wore a black T-shirt sporting the Grim Reaper swinging a scythe and riding a stallion. The caption read, "Too Old to Die Young."

"So you're into heavy metal?" I asked, pointing at the shirt.

"Oh this? Nah, it's a crime drama my wife and I are binge watching on Amazon Prime. Well, my wife is binge watching to be more precise. I watch it here and there. If I get too comfortable, I'll be like her and never leave the house ... So, that's the red beauty. Is it easy to use the sail?"

"Yes, not too bad on moderate wind. I'd be a little careful with it when it's blowing hard. You don't want to lose control. It's a welcome reprieve, however, if you have to paddle for ten hours or more in a day."

"I don't have any sailing experience."

"You soon will then."

I showed him how to hoist the sail and how to stow it on the deck. He inspected the hatches and ran his palm over the hull and deck to feel if the scratches told any stories. "I'll take it."

He paid in cash, we lifted the boat onto his car roof, and he fastened it with a set of black straps. At that moment I asked him if we could take a few photographs. Although I had not paddled the Tempest ever since I bought the Taran and it had been sitting in the garage for over a year, I felt a pang of nostalgia at the realization that this would be the last time I'd lay eyes on this kayak which over the years had been so generous to me.

"You know, this kayak taught me to roll, and took me on camping trips in the Florida Keys. It was my companion through storms and swells on my first expedition from Miami to Marco Island through the Florida Everglades. Even when I saw an alligator as I was paddling I didn't feel afraid when I was in this boat. Granted, it wasn't a very big alligator, but I'm sure it will be a boat that will give you confidence and you'll make fond memories with it. Take good care of it."

He drove off with the boat on the roof rack, took the right bend on the street corner, and soon vanished from view. I stood in the middle of the parking lot for a while as the evening was setting in when a thought crept into my head, *You shipped the Taran this morning to Seattle, and now you just sold the Tempest. Technically, you don't have a kayak anymore. You better hope the shipping company does what it promised.*

When I paddled around Puerto Rico I had a few close calls with reefs and submerged rocks. On more than one occasion I was surprised by a wave breaking over a hidden boulder which I managed to avoid only by timing my strokes with the wave crest. A rock covered with jagged barnacles and oysters is the kayaker's most terrible enemy and I fear them more than a hungry great white shark. There's always a chance the shark is just curious.

Because of that I've always carried a fiberglass repair kit with me, but somewhat irresponsibly, I've never taken the time to learn how to do a field repair. It's been buried in the front hatch providing nothing more than emotional support. But in practice, it has been as useless as a can of fish with no can opener.

I've always been one to think, *It will never happen to me.* My beach landings have almost always been on sandy shorelines and I've had the foresight (or luck most likely) to check that the landings would be in calm bays sheltered from the wind. In the chance that a quick repair was needed, I've had some waterproof tape with me that would hopefully get me to safety in the short term. In Vancouver Island, however, relying on hope and optimism just seemed too imprudent and disrespectful of my good fortunes thus far in life.

From photographs I'd seen, many of the landings on the Pacific coast are rocky, exposed, with countless scattered reefs. Out on the ocean, you only need to be unlucky once to be unlucky for the rest of your short life.

I concluded that learning how to execute a successful fiberglass field repair was a skill I must have. To do that I called up the man I call the "Kayak Whisperer", out in Naples.

"Hi Jay! I've decided that the Vancouver Island adventure is a go for this year. You mind giving me a class on fiberglass field repair. I got a feeling I might need it this time."

"Yes, of course, come on by next weekend.

I've known Jay for four years ever since I bought the Taran kayak. Meeting him is every kayaker's most fortunate life encounter. Mine happened because when I purchased my kayak, it came with a small but critical production defect. The stern opening for the rudder deployment cable was placed in a location that made it inoperable. The existing hole had to be patched and closed, and a new one drilled farther back. Looking at a $6,000 kayak about as useful as a pile of driftwood in my living room, I was feeling extremely distraught. For nine months I had anxiously anticipated the delivery watching YouTube videos and reading blogpost reviews about my new kayak. And now that it was here, I couldn't take it out on its maiden voyage.

I posted on the Strictly Sea Kayaking group asking for recommendations on kayak repair shops in South Florida. The recurring responses from as far away as Newfoundland were, "Call Jay Rose!" or, "Jay is the master of fiberglass!" and, "Oh, you are so lucky you live so close to Jay."

I called Jay and after briefly explaining the work, I was driving to Naples cross-state with my three-piece kayak crammed inside the Prius.
When I arrived at Jay's shop I was a bit concerned. There was no shop. I had just driven down a potholed street to an old warehouse park on the outskirts of town. Surely the address must be wrong, I thought, wondering why there were no kayaks anywhere to be seen.

A few minutes after I arrived, another car with a kayak on the roof rack pulled into the parking lot and a man wearing gray wife beaters stepped out. He was not very tall, but he was built with broad toned shoulders and wore a trimmed beard black as coal that seamlessly merged into his short curly hair.

"Hi, I'm Jay. You must be Felipe. Holy cow! Is the kayak inside the Prius?"

"It's a little tight, but I can just about drive safely on the highway with this setup. If I can manage without the central rearview mirror, and don't mind being a little too close to the steering wheel."

"Don't think I've ever seen something like that. Well, let's get it on the work stand."

As he said that he unlocked one of the overhead rollup warehouse doors, coiled it up with a clatter, and revealed a garage workshop with several stacked kayaks on a rack.

"I have five units like this one. It's been getting crowded, people keep sending me their boats, and I need to rent out more and more space."

He looked at the stern piece with the opening for the rudder cable, and immediately gave the diagnosis.

"Yeah, looks like whoever was making this goofed it. You rarely if ever see three-piece kayaks. Fortunately, this is easy, oh, and you already have the right dye pigment for the gel coat. It will look flawless. You can come and pick it up next week."

He wasn't overstating things like a used car salesman. When I picked up the kayak the following weekend, the defect looked as if it had never existed.

I was reading a book about the ancient Greek myths when I came across the story of Hephaestus (Vulcan if you prefer his Roman name). He was the first-born son of Hera and Zeus,who by some cruel twist of fate, had such an ugly distasteful appearance that when he was born his mother hurled him down the mountainside of Olympus in disgust. When he landed, he broke his foot and was forever lame and walked with a limp. During his exile, he learned from the Cyclopes how to work metal forges and became renowned for his ability to turn metal ores into shields, swords, spears, and armor.

Yet, had the ancient Greeks ever asked one of their many oracles what kind of materials man would invent some 25 centuries in the future, they would surely have included fiberglass, carbon fiber, Kevlar, and epoxy glue to Hephaestus' suite of industrial equipment. The magic of modern chemistry can take a fabric, soak it in a potion, expose it to the sun and transform it into a hard but lightweight shell of any form imaginable, tough like a metal, yet light as a breath of air.

I arrived for my boat repair lesson with Jay early on Saturday. He gave me a full explanation of the types of glass fabrics that are available. Immediately, he pointed out that the one that comes in the boat repair kit I purchased was not the best.

"You see, the fiberglass they provide has loose ends and is going to fray into thousands of loose strings of glass filaments the moment you cut into it. What you need is a fiberglass roll with the sides weaved together so it looks like a lace ribbon.

"Before you even start to do anything, I'd say the first thing you have to make sure of is to be somewhere that you know you can camp. If you can't, you might as well throw in some layers of the marine tape both on the inside and outside of the crack and get somewhere you can spend a couple of days because you don't want to do this in the rain. If you do a rushed job, it's going to come out bad …

"Okay, so once you're in a calm, clean place, you'll need to clean with acetone the whole area of the crack. You don't want any dirt or salt water on it. After you've done that, you must sand the crack to remove all the gel coat at least one finger's width around the fracture. That will give the epoxy glue more surface to bind to."

For this part of the lesson, he brought out a fiberglass panel which he promptly folded until it fractured down the middle so that the two pieces were only loosely held together.

I used a rough number 40 sandpaper and scrubbed the cracked area clean of the gel coat until the underlying fiberglass was exposed.

"Make sure you also scrub off any loose fibers from the panel. That way the fiber will lay as flat as possible. Okay, you're good. Now blow off all the dust, but make sure no one else is in front of you when you do that; you don't want anyone to breathe glass dust into their lungs and for good measure, clean everything with acetone one more time.

"The next step is the most crucial. Before you mix the epoxy, you have to plan how you are going to lay the fiberglass and have the fiber sheets pre-cut. You almost always want to have three overlapping layers and make sure you alternate the direction of the fibers by ninety degrees in each layer to maximize the fabric strength. The top layer should also be the widest to cap over everything below and leave no loose ends."

"Got it!" I said while taking notes.

I looked at the longitudinal fracture on the panel and decided to make one long strip for the base layer to go along the length of the fracture, then several smaller roughly square pieces to be laid perpendicular to the first, then followed by a final long strip to cap it all in the third layer. I used a serrated pair of scissors to cut the fiber and immediately noticed that the fibers started fraying at the ends.

"Don't worry too much about that," Jay reassured me, "if you start pulling the loose strings, the whole thing starts to unravel like a sweater.

"Now that you have the sheets premade, it's time to mix the ingredients for the epoxy."

Out of the repair kit he pulled two small clear bottles labeled Chemical A and Chemical B.

"Chemical A is the resin; this is what is going to bind the glass fibers together with the different layers. Chemical B is the hardener which will cure the resin into a solid. It's important to get the correct ratios in the mixture. Too much hardener and the solid will be brittle; too little and it will not solidify. Two-to-one of A and B. Use a measuring cup you don't mind throwing away.

I mixed the two chemicals being very careful to measure out each amount. As I stirred the potion together, it soon started to give off heat. "Go slow on the stirring, you don't want to have bubbles."

I stirred the mixture for about two minutes.

"Okay now, get a paintbrush you also don't mind throwing away. Let the liquid soak up on the brush head and then apply to the sanded area. Not too much, you don't want to drench it. Just brush tap all the areas we'll be laying the fiberglass on until it all looks even."

After wetting the entire area with glue, I laid the base sheet of fiberglass over the fracture. The white material immediately became translucent. "There you go, you got it. Now, those small white dots in the fiber are bubbles; you must sweep them out with the brush because they will become points of weakness otherwise."

We repeated the process for the next two layers and then placed the panel in the sun to speed up the reaction. After half an hour, the crack was no longer visible and the panel was again one solid sheet. "Well, that's it! In the kayak itself, you will also want to lay some fiberglass on the inside of the crack as well if the crack goes all the way through; it gets kind of tricky to sand and layer in the fabric if you need to get deep inside the hatch. Much easier to do it in the shop than on a beach."

"Thank you so much, Jay! Hopefully this is the only time I will ever have to do this."

"Oh, trust me, it won't be. Paddle enough miles and eventually almost everything that can happen happens. It's one of those things you can never be in control of, only be prepared for when it happens."

"At least I hope that when it happens there will be phone reception so I can video conference with you to check up on my work. A thumbs up from you will be a huge confidence boost before I get back into the elements."
"I'll keep an eye out for any messages while you're out there."

It hardly felt like it, but in a week I would be pushing my kayak from a boat ramp in Seattle. My mind began to shift from thinking about work and the daily hassles like reviewing contractor submittals and attending meetings, to thinking about how the journey would unfold. For the first time, the weather forecast in Seattle now included Sunday, May 29, my tentative departure date. It called for rain and a maximum temperature of 59°F; it didn't seem like it would be too windy, but Mom was right to insist I bring a jacket.

The light wind will make it an easy first day to get in the swing of things, I thought.

There were still a few items to wrap up such as activating my monthly GPS plan with inReach. When I was packing the kayak and gear for shipment, I specifically remembered placing the GPS unit in my living room cabinet so I didn't accidentally ship it with everything else. Or at least I thought I remembered specifically doing that, because when I went looking for it, I couldn't find it. Exasperated, I took all the clothes out of the drawers, rummaged through the kitchen cabinets, checked the cracks between the sofa cushions, looked under the bed, flipped over the seats in the car, and checked a thousand other places but found nothing.

I sent a message to my contact in Seattle who would be receiving the kayak.

"Hey David, need a big favor from you. Can you look for my GPS unit in the kayak gear? I don't know which hatch or which bag it's in, so you'll have to unpack everything; it will probably take a while to find it."

"Yes, no problem. I'll be home in a few days, will look for it then and let you know."

A few days came and went, I heard nothing from David, and began to worry. I messaged him and got some bad news. "Hey man, I got into an accident, got several cracked ribs. Can't lift anything."

"Oh darn. No worries then. I'll buy a new unit and if the old one turns out to be there, I'll find a way to return it." Like any normal person, I hate to spend money to fix a mistake, especially a $400 mistake which is how much the GPS unit cost, but it was worth it for the peace of mind.

Fate sometimes sends a rogue wave out of nowhere and you have to roll with the swells. On the weekend before departure I started getting a sore throat. At first I thought I had swallowed a rough Doritos chip or some other coarse food morsel. *It will go away soon enough,* I thought.

It didn't. On Saturday afternoon I was lacking energy and went to sleep early hoping that it was a result of the rough workweek. *Some ten hours of quality sleep should do the trick.*

Again, it did not. *Oh darn, I hope I'm not coming down with the flu, or worse yet, Covid. Not now of all times ...* I did a home antigen test on Sunday and it came back negative. *Another good night's sleep and rest should clear this, I hope.*

On Monday morning I was a little better and went to work at the office, but planned to take things easy. There would be no lunchtime workouts at the gym this week.

Compared to the start of my journeys around Puerto Rico and Florida, I was only mildly fitter than before. In my 20s and early 30s, I had the physique of a top athlete and would do 100-mile bike rides from Miami to Key Largo just for fun, or paddle a 20-mile course from my house in Key Biscayne to Miami Beach in the late evening after work only to then arrive home and consume a 32-ounce jar of Greek yogurt with Nutella before heading to bed. Gaining weight was something I never had to worry about. As I got older, however, my time spent at work increased, the exercise frequency went down, and the food intake stayed about the same.

These long-haul endurance expeditions have been the ace up my sleeve to rejuvenate in a short amount of time; I lost 15 pounds in the 24 days around Puerto Rico, and 20 pounds during the 47 days around Florida. My physical appearance was so transformed by that trip that one of my female coworkers joked that my looks had improved from a six to at least an eight and a half. My mother, however, thought otherwise.

"This yoyo thing you do with your weight is not healthy. You're not a bear going into hibernation for the winter."

"When I come back from this journey I'll try to be more diligent about it," I told her. "The work schedule is the problem. They keep scheduling lunch meetings when I want to go work out, and the meetings move around from week to week."

"I think the problem is that celebratory pint of chocolate ice cream you give yourself at the end of each trip ..."

"It's not every trip, it was only on the Florida trip, and only because the people I rented my house to had left it in the freezer."

By Monday afternoon I felt considerably worse and went home. I started feeling joint aches in my elbows, knees, and ankles; the same aches from the Covid vaccine. I took another antigen test, and this time it came back positive.

Oh rats, I thought. *I'll never be allowed to board the flight like this.* I called my primary care doctor and asked if he could prescribe some antiviral Paxlovid tablets to get me out of the hole as quickly as possible.

"Sorry, but that's only for the elderly or people who are immunocompromised, which isn't your case. You'll have to do what everyone does. Isolate for at least five days or until your symptoms go away, whichever is longer."

I pleaded for him to make an exception. I said I was going on vacation; I had a flight booked for the following Saturday and I needed the strength to start paddling the day I got to Seattle. All to no avail. "For these things, time and rest are best. You're young, you're fit, and you got the three Covid shots, so you should be fine. Drink lots of fluids.

It was a hectic week before departure. I had rented my house for the two months I'd be away, the renter had already checked in, and I was staying at my mother's house, who unsurprisingly was none too pleased to find herself hosting the plague.

"I'm seventy, you know," she said, "that's the high-risk group they're always talking about on TV. One day you're fine, and then five days after you start sneezing you're in the hospital with a ventilator. I hope to be around long enough to one day see grandkids from you. I'm going to put you in the guest bedroom and you're staying in there until the day you catch your flight."

That Monday was the worst day; I could do nothing except lie in bed. By Wednesday, however, the joint aches had receded and my strength was on the upswing. On Thursday I felt fine save for some mild coughs, but the home antigen tests were still coming back positive. I called American Airlines to explain my situation and try to postpone my Saturday flight. To my great fortune, the flight was overbooked and they were happy to bump it to Sunday night.

On Saturday, my antigen test came in negative. *Yay! I'm really going! It's all going to work out.* I felt relieved.

When I walked out of my room the next day the house was dead quiet. My mother had left me a note on the kitchen table.

Dear Son,

I'm so happy for you that you are heading out on your trip which you had been planning for so long. It is bittersweet that I can't be there to give you a big hug and a kiss to see you off. But before you leave, please do a few things to take care of me.

1. Throw away all the trash you accumulated in your room directly into the dumpster.

2. Use the Lysol spray to disinfect the door handles, the bed sheets, and anything else you might have touched on your way out.

3. Keep your room door closed and leave the window open. I won't be going in there to have the sheets washed for at least the next three days.

I am so sorry to have to say goodbye to you like this. This terrible virus has taken five wonderful days which I could have spent with you, my only son, before having to miss your visits for the next two months. Will think of you and call you every day.

Watch out for the bears!

Love you!

Mom

I felt a pang in my stomach not being able to say a proper goodbye to Mom before heading to the airport. She has been the person who has given me the most emphatic support for my adventures. "You have to live your dreams while you have the ability to do it; if I can help you make it happen I will," she'd often say. "At least you don't go skydiving anymore like you did when you were in college. That really put my heart in my throat."

I ran through my thoughts from the day I had shipped my kayak to the present trying to think of anything I might have forgotten. Work at the office was wrapped up, my documents, wallet, and Mom's jacket were in my travel bag, and the kayak was waiting for me in Seattle. The only thing left to do was to push off and paddle a thousand miles.

CANADA UNITED STATES
MT BAKER
EVERETT
MT VERNON
CAMANO Is.
BELLINGHAM
ANACORTES
WHIDBEY Is.
DECEPTION PASS
ROSARIO STRAIT
FRASER RIVER
SAN JUAN ISLANDS
PUGET SOUND
PORT TOWNSEND
LOPEZ Is.
ORCA Is.
THE SALISH SEA
SAN JUAN Is.
ROCHE
NEW DUNGENESS
HARO STRAIT
BRITISH COLUMBIA
STRAIT OF GEORGIA
GALLIANO Is.
VANCOUVER
VICTORIA
PORT SIDNEY
PORT ANGELES
RACE ROCKS
GABRIOLA Is.
SOOKE
NANAIMO
VANCOUVER ISLAND
BALLENA ISLANDS
LASQUETI ISLAND
JUAN DE FUCA STRAIT
OLYMPIC PENINSULA
TEXADA ISLAND
PARKSVILLE
PORT RENFREW
POWELL RIVER
GILES BAY
AHGYKON Is.
NEAH BAY
DENMAN & HORNBY Is.
PORT ALBERNI
CAPE FLATTERY
LUND
DISCOVERY
HERNANDO Is.
CORTES Is.
ISLANDS
COURTENAY
MARINA Is.
CAPE MUDGE
BAMFIELD
HERIOT BAY
QUADRA Is.
CAMPBELL RIVER
N

PART 2 - SEATTLE TO HERIOT BAY

May 30 – Day 1

The afternoon cab ride to the Miami International Airport was surprising for its uneventfulness. If there was one benefit from the pandemic, it was the death of the Miami rush hour traffic jam when millions of daily commuters left the downtown waterfront business district for the western suburbs of Doral and Hialeah via the forever-under-construction Dolphin Expressway. Crashes and pile-ups happened nearly every day here; you would likely be turning off your engine at least once, and pass the time counting how many rumbling jets skirted over your head as they came to land. It didn't matter if the accident was on your side or not; there'd always be onlooker delays in both directions. Seeing the nearly empty highway on a Friday afternoon, arriving at the airport in less than 10 minutes, and not being harassed by airport security for double parking was a surreal experience.

Heavy downpours delayed my flight for three hours and I would not be in Seattle until the early morning. Even though the airport was much emptier than normal, the flight was full and I was assigned the dreaded middle seat in between two fleshy passengers hogging the armrests. After settling in I closed my eyes hoping to sleep for most of the flight and prayed that the rotund individual in the window seat would not be getting out to use the bathroom - or clog the emergency exit door in case we made a water landing in the middle of Puget Sound.

I was jolted awake when the plane wheels bumped the runway of the Seattle-Tacoma International Airport, and the cabin lights were suddenly turned on. There was a very faint purple twilight of sunrise visible out the plane window and the silhouette of a large conical mountain I assumed must have been Mount Rainier, a big dormant snow-capped volcano which on a clear day can be seen all the way from Canada.

Out of the airport I took another cab to Lake Stevens, a small suburb in the north part of the Seattle-Tacoma metro area separated from Puget Sound by a wide-open marsh and a winding lazy river called the Snohomish.

David was waiting for me outside a two-story house in the residential neighborhood. His front garage served as the depot for his kayak shop and had a rack of neoprene wetsuits and paddles. "Welcome to Seattle! I'm excited for your trip! I wish I could be doing that, but I'm afraid I'm getting married in July."

"Oh, my condolences to you!" I said, faking a sad face. Perhaps this was not the best way to make an introduction with someone you've never met and has given you tremendous help, but thankfully he cracked with laughter at my dark humor.

"We'll go to my warehouse and get a look at your boat. I didn't get around to opening any of the bags. I'm curious to see what a three-piece kayak looks like

We had a quick drive to the warehouse where, to my great delight, I set eyes on my familiar kayak bags wrapped together in plastic film exactly as I had dispatched them in Miami.

"Oh, and here are the things you ordered," David said as he handed me a box with the new GPS unit and fiberglass repair kit.

I immediately thought back to the missing GPS unit I had been looking for all over my house. I opened the kayak bag with the cockpit section, found the dry bag with the electronics, and poured out the contents. The original GPS unit wasn't there.

"I was totally convinced it would be here. How could it just vanish?" I mumbled. "I guess I really am out $400." Even after the journey when I returned home, I never found it.

I started unpacking the other items.

"How are you getting to the water?"

"Oh, I marked a boat ramp on the north bank of the Snohomish. It's about six miles from here. I figured that I would make a portage there." I showed him the marker on Google Earth in a place called Ebey Park near the river mouth. David looked at my phone screen with a frown.

"You guys in Miami must not know what a hill is. That ramp is a good four-hour walk with your kayak and probably not the best place if you decide to spend the night. It's right next to a sewage treatment lagoon so you'll be catching a nasty whiff in the tent all night. Let's do this, I'll drive you down to Everett. There's a big marina there, and the waterfront has several hotels. You can then decide what to do."

That was wise advice. Having barely slept the night before, my body rhythm had been running on adrenaline fumes. After we loaded the kayak on the roof rack of his pickup truck and were on our way, I immediately fell asleep in the backseat.

"You know David, I think I'll launch tomorrow," I said, struggling to keep my eyes open. "I'm pooped and jet lagged. I have to think through things when I pack the kayak and not forget anything. Best I don't rush out on the first day."

"Yeah, I agree. That's when bad stuff happens. I'll drop you off at this really nice hotel called the Indigo. It's where most of the folks at my wedding will be staying. I'll tell the front desk you're a friend and they can probably get you a deal and handle the kayak for the night."

David was right. Tucked on the banks of a picturesque bay the hotel was a very fancy place. The lobby had a shiny granite floor with a walk-around glassed-in fireplace lit with dancing orange flames. It was surrounded by inviting couches with colorful pillows where you could lounge and lazily admire the sailboats docked in the harbor through a floor-to-ceiling glass window. I navigated my way to the front desk pulling my 18-foot-long kayak behind me through the sliding doors leading in from the valet parking stand. I then made a hard 90-degree turn in the hallway to the reception desk, only missing a good whack at the glassed-in fireplace with the rudder by a couple of inches.

After some initial awkward looks from the front-desk lady, she turned out to be extremely accommodating and had me back-wheel the kayak down a long winding corridor to the hotel ballroom where I could spread out all the gear on the floor to get organized.

"Only a little more complicated than a guest asking for an additional towel, right?" I joked.

"Yeah, not the worst thing I've ever had to deal with. Just be careful on your way out tomorrow."

May 31 – Day 2 – Launch Day!

I had a restful sleep the rest of that afternoon and most of the night before waking up at 4 a.m. My biological clock was still running three hours ahead.

The first day of any expedition is best spent getting the rhythm of things that will need to become routine. My first task was to set up the new GPS unit. I called inReach at 5 a.m. (8 a.m. on the East Coast) and had the operator run through the activation and syncing process. To my delight, there were no issues; this could easily have delayed me by an additional day or more and I felt upbeat to have ticked off the first item on the list without a hitch.

The next task was to do one last run through all the gear to confirm everything was there, and to do a dress rehearsal pack job making sure that every item was in the correctly colored dry bag and fitted into the right hatch in the right order. I was again grateful to be able to do this in the comfort of the hotel ballroom, rather than out in the wind and drizzle on the boat ramp. If there is a saint or deity that looks after kayakers, they must have been watching over me. Everything fit inside just right and there was even a little bit of room to spare in the bow hatch. I put the kayak on the cart, and was just about ready to walk out of the building with the kayak in tow, when I noticed that my GPS charging cable was still attached to the plug socket in the hotel lobby next to the reception desk.

That would have been a terrible headache, I thought.

I pulled the kayak behind me through the hotel lobby, out through the sliding doors into the parking lot, and gave a friendly goodbye wave to the gentleman starting the morning shift at the front desk whose puzzled looks told me no one had informed him of my situation.

"Good day for a little paddle on the sound, eh?" he said.

"Looks like it. The sun's coming out."

"How far are you going?"

"Canada!" I exclaimed, and he gave out a laugh unsure whether I was pulling his leg.

"Well good luck then."

A few weeks earlier I had the entire 1,000-mile route annotated with markers for potential campsites roughly every 10 miles. This would ensure that I would always have at hand a nearby put-out point in case of bad weather, along with locations of accessible boat ramps, hotels, supermarkets, and general stores for resupplies. My plan for the initial section was to make my way through the sheltered waters of the Puget Sound before exiting through Deception Pass into the Juan de Fuca Strait. From there I would find the safest traverse point to the island maze of the San Juans, cross the border into Canada, and make my way up the coast to Quadra Island where I would take a well-deserved first rest day at the Heriot Bay Inn. I picked up the cell phone to see where I had marked the first few campsites. If I had started in the afternoon the day before, I would have planned to stop on Hat Island, a small islet 10 miles from the original launch point on the Snohomish River, but given that it was now barely past 7 a.m., I could put in a full day's paddle as far as somewhere on Camano Island.

It was a 10-minute walk from the hotel parking lot to the harbor boat ramp where there were already a few early risers putting their fishing boats on the water. I found an empty slip, unloaded the gear stored in the cockpit, and eased the kayak stern first halfway into the water. After re-stowing everything into the hatches (though not in the same way I had done back at the hotel), I walked up the ramp to find a bench to sit and dress into the dry suit. When I returned fully dressed after 10 minutes, I got taught a valuable lesson on how quickly the tides in the Pacific Northwest can change. My kayak was floating in the turbid knee-deep water and slowly drifting away.

That could have been the second terrible headache of the day, I thought. *Let's get going.*

I waded into the water to grab the boat before it drifted any farther and slid my legs into the cramped cockpit. After struggling to get the spray skirt around the comb, I released the rudder line, tested the steering foot pegs, and then finally, made the first of the 1 million forward strokes I would need to arrive back at the same boat ramp two months hence.

Oh God damn it! I have two right-handed gloves, I noticed as I slipped them on. *I must have put both the left hands in the stern hatch. Well, they're staying there today. I'm not getting out to do a relaunch.*

I had to stop paddling after a few minutes as I was gasping for air.

"This life jacket is too tight," I moaned aloud. Obviously, I hadn't adjusted it to account for the extra bulk of the dry suit. I reached behind my back and released the tension on the straps with instant gratification.

Finally, I felt comfortable enough to get in a paddle rhythm. The water was flat like a mirror. I was gliding effortlessly along like a sharp knife cutting a paper-thin slice through a salami stick when I suddenly noticed three seals attentively observing me with their black, round eyes like the periscopes of a submarine.

"Well hello! Good morning to you. How are the fish?" I said to them.

Once their curiosity was satisfied and they concluded that I was neither food nor predator, they swooped into the dark water to look for shellfish and didn't reemerge again. I learned from my guidebook that they were harbor seals because they are most often seen around harbors and marinas, sometimes snacking on fish scraps tossed out by fishermen. I would venture to rename them burrito seals as their brownish, dappled skin and chubby, puffy bodies make them look like tortillas filled with black beans, rice, and delicious pulled pork. Perhaps I gave the seals a wolfish stare and they thought better than to stick around and find out that orcas aren't the only things that would make a meal of them.

After my meeting with the seals, a strong northern headwind started blowing and didn't let up the entire day. The paddle went from a leisure stroll to a determined but agonizingly slow plod, headfirst, into an assembly line of ramming waves only easing slightly once I secured a toehold on Camano Island. I hugged the shore along pebblestone-washed beaches rimmed with an unbroken line of driftwood neatly laid against an alternation of impenetrable treelines and steep escarpments. I wondered if that marked the extent of the previous high tide and if there would be any safe stretch of beach to camp on. In Florida, I had more than once been surprised to find that a spot I had identified on Google Earth and marked as a campsite was submerged in the peak of a spring tide.

After paddling for 17 miles past many unsuitable landing spots, I arrived on a pebbled beach where three feet above the driftwood was a picnic table on a grassy field. I checked the GPS and saw that I was almost on top of a marker I had put down with the boat ramp symbol and the note, "Camano Park." After stretching my neck around the bend on the beach I sighted the concrete boat ramp exactly where I expected it to be.

Good enough for the first day, I thought.

June 1 – Day 3

I slept better in the tent with the air mattress in my sleeping bag than on many nights I had in my bed the previous month. I can only reason that it was because I hadn't given myself a full day of nearly continuous and strenuous exercise in a while. It's far more fulfilling to be physically spent from an exhausting day paddling than being mentally exerted by a day-long stretch in front of a computer screen.

I thought about the journey and all the weeks and days still ahead and had a strange feeling. Barely a weekend had passed since my last day working, but it felt so much longer than that already. I've experienced this time dilation effect before during the beginning of the Puerto Rico trip. It's like driving with cruise control on a highway, then suddenly killing the engine. Your mind, only tediously awake, gets jolted into the immediacy of the present, aware of everything that's happening. So much feels like it has already happened, yet there's so much more left to happen. *Hopefully, by the end I won't even remember what my job was, I thought. By then, maybe, the journey will feel like the mundane, and the daily job will feel like the new. Or maybe not. Maybe I will just start planning the next journey.*

After I had set up camp that night, a group of fellow campers offered me a dinner of rice and black beans, tortillas, and steak. I gladly accepted, but later concluded that kayaking in cold climates should not be combined with a heavy serving of Mexican food. I farted all day long inside my dry suit, and the couple of times I bled out the air the smell was particularly foul.

There was almost no wind or any trace of the blunt waves from the previous day. The only waves came from the motorboats buzzing along the sound. By midday, the sun had come out leaving me feeling hot and overdressed.

Time for a few practice rolls with the loaded kayak and a little cooling dip in the water, I thought.

The kayak roll (also called the Eskimo roll) is the trickiest skill for any principiant kayaker to master. It consists of capsizing until you're completely upside down and then righting yourself and your kayak back up using a body motion called "the snap." The most skilled kayak rollers are whitewater kayakers who navigate down cascading mountain rivers with rapids, overfalls, and whirlpools where exiting the boat could leave you exposed and battered against shallow rocks and boulders. For the touring sea kayaker, the roll isn't quite as essential for protection against boulders and rocks, but it is a useful skill for paddling in the surf zone where thrashing waves and swells can easily send you swimming. It gives an immense boost of self-confidence to know that you can dodge a breaching barrel tumbling over your head by ducking tightly under the safety of your hull and letting the commotion upstairs wash away before you peek back up.

As these were to be deliberate rolls, rather than part of a real spur of the moment combat roll against the sea, I performed my preparatory rolling ritual by putting on nose and ear plugs (last thing I wanted to get on this trip was an ear-canal infection like I did in Puerto Rico), storing my prescription sun goggles into the front day hatch, and slipping the wide-brim hat under the deck bungees.

I then clamped my paddle against the starboard side of the hull (the right side), crouched my head against my torso, and let myself tip over. Immediately I felt a rush of chilled water against the back of my neck. Usually I would have paused for a second or two completely upside down while I cooled off from the heat. However, I wasn't prepared for the sudden cold shock against my naked scalp and my chest which was very much dry inside the dry suit. I quickly swung my paddle wide while unwinding my body with a long and deliberate hip snap to right the boat back up before bringing my head out of the water.

Brrrr ... that was really cold, I thought, gasping. I only managed to do three more rolls on either side of the kayak before my head began feeling like I had swallowed three scoops of ice-cream all at once. I concluded that I wouldn't want to be rolling again anytime soon unless I had to. Ironically, that was just 30 minutes later when I was again feeling baked like a bread loaf in my dry suit by the scorching midday sun above. Unfortunately, when you paddle in cold water there isn't always a way to be adequately dressed both for a swim and a paddle at the same time.

Some 20 fighter jets buzzed over the afternoon sky thundering just above the trees. They flew in pairs, first appearing from the northwest, then crossed over the sound and after a sharp turn to the southwest, skirted along the opposite shore before vanishing back from where they first appeared. On their closest approach I could make out the vapor clouds forming over their wings, and they were so loud that even the noise from the nearby motorboats was drowned out. I checked my phone map to see where they might be coming from and found an airfield roughly eight miles to my west called the Whidbey Island Naval Air Station on the Juan de Fuca Strait shore.

Either there's a big airshow going on, or Canada must be invading Washington, I thought.

I continued for another 10 miles and arrived on the north shore of Hope Island near the northernmost point of the north arm of Puget Sound. Along the way I noticed a current pulling me along gently, but with ever so slightly increasing strength with the passing hours and the further north I got. No doubt it was the ebbing tide on Deception Pass making its presence known.

Twice a day nearly all the water in the northern third of Puget Sound is tugged back and forth through a narrow slit scoured into the basaltic deposits that separate the long and crooked Whidbey Island from Fidalgo Island where a channel has been dredged so fishing boats can sail around the treacherous tidal rapids and whirlpools. The current on the channel throat flows as fast as nine knots and even motorboats can have difficulty making headway against the current.

"When you get there, you'll see that there is an island right in the middle of the pass," David told me before I left. "One side is narrower than the other. The narrow side is rougher, but that is the side most kayakers go through as motorboats favor the wider side where there's some room for maneuvering. Once you pick a side there is no going back, you can't fight the current."

It was Captain George Vancouver who gave the pass its name. In 1792 he sailed into Puget Sound with two ships, the *Discovery* and the *Chatham*, to explore the bays and inlets, and sent a crew of sailors that included a certain Joseph Whidbey, for whom the island is named, up the north arm of the sound to map the land. The crew went as far as they could until the waters became too shallow for navigation, and returned with news that the land to the west was a large peninsula. When the expedition continued north it happened onto a waterway with a strong outflowing current which they believed to be the mouth of a great river. Captain Vancouver again sent Whidbey to explore this river who after much effort and difficulty succeeded in making it past the narrows. Unfortunately, Whidbey and the crew soon realized that they had been in those waters before, and concluded that what they had thought was a peninsula was in fact an island, leaving Captain Vancouver sorely dispirited.

"How disappointing to not find a river here; I have been deceived by the tide," he must have said. "Deception Pass it is then. Well Whidbey, at least you get an island named after you."

There is no mention of how Hope Island got its name, but I'd venture to guess that it could have been a sailor with the Whidbey crew thinking, *I hope we don't miss the tide or we are going to be stuck on this island for at least half a day.*

June 2 – Day 4

I wondered if I should do a visual inspection of Deception Pass from the bridge crossing over the strait to see what I was about to get into. It was, however, 6:30 a.m. and the tide had begun to ebb an hour earlier.

By the time I paddle into the Deception Pass marina, hike the trail to the bridge and back, and get going again it might be well past midday. The tide will have turned, and I'll be stuck.

From my campsite in the dense woodland on the north shore of Hope Island I could barely perceive a ripple in the flat water shining under the morning sun. But the rapids and whirlpools at the pass would most certainly be getting stronger with every passing hour and I was eager to get going.

I decided to switch paddles for the day. Up until now I had been using a wing paddle which I tend to favor as it's shaped like an ice cream scoop and cuts smoothly through the water, giving greater speed in flat conditions; it also has less surface area when your stroke brings it out of the water against headwinds. In confused seas where waves break in the surf zone and in white-water rapids with whirlpools and overfalls, the wider and flatter Euro blade gives more stability for bracing, turning, and explosive acceleration when needed. It's also easier to learn to roll with, but the technique is slightly different with how you skim the blade over the surface of the water, and sometimes requires a little practice when switching paddles to refresh the muscle memory, as I was soon reminded.

I quickly performed my pre-roll ritual with the ear and nose plugs, and tipped into the water with a deep breath; and to my disappointment, did not roll back up, even after three attempts, and reluctantly pulled open the spray skirt for a swim. The water was frigid like a cold shower in winter, and in less than a minute I was feeling chilled to the bone. After a couple of jumps on the stern for a wet cowboy reentry, I finally settled inside the waterlogged cockpit and began bailing out the water. The whole ordeal barely lasted more than 20 seconds, but I was left gasping for air and reminded of my first cold-water exit when I went kayak surfing on the Oregon coast. I was astounded how it took monumentally more effort to climb back into the kayak by myself in 55°F water than in a tropical Florida beach. My body just could not generate enough heat fast enough to overcome the loss to the water, even in a dry suit. It was like giving my all in a 100-meter sprint, only to find out that I needed to run a mile.

After a few minutes spent catching my breath and letting my body warm up, I readied myself to try again, if for nothing else than personal pride. *How embarrassed would you be if one day you realized that you forgot how to ride a bike?* asked a voice in my head.

I visualized the entire movement sequence in my head, and after an especially deep breath, dipped in on the starboard side. This time I made sure to deliberately push the paddle up against the hull, angled the leading edge to skim over the surface of the water, and kept my eyes fixated on the sweeping blade tip as I hip-snapped right back up

I wonder why it was so difficult the first time, I thought. When the technique is finessed, the kayak roll is almost effortless, and even the paddle becomes irrelevant. I decided that for now at least, I would not try rolling on my weaker side with the Euro blade. Even personal pride has its limits, at least when no one is watching.

I inched my way to the pass slowly and carefully observed the water to assess the conditions. When I got sight of the bridge, I extended my neck as high as I could to catch a glimpse of any tidal rapids. I couldn't see any on the wider south side of the pass, and early in the morning there were also no large vessels navigating through. I decided to take that route.

To my good fortune, the Deception Pass wasn't living up to the hype. I crossed under the bridge about two hours after high tide. There were a few whirlpools spinning and tossing driftwood, but nothing scary. The wind was calm and the air was silent. Only after I checked the GPS later that day did I realize that I had a maximum speed for the day of just over 10 knots. When the wind blows against the current this place would look very different from the benign conditions I had just paddled through.

Reaching the Juan de Fuca Channel was like entering a football pitch through the tunnel of an empty stadium. The landscape widened in all directions and I had a clear view of the horizon with a few mountain summits in the San Juan Islands visible above the low clouds. I could also hear the rippling sound of the current.

I hugged the coast and paddled north up to a town called Anacortes. When I was planning the route I specifically intended to spend a day here to go to a local pharmacy and get a PCR Covid test before crossing into Canada. However, the testing requirement had been lifted just a few days prior. Instead I stopped in town for a more urgent need. I desperately had to find a bathroom, and a clean one.

I spotted an outhouse at the local marina, but to my dismay, it had an electronic combination lock. I sat by the door for a while hoping some local might pass by to use it. My luck was in full swing as someone did after just a few minutes. I gazed out the corner of my eye to try and glance at how the man typed the numbers on the keypad. It took me five tries but I eventually got it: 9-1-3-7. *Yay!* Deception Pass may have had disappointing whirlpools this day, and Captain Vancouver was bummed for not finding a river, but I was feeling extremely satisfied.

With my kayak now much lighter, my attention turned west over the Rosario Strait and San Juan Islands less than five miles away. Given that it was still early afternoon, I thought maybe I should shoot for as far as Orcas Island in the middle of the archipelago, but I wasn't yet feeling fit enough to put in a 30-mile day. Instead, I stopped a little closer at Lopez Island which I could see across the strait and where I had marked a campsite called Spencer Spit. It was a stretch of sand in the shape of a triangle with a wide beach on either side reaching into the sea to a small rocky islet. I have noticed these kinds of formations before but only on open coastlines. They are called tombolos and they form where an island close to shore becomes connected to the mainland as waves immediately behind the island are calmer, and progressively deposit sand until an isthmus is formed. This was the first time, however, that I had ever seen a tombolo form so far away from the main coast. The meandering tides through the Juan de Fuca Strait and its many islands must make some very peculiar currents to carry the sand all the way here.

I approached the spit from the south shore before noticing a few tents immediately to the north, and so continued on passing right in between the tip of the sand spit and the island it was nearly touching.

There weren't just a few tents, but an entire tent city with nearly every patch of grass spoken for. Strangely, there was no one around. It was as if I had arrived in a ghost town.

I climbed out of the kayak, pulled it above the high-water mark on the sand, and walked up the short path through the tall grass to the campsite. The tents were all neatly arranged two or three per plot. Some plots had wooden benches and on top of them were dry bags and coolers which I presumed had food and drinks. On one bench was a plastic sack full of hotdog and hamburger buns ready for a barbecue, and on another was an enormous bag of colored marshmallows with a sack of Hershey's chocolate bars and crackers. Next to the benches was a clean set of chopped logs in a nearby fire pit, and a clothesline stretched between two poles with five wet swimming trunks.

As I walked from plot to plot trying to find an empty spot and pitch my camp for the night, a person walked out from behind one of the tents to meet me. He was a boy who couldn't have been more than 15 and he seemed to walk with a slight limp.

"Hi there, where is everyone?" I asked. He seemed a bit hesitant to speak and answered me in a low voice.

"They're not here."

"I can see that. Where did everyone go? There are enough tents here for 50 people, maybe more.

"Everyone went cycling. They'll be back soon."

"How come you didn't go cycling?" I asked before realizing that the question might offend him. He didn't answer me.

I found a plot that was a little emptier than the others at the edge of the campsite and began to pile my gear there. Whenever the other campers arrived I would ask for forgiveness at my intrusion and beg to keep the small spot I had claimed for the night

Thirty minutes later a few cyclists on mountain bikes began rolling in. They were middle school kids and the eerie quiet that had hung over the campsite like a fog dissipated with the chatter, laughter, and shouting of a dozen little voices. One of the boys grabbed a football and a group formed begging him to throw a pass so one of them could catch it and run down the camp. Eventually I heard an adult telling the rowdy troop that they would be preparing dinner, and that if everyone ate their tomatoes, they'd get an extra smore. I approached the gentleman to introduce myself and explain my situation

"Oh of course, please do camp right here for the night if you'd like," he said, chopping the vegetables. "We are a school group from Utah and every year we take the kids out on a weeklong summer camping trip. This year we decided on the San Juan Islands. There are about a hundred of us in total, half here and half in Odlin Park on the other side of the island. Today we all went mountain biking. Tomorrow we might go kayaking if the weather is decent. It gets a bit crazy but the kids love it. Wow, you're on the beginning of a big trip!

I quickly grabbed the rest of my gear, set up my tent, and started eating dinner which on this day was canned tuna and canned salmon for the main course, followed by canned pineapple for dessert. After changing clothes I laid my used socks and undergarments over the tent to give them a chance to soak up the remaining afternoon sunshine, and then slumped in my folding chair to rest and watch the kids chasing after the football.

At that moment one of the other adults in the group, a man wearing a small silver crucifix around his neck and a scruffy beard down to his chest, approached. He didn't look happy to see me.

"I'm sorry, but you're going to have to move. We booked the whole campsite for the week, and we don't want outsiders.

"Your colleague said I could camp here for the night."

"Well, he is wrong. I'm the one in charge and you have to go. There's an open site for walk-ins next to the pit latrines down the trail. You can go there."

I wasn't going to argue, but there was no way I would sleep next to a smelly toilet. I disassembled the tent, packed up my gear, moved to the beach next to my kayak, and waited until darkness to pitch the tent.

June 3 – Day 5

Nothing soaks your will to start the morning more than waking up in your tent and hearing pouring rain. *Oh, do I have to? Everything is so damp ...*

I delayed getting ready until nature forced my hand to unzip the tent, put on my shoes, and find the outhouse on the trail. The tent city was quiet. If any of the school kids were awake, they must have been huddled in their sleeping bags. I then decided to return the hospitality to yesterday's gentleman in charge. After finishing my business at the outhouse, I left the lid on the toilet seat up to release the noxious aroma from the latrine pit and took with me the only roll of toilet paper there. *Have a good day, sir!*

After dressing in the dry suit, packing the gear, and eating a breakfast of cereal and chocolate bars, I pushed off the flat beach by the camp and paddled northward toward Orcas Island barely visible in the drizzly fog. Finding the way in these hazy conditions through a labyrinth of islands, narrow passages, and currents can be challenging even with a GPS. You can easily end up down the wrong channel only to have to backtrack against the wind and current.

Fortunately, there was an easy cheat code for me to take advantage of. I just had to keep an eye out for the ubiquitous BC Ferries plodding along, and if I had one of them in view at all times, I would know the way. The ferries are enormous barges, hundreds of feet long, carrying thousands of passengers and cars. There are dozens of them sailing the Inside Passage from Seattle to the Alaskan border, connecting coastal towns and villages, some for which the weekly ferry is the only link with the rest of Canada. On a sunny day, the tourists waving at you in your kayak from the five-story deck would have you think it was a cruise liner on its way to Alaska – if it weren't for the rumbling diesel engine drowning out your thoughts. Today, however, there were no tourists braving the rain and wind on the ferry in front of me, and my concerns were fixated on the thundering roar a hundred or so yards behind me.

I hope he sees me, I thought.

The rain stopped and the fog lifted a little and after following the ferry for seven miles, I arrived at a village called Orcas perched on a steep cliff some 50 feet above. There was a narrow beach at the foot of the cliff that had been exposed by the low tide, and a zigzagging dirt path to the street and the ferry dock parking lot. Next to the ferry dock was a general store which to my great delight served chocolate croissants and made-to-order sandwich toasts with ham and cheese. After eight fish meals in the past four days, that was a pleasant lunch which I paired with potato chips and a $4 chocolate almond Magnum ice-cream bar which I felt was very much worth the inflated price.

I sat on a bench outside the general store next to the ferry ramp as a column of vehicles and passengers boarded the ship. After less than a minute, a flock of seagulls landed at my feet giving me eager looks.

"No, not for you!" I told them, but one was already swooping over my head so I offered a few potato chips to get them to leave me alone. That immediately started a seagull riot with the birds kicking, screaming, and jumping over each other until one of the more clever birds nibbled two big pieces and made a getaway with his friends in pursuit.

I continued from Orcas along a narrow passage that flowed out into the main San Juan Channel that cuts through the archipelago from north to south, and after another 12 miles battling head currents, I arrived late afternoon at Roche Harbor on the northern tip of San Juan Island, just a short hop across the Haro Strait from Canada.

The Roche marina was packed with large expensive yachts in almost every slot, and the seaplane terminal had two Twin Otters moored on the dock, with a third taxiing into the harbor having landed over my head. In the back of the harbor next to a pedestrian street was a two-story white wooden building with a general store and a laundromat from which ran a boardwalk overhanging the water; there was also a flowery garden filled with buzzing bumble bees. Behind the garden on a cobbled street was the Hotel De Haro Resort, with a two-story balcony overlooking the marina. It was the only accommodation close enough to the boat ramp where I could walk with my kayak now nestled on its cart with all the gear piled in the cockpit.

The word resort is misleading and deliberately overused nowadays by almost any hotel that can get away with it. It means they will whack you with an additional daily resort fee at the check-in after you've booked the room through an online travel site. What does the resort fee include? Well, nothing.

"Is breakfast included?" I asked the front desk.

"No."

"How about laundry?"

"No."

"Is there a spa?"

"That costs extra."

"Like resort fee extra?"

"On top of the resort fee. We waive the fee once you accumulate enough points or if you book a wedding package."

"Fantastic, I'll remember it for the next time I come on a Twin Otter," I said. "How much is it for the most basic room for one night?"

"We have one remaining room for two hundred and forty-nine dollars plus the twenty-dollar resort fee, plus tax. There's a sink in the room, but the showers are in the communal bathroom on the third floor."

That raised my eyebrows and I gasped deeper than when I was doing the wet cowboy reentry into the kayak after my bad roll at Deception Pass. "And the kayak, where can I put it?"

He looked over my shoulder seeing the boat parked on the patio outside the entrance door. "Eh, you can put it in the back next to the golf carts."

"Okay then. Swipe my card, and please show me again where the showers are. I want to get out of this sweaty dry suit."

I did not tell the front desk, but I planned on washing all my equipment in their communal shower.

June 4 – Day 6

A little over three miles south of Roche Harbor, away from the bustle and popular shops on the boardwalk selling souvenirs to passing tourists, is a little-visited place by the water's edge tucked in between two embracing peninsulas with a narrow opening to the Haro Strait. It's called Garrison Bay. There is not much to greet the few daily hikers who make it here through a winding dirt trail that climbs over a hill overlooking the straits and past a cemetery long ago reclaimed by the surrounding forest. There are a few white painted sheds, a circular hedge garden with a white picket fence, a couple of wooden benches facing the bay where sailing ships hide anchor away from storms in the Juan de Fuca Strait, and a seemingly out of place flagpole flying the Union Jack. The flag makes a little more sense once you learn that this field nestled in the forest by the waterfront is called English Landing, and has a plaque noting that it is "a gift to the San Juan Island National Historical Park from the People of the United Kingdom, in recognition of the long friendship between the United States and the United Kingdom."

Had there been anyone else here in the early morning appreciating the sight of the sailboats anchored in the calm waters, they might have also seen a small black-and-yellow kayak with a paddler sweating in his baggy green dry suit, pulling into the beach, and feeling a little disappointed to have made such a detour to this nearly empty field that the front-desk lady at the Hotel De Haro said was the most important historical site in the San Juan Islands, and perhaps even the entire Pacific Northwest.

It is a quirky story, unknown to most outsiders but common knowledge among locals in San Juan Island, that British Columbia nearly fell into American hands because a few hot-headed men nearly escalated a dispute over a pig and a potato farm into a full-blown war, and gave me some good laughs the more I learned about it.

In 1846 the United States and Britain signed the Oregon Treaty to extend the border west of the Rocky Mountains along the 49th parallel to the Pacific Ocean, and then down the middle of the "channel which separates the continent from Vancouver Island." But which channel that was supposed to be was unclear as both the Rosario and the De Haro Straits fit the wording of the treaty, leaving possession of the San Juan Islands in doubt.

The British proposed drawing the border down through the not-so-navigable San Juan Channel giving themselves San Juan Island and the remainder to the Americans. But the Americans, when offered a fairly reasonable compromise, flatly refused.

Settlers from both countries continued moving to the islands, but tensions ran high. Each government claimed the other was infringing on sovereign territory and confiscated goods and livestock from each other. The future first governor of British Columbia, a certain James Douglas, who was already vexed from having to pack up from Fort Vancouver on the Columbia River after the Americans got the better deal in the Oregon Treaty, was livid on hearing that the Americans were demanding taxes from British subjects on San Juan Island.

The spark that nearly lit the powder keg happened in 1853. The story goes that an American potato farmer named Lyman Cutler was very unskilled and lazy and incapable of building even a rudimentary fence around his plot. His farm was in the middle of a sheep run used by a British settler named Charles Griffin. The two men were not on good terms. On previous occasions Cutler complained to Griffin about his pig trampling through his farm and uprooting his potatoes, to which Griffin replied, "Keep your potatoes out of my pig!"

Pigs and sheep belonging to British settlers on San Juan were free to roam the island and often trampled over American plots. The Americans, in turn, confiscated the wandering animals, demanding compensation from the British who saw such acts as nothing short of kidnapping and extortion by trespassers. Griffin felt he had an axe to grind with the Americans. Sometime before, he had 49 breeding rams confiscated at gunpoint on orders from the Washington Territory Legislature for unpaid taxes.

One day, the story goes, Cutler found Griffin's Yorkshire pig uprooting his potatoes (his plot supposedly only had fences on three sides), and immediately shot the animal in a fit of rage. After cooling off and realizing what he had done, he went to Mr. Griffin's house to offer compensation. Mr. Griffin was livid and emotional, claiming what had happened was akin to murder, and demanded $100, half the yearly wage of an unskilled laborer at the time. Lyman, offended, countered with a take-it-or-leave-it $10, and the two nearly came to blows.

The situation escalated. When Governor Douglas heard of the incident, he ordered Cutler arrested and taken to Victoria. Whether he was or not is unclear, but on learning that the British were rounding up American citizens, U.S. General Harney ordered a military contingent to occupy San Juan Island. Leading the operation was a captain named George Pickett, whose distinguishing trait was questionable intelligence and a lack of wit. He was the same George Pickett who would later lead the infamous Pickett Charge in the Battle of Gettysburg when Confederate soldiers were slaughtered by Union troops, marking a turning point in the American Civil War. General Harney was also hot headed and had a huge ego; it was rumored that he cared little for the plight of American settlers in San Juan, and his real intention was to goad the British into starting a war with the United States. To this end, Captain Pickett was the ideal useful fool for a suicide mission. The General had his fingers crossed that the British would shell the American camp on San Juan, giving him the excuse to start a full-blown war in which he could conquer British Columbia, and be catapulted into a successful run for President.

If those were the intentions, the British nearly swallowed the bait. Governor Douglas opted for gunboat diplomacy and sent the British Navy to San Juan with orders to take back control of San Juan Island. Were it not for the level headedness of British Navy Captain Geoffrey Hornby in command of the fleet, things might have come to blows. Hornby requested a meeting with Pickett who soon realized that the cannons were cannons pointed at his head from all sides. The two agreed to a tenuous peace which led to a compromise that included joint occupation of the island, until final status could be settled.

The reaction in London and Washington to news that they had almost gone to war over a pig had alarm bells ringing. The Americans recalled General Harney, and later during the American Civil War, forced him into retirement as he was thought to be a Southern sympathizer. Governor Douglas continued in his post until 1869 before retiring and returning to England. He mustn't have been happy with the outcome of the Pig War, however. In 1872, Britain and the United States agreed to international arbitration by the King of Prussia, who sided with the Americans, giving them full control of the San Juan Islands.

I felt a little disappointed having made the detour here, given how little there was to see. After securing my kayak above the tide line I walked with some clumsiness in my dry suit around a mostly empty grass field. A plaque written in green ink noted that the English had their encampment established here as part of the joint occupation, and that the American camp was at the southern end of the island. A few information panels scattered around told the broad strokes of the Pig War, and the ruins of a long-gone stone building were the only remnants of anything that might have stood here at the time of the dispute. Even the flagpole with the Union Jack had a note that it was erected in August 1998. Another sign near the trail warned that scanning the ground with metal detectors was prohibited.

The largest building on this field, a white stone shed with two chimneys, served as the visitor center. It was the original building, and several black-and-white photographs showed it had changed little over the years. The building had two rooms; one decorated with British flags and stripes hanging from the walls and ceiling, and the other had mannequins of British officers in uniform alongside a gift shop with books and trinkets.

"I'm surprised there's no statue of the famous pig that was the cause of the war," I said to the park ranger sitting at the kiosk desk, an elderly lady in the typical ranger uniform of a brown shirt, green jacket, and wide-brim hat.

"Oh we do," she said. "We call him Kaiser Will-Ham. He is at the American camp which gets way more visitors. You might be the only one today." She showed me a picture of the statue on her phone of the plump swine with a large potato in its mouth which had me laughing at what Kaiser Willhelm would have thought of it.

"Ah, I guess that makes sense."

Betty had been working at the park for the past 10 years after she retired as a high school history teacher in Seattle. She must have spent most of her days there alone as my presence got her in a talking mood.

"There would almost certainly have been mutinies on both sides if war had broken out," she said, giving me a crash course on the Pig War. "Both armies were made up almost exclusively of Scots and Irish. Mostly conscripts on the British side and recent immigrants on the American. There were folks on opposite sides who were from the same home towns, and even first cousins. After the joint occupation was agreed to, they all got along over the years. The Americans came to the English Camp to celebrate Queen Victoria's birthday, and the British went to the American Camp on the Fourth of July. They even held cricket games together."

"And what was the reaction when the decision was made that the islands were to be American?"

"The British left peacefully back to Victoria. Well, almost peacefully. The officer in charge had a bit of sour grapes and took the original flag pole with him so the Americans had no place to hoist their flag on the date of the handover."

Having seen all there was to see at the English Landing, I set off for Canada. My crossing of the Haro Strait went without incident. The conditions felt so exceedingly calm that whenever I stopped to catch my breath, the silence was so absolute that I thought I could hear people whispering, cars rumbling, and the drumbeats of a musical band far away on the Port Sidney boardwalk.

Even with all this calmness, the flooding tide was busily working the waters beneath me, though I would have never known it from my quiet surroundings in the middle of the strait. Although my compass bearing pointed due west, my relative movement according to the GPS was closer to northwest, forcing me to adopt a slight ferry angle to the southwest or I would miss my intended landing near the Sidney Marina by at least a half mile.

The trance-like silence was eventually ruptured by a loud horn. Rounding the western tip of a small group of islands to my north there appeared a blue-and-red container ship which slowly turned southward heading roughly in my direction. No doubt the ship had left from Port Vancouver on the mainland and I wondered if it was bound to somewhere in Asia or farther afield. The stretch from Neah Bay in Washington on the mouth of the Salish Sea to Vancouver, Canada, is one of the one of the busiest shipping lanes in North America with some 11,000 container ships per year traversing through the Juan de Fuca Strait to and from the ports in Seattle, Tacoma, and Vancouver. On a sunny day like today, these 300-foot-long vessels are easy to see from a fair distance, and even a small kayak like me would have enough time to give them their space. However, they can easily be hidden in dense fog and quietly sneak up on you.

The ship was about 10 minutes to my north, though how far in front and whether I could cross ahead of it were much tougher to tell. The safest thing to do was to aim for the ship's stern rather than wait for it to pass, as I would at least make some headway and crucially, not get caught in any sudden change in the ship's direction.

When it finally crossed one boat length ahead of me, I was surprised by the small size of the wake. On the government cut at the mouth of the Port of Miami between Fisher Island and Miami Beach, the departing container ships and cruise liners displace enough water to momentarily change the direction of the flooding tide which makes for a fun, if a little dangerous, way to paddle out into the ocean without the effort of paddling. But here, the wave was barely noticeable. *He must be light on cargo*, I thought.

I landed at Port Sidney on a beach south of Beacon Avenue and the Sidney Marina. A building just beyond the beach with a bright red sign and the word "INN" seemed to have been placed there especially for me. *I won't have to walk far with the kayak for a place to stay tonight.*

This was my first time crossing an international border by kayak and I was a bit unsure how the immigration process should be carried out. Google Earth noted a customs office station at the marina and I walked there to check. The marina guard advised me to continue all the way to the end of the dock where I would find the customs office shed.

There was no one there, but a sign on the window noted that international arrivals should either call the number written on the window or use the designated red phone beside it. The phone was dead, so the phone number was the only option. After a 15-minute hold, I was put through to an operator.

"What's your boat registration number?" said a male voice.

"I don't have one. I came by kayak."

"Hmm ... Okay, let me put you on hold and check with my supervisor how we handle that."

After another five minutes of silence the same voice spoke again. "Okay, we'll make your registration your last name and the word kayak. What was your port of departure?"

"Roche Harbor, in San Juan."

"Is that Puerto Rico?"

"What? No, it's across the channel in Washington."

"Right, of course," he muttered, a little embarrassed.

We went through a standard list of questions about what I was carrying (no guns, pets, perishable foods, or marijuana) plus the standard Covid questions, and after signing off with a "Welcome to Canada," I was free to go.

June 5 – Day 7

My first afternoon in Canada coincided with the completion of the first 100 miles of the journey, and I thought that this was reason enough for a small personal celebration. After pulling the kayak to the top of the beach and butting it between the sea wall and some driftwood piles where I presumed it would be safe from both the rising tide and prying eyes, I went for a stroll in town looking for something to eat that didn't involve canned tuna or pasta.

Some six blocks down Beacon Avenue I found a local pizzeria and seeing that it had good reviews, ordered a large pepperoni to go. Upon opening the box in my hotel room, I was horrified to discover that Canadians like their salami cut in one-inch-thick slices, and only lay them on the pizza after it's been baked. I tossed out the offending meat and grudgingly ate the now meatless cheese pizza.

I was concerned about leaving my kayak on the beach for the night and relying on only the good character of Canadians to keep it from growing legs and wandering off. Those thoughts led to a strange dream. I was looking at my kayak floating away in the ocean, filled with water, and rolled upside down so that only the stern was above the surface. Somehow, I fetched the kayak out of the water with one hand, lifted it above my head, and poured all the water out in a long cascading waterfall into the sea. The kayak, however, was slippery, slid out of my hands, and now that it was empty, sat high on the water where a breeze blew it away out of reach. My hands swooshed the water toward me hopelessly trying to make it change direction. "Don't go," I said, but the boat could not hear me.

What the dream was supposed to mean I wasn't sure. Was the upside-down kayak a failed endeavor, and the water pouring out my feeble attempt at a remedy only to be thwarted by the breeze? Something fated to be let go of despite my efforts and reluctance. Or perhaps a deep-rooted fear kayakers have of getting marooned? Dreams are hard to interpret and start to fade as soon as you wake up. Perhaps I had already forgotten some important part of the dream.

All said, I was relieved to find the kayak on the beach next to the driftwood piles exactly as I had left it, save for some water in the cockpit from the night's rain. *You certainly didn't think to go it alone, did you? Of course not, you're a kayak.*

North of Port Sidney the coast of Vancouver Island is shielded from the Strait of Georgia (the name changes north of the San Juan Islands from Juan de Fuca to Georgia) by hundreds of small, forested islands scattered over the sea like green glass beads. If Vancouver Island had been a pirate den in the 19th century, then this would have been the perfect staging point to ambush a lumbering treasure ship leaving Port Vancouver loaded with gold panned on the Fraser River. From the mouth of one of the many inlets into the Strait of Georgia, a nimble boat could easily spring on an unsuspecting victim like a trapdoor spider, grab the loot, and quickly fade back into the maze of bays, coves, passages, and tidal currents. Anyone giving chase without a mental map of the place and a good sense of direction in bad weather would be hopelessly lost.

Fortunately for me, I had fair weather with a slight tail breeze and the islands north of Port Sidney quickly rolled past, one after the other. I eventually came to a channel almost two miles wide running parallel to the Georgia Strait with a continuous line of trees on both banks down to the water's edge. The only break in the trees appeared when I came by a narrow inlet leading either to the Georgia Strait in the east or other hidden coves further in. I could deduce my position relative to almost every inlet from the strength of the ebbing tide and the wind. At first there would be a slight tug from the water pulling me forward. This tug got stronger the closer I got to the inlet and eventually I would catch sight of some rough water whipped up by the wind squeezing in from the Georgia Strait 200 yards ahead. This was my cue to increase my cadence on the paddle strokes and make the most of the following current; as soon as I was level with the inlet, the funneling water would change direction and become a drag on my efforts to keep moving forward. This would happen about halfway to the next inlet where the process would repeat again.

On one of these efforts some way between Galiano and Valdes islands, I came across a sleeping seal bobbing just above the water. At first I thought that it was a gray mooring buoy until I saw two tiny, closed eyelids and an ambiguous Mona Lisa smile. I wondered if seals have dreams about chasing fish, doing shenanigans with their friends underwater, or recollecting the times they played a prank on a human when they climbed on the back of their kayak. Whatever the seal might have been dreaming about, it had no idea I was floating two or three arm lengths beside it.

"Good afternoon, sleepy head," I said to the drowsy seal.

Its eyelids cracked a little like someone had just opened the curtains and let the sunshine in, and it took him a moment to realize I was there. But as soon as he did, his black eyes widened, and looking somewhat startled and perhaps a little annoyed, dove off and went to find a more tranquil place to hide.

I camped on the southern end of Valdes Island next to an abandoned barn. The grass was stalky and overgrown, and the collapsed barn roof had rotten away long ago. On the broad side of the barn was scribbled some graffiti reading, "Native American Land, No Trespassing," which reminded me of a story a friend told me about a kayaking trip he'd done in the San Blas Islands in Panama. He could camp on any island he wanted, but come sunset or at the crack of dawn, no matter how small the strip of sand he'd pitched his tent, the owner, an indigenous Kuna man, would show up in his dinghy powered by a single-stroke engine to collect the rent, which had to be haggled down to the penny.

There wasn't a single boat in any direction I could see, and I sincerely hoped no one would show up asking me to pay up, especially considering that I didn't have a single Canadian dollar on me.

But this beach did have a portly master who was having a swim and he gave me a disgruntled bark whenever he poked his head out of the water to look at me. The California sea lion weighed a good 500 pounds or more, and his puffy face and grumpy demeanor reminded me of a bouncer at a nightclub.

"I don't think you`ll want the rent paid with canned spaghetti and meatballs," I said looking straight at him.

I must have put on a brave face as he took a dive and reappeared a little farther along the shoreline with another grunt as if to say, "But it's my beach."

"The beach is big enough for the both of us," I yelled out to him. "You won't even be seeing me once I'm in the tent and if you're sleeping tomorrow morning, I'll tiptoe around you and try not to wake you up."

June 6 – Day 8

The sea lion snored outside my tent but that didn't wake me that night. Nothing could have. The previous day I had covered 32 miles against both wind and current and I woke up feeling both exhausted and sore on the shoulders. The remaining 18 miles to Nanaimo would be done at a more leisurely pace.

After clearing the northwest shore of Gabriola Island, I got my first view across the whole width of the Georgia Strait to Vancouver on the mainland some 30 miles distant. The continuous wall of mountains silhouetted by the sun made them look like small hills, and the opposite shore did not seem so far. Only after catching sight of one of the giant 300-foot-long, 10-story-tall container ships - and seeing only the bridge deck and bow with the rest below the horizon - was it clear how far away the mountains were. The skyscrapers in downtown Vancouver, farther still, didn't even poke above the curvature of the Earth.

I paddled through the mouth of the harbor dodging around several fishing boats and two large ferries, one arriving from Vancouver which I had my eyes fixated on, and another that had just left the Gabriola Island Terminal, hidden behind a headland to which I was completely oblivious to until it blared its horn at me.

I landed at a park immediately north of the harbor on the steps of a wide concrete boardwalk where teenage kids were rolling on their skateboards and electric scooters around the statue of a pirate with a feathery hat and a blunt sword. A certain Frank Ney, who was mayor of Nanaimo for many years, and had he not died in 1992 at the age of 74, would have certainly enjoyed a cameo appearance as one of Captain Barbossa's mutineers in *Pirates of the Caribbean*.

[ABOVE] *A cautious approach to Deception Pass. Its ominous reputation should not be underestimated.* [BELOW] *Hotel De Haro at Roche Harbor, San Juan Island.*

Taking stock of the expedition gear at the Indigo Hotel the day before departure.

[ABOVE] The Author, washing his equipment in the common showers at the Hotel De Haro.
[BELOW] Backing up the kayak in to the hotel ballroom, Best Western Hotel, Nanaimo.

A break from the portage at the Nanaimo Provincial Courthouse

[TOP LEFT] A view of Lund Harbor at low tide. [TOP RIGHT] If you are ever in doubt about the way forward, you can follow one of the many BC ferries to find the way. [BELOW] Arrival in Canada.

[ABOVE] A Calm morning leaving Nanaimo Harbor...
...followed by rough weather just three hours later [BELOW]

Once in town I had an important thing to do: change my U.S. loot into Canadian money. Any settlement north from Nanaimo would be remote and possibly not have the means to accept credit cards. Unfortunately, I discovered that none of the Canadian banks would exchange your money if you weren't one of their clients, - a huge inconvenience for tourists from south of the border for no apparent benefit to anyone.

I searched for an exchange house on Google and found the closest one was a Quickie Mart two miles away in a strip mall. I called ahead to make sure they did indeed exchange money and was assured that they did.

"What's your exchange rate?" I asked.

An East Indian voice told me that it was 1.22 Canadian for one U.S. dollar, plus a fee of $4 Canadian.

The official exchange rate was 1.33 Canadian. "Okay, I'll be there in an hour."

I exchanged about $250 to which the teller at the register gave me several $20 Canadian bills and a few fives that I particularly liked. Their backside showed the robotic arm (Canadarm2) in the International Space Station stamped with Canada's name and a maple leaf.

"You want loonies or toonies?"

"What are those? Looney Tunes? Like Bugs Bunny?"

"No, loonie is the one-dollar coin. It has the loon bird on the backside so we call it the loonie. The two-dollar coin has the polar bear, so I guess we should call it bearnie, but since it's worth two bucks we call it the toonie to rhyme with loonie. Yes, confusing I know, took me a while to get used to it too. Live here long enough and you'll start talking in Canadianisms."

"Ah got it. So, what's a good place to eat here?"

"You want a Canadian experience? Check out the Tim Hortons across the street."

I've seen at least a few of these chain restaurants the previous three times I've been to Canada (there's definitely one in every airport). They are ubiquitous with one on every corner, like Starbucks in the United States. In fact, it has been described to me as the Starbucks of Canada. And yet, I had never been to one. I Googled the name to read up about the restaurant chain.

Tim Horton was a real person; a man who played in the Canadian Hockey League from 1950 up until the 1970s, mostly for the Toronto Maple Leafs. Another search for his name turned up hundreds of vintage photographs of a handsome young man with short spiky hair, chiseled jaw, and comically broad shoulders. His expression while in uniform isn't at all intimidating for a hockey player; he looks like a good mama's boy. However, a short biography described him as a formidable defenseman/enforcer. In hockey, such a role is to prevent the opposing team from scoring, and also doling out a large can of whoop-ass on the adversary players if they try some underhanded tactics against the goalie, (apparently a little violence isn't against the rules in hockey). Yet even in this role, Tim Horton was a legend. He was nicknamed the Superman on account of his baby-face good looks combined with superhuman strength (he was also extremely nearsighted and wore thick-framed glasses when off the rink which made him look like Clark Kent). The feats of strength credited to him are comical and yet borderline plausible. He could lift a 40-gallon beer drum over his head, toss a railway tie like he was playing fetch with a dog, and push over cement barricades to drive his car across a blocked intersection. He was feared and respected; a glance from his eyes was all that was needed to keep the game a clean affair. In the United States, there's a saying from President Theodore Roosevelt, "You can afford to speak softly if you carry a big stick." If you were Tim Horton and you carried a hockey stick, you could be extra soft with your speech.

The restaurant franchise came about because Tim Horton, despite his toughness, had a sweet tooth and a culinary talent for baking muffins.

"So, which one of these is Mr. Horton's favorite?" I asked the lady at the cash register, pointing to the different flavored muffins on display.

"Oh, he definitely was a fan of the carrot muffin with cream cheese filling. He invented it," she answered with a laugh, noting that she was in on the joke.

I got a box so I could try one of each. One chocolate, one raspberry, one carrot, one fruit explosion, and one blueberry. "Since there are only five flavors, but the box fits six, I'll get a second carrot muffin to honor Mr. Horton."

"I'm sure he would be very pleased if he were still alive today."

"He's dead?" I said surprised.

"He died in 1974 in a car crash. Kind of a weird story. He was flying down a highway when he flipped over on his own. Nobody knows what he was up to."

After arriving back in the hotel I decided to eat one of the muffins before bed. If I had a hat with me, I would have taken it off to Mr. Horton's baking skills. The carrot muffin was delicious.

June 7 – Day 9

There wasn't a cloud in the sky all morning and as I looked toward the southeast, down the middle of the Georgia Strait, I could just about make out the conical snow-capped top of Mount Baker in Washington nearly 100 miles away.

To leave Nanaimo I paddled through a narrow channel north of the main harbor sandwiched against a long mooring line of yachts along the Trans-Canada Highway and an island with a dense and dark forest which in the morning, cast a pleasant shade over the clear water. I made a stop on a ledge as this would be the last opportunity for several hours to run the yellow faucet, but was rudely interrupted by a family of raccoons.

"Shoo! Go away!" I said. And they did in fact keep their distance, unlike their cousins in Florida who aren't shy about stealing from your hatches.

A little further on the water I crossed paths with a couple paddling a double kayak into the harbor.

"Did you see the bear on your side of the island?" the man asked.

"No. Only a bunch of racoons. There's a bear in the town?" I said surprised.

"Yeah, he lives on the island, though sometimes he swims to the mainland and wanders around the marina looking for open trash cans."

I wondered if he was pulling my leg. The island didn't seem big enough to support a bear on a diet of squirrels and raccoons, unless he was also adept at stealing picnic baskets from unsuspecting tourists. Nonetheless, if a bear did live on the island, I was glad he didn't catch me with my pants down.

I continued up the coast for about 10 miles and then veered into the Georgia Strait for a crossing to Texada Island. About a third of the way I stopped at a small group of rocky islets called the Ballenas Islands which had a lighthouse and a few scattered dwellings connected by a narrow road. I was somewhat puzzled that these islands were not shown on my GPS map, and the aerial view had a light-blue pixelated smudge in the location where the islets should have been. When I approached the mooring dock where two seals were lazily stretched out sunbathing, I noticed someone driving down the road to the dock on a golf cart.

When he reached the dock I saw that he wore military fatigues. I waved at him and he waved back, but when I gestured that I would like to step out on the dock, he was quick to stop me.

"So sorry but no visitors. This is a military base."

"Can I just stand up out of the kayak for a little bit? I need to pee really badly."

"Be quick about it. When you leave, go by the west side. The east is the hazardous area."

A Google search for "Strait of Georgia military base" turned up several articles about something called the "Whiskey Golf Hazardous Area" that serves as a torpedo firing range for the American military. Here it does more than 300 tests every year from land, submarine, ship, and even from airplanes. When a test is about to happen, the area is cordoned off; the torpedo is then launched and runs on the water surface before dropping to the sea bottom where it gets retrieved by a diving crew nearly 1,000 feet down. Disruptions to boat traffic are common and make for a running complaint at the provincial government in Victoria. The federal government of Canada promised to pay British Columbia $125 million for the inconvenience, but so far has paid them less than $2 million since the 1960s.

I doubted that a torpedo would ever be a problem for a kayak. Even fully loaded for a multiday journey and low on the water, my draft could hardly be more than a few inches, and I would likely mistake the whizzing underwater missile for a dolphin swimming under the hull.

June 8 – Day 10

I had paddled about a quarter of the way along the western side of Texada Island before finding a reasonable spot at a clearing in the forest, next to the water, to pitch the tent for the night. Yesterday's bear story had me looking over my shoulder from time to time and I decided to hang all my food in a bag over a tree limb eight feet off the ground. It would probably not have been high enough to dissuade a hungry and persistent bear, but it was the best I could find. All my food was either canned or factory sealed, and I made sure that the trash salmon cans from dinner were thoroughly washed until I felt confident that even a keen-nosed bear wouldn't catch a whiff of anything. Even so, the woods just immediately above the beach were dark and foreboding, and my ears kept watch all night wondering if the shrilly wind on the branches and the shivering grass outside the tent were the tippy-toes of an uninvited guest.

The next morning, however, there was no evidence of anyone or anything. The food bag hung from the tree branch just as I had left it. There were other creatures though, and lots and lots of them: famished mosquitos for whom my emergence from the tent was the breakfast bell they had been waiting for.

I hadn't thought to bring any repellent, and as far as I knew, mosquitos in British Columbia were no worse than anywhere else and certainly nothing close to a summer evening in the dead still air of the Florida Everglades. The morning became a reminder that although bears and cougars may be the biggest predators in the forest, the mosquitos get most of the meat; and they have no qualms or shame in biting your most vulnerable parts when you are forced to tend the garden.

The morning brought a strong and constant breeze from the southeast that persisted along the whole length of Texada Island. I decided to use the sail for the first time on the journey. As soon as I was settled on the water, I pulled the hoist line lifting the mast and the wind immediately filled my sail and had me gliding from swell to swell. I only needed occasional stern braces to keep the kayak in the right direction at a steady seven miles per hour.

At the northern end of the island near Gilles Bay I caught up to another kayaker who must have camped a few miles ahead of me the previous night. I was surprised how difficult it was to see his boat, even when I was only 100 feet behind him. Whenever he slipped into a wave trough he disappeared and only became visible again when both of us were on separate wave crests.

"Lovely day, is it not?" he shouted.

"It sure is! Good luck. Where are you headed?"

He responded with something but the wind muffled his words and moving at least twice his speed I was soon out of hearing range.

The exhilarating downwind run propelled me for 38 miles to a small village on the BC mainland called Lund where I had marked in my GPS that it had both a boat ramp and a lovely marina hotel and restaurant overlooking the Georgia Strait and Vancouver Island. It seemed almost too convenient and I was looking forward to spending an evening sitting on a bench in a green field with legs stretched and resting from having spent a full day in the crampedness of the kayak. Here I envisioned watching the ruby-red, ginger-orange, and wine-violet sunset over Vancouver Island in the distance, and deciding what shapes the passing clouds were making.

Alas, those thoughts were a little premature. I pulled my kayak to the hotel entrance and found it locked. A waitress at the pub next door informed me that it had been closed for the past two years because of Covid, and the only campsite was a 30-drive away.

"Drive? I'm certainly not walking a distance that would take a car half an hour."

"You know, what you should do is camp in the marina parking lot. Pitch your tent after dark and be gone before sunrise. It's a little busy now, but this place turns into a ghost town at night. You can also use the marina rest area; there's a clean bathroom there with a shower. The combination for the lock is #3-6-9#. Yes, with the two hashtags. Don't tell anyone I said that though."

I enthusiastically thanked the waitress, ordered a lime soda with a smoked salmon sandwich, and gave her a 100 percent tip. If ever I can claim to have received exceptional service, this was the occasion. I sat on my now favorite bench overlooking the water and for the next hour, just appreciated the moment. It was a very lovely sunset and I thought the clouds had shapes of sea lions, dolphins, and sailboats.

June 9 – Day 11

I sat on the bench watching the last twilight shades of red and purple give way to stars, waiting for the last vehicles in the parking lot to finally head off, when suddenly a thought sprouted in my head.

Why don't I sleep in the marina bathroom instead of pitching the tent?

It was a spotless public bathroom, so much so that I would have been happy to pick up a slice of smoked salmon off the floor and put it back into my dinner sandwich. And there was plenty of room to lay out the mattress. *A hobo's dream*, I thought. I would also have less gear to pack up in the morning so I'd be gone before anyone noticed. I made myself comfortable and slept the whole night.

Perhaps I slept a little too well. I snoozed right through my alarm clock set for 4:30 a.m. and was only jolted awake when a car rolled into the gravel parking a half hour later. I frantically started to pack up before someone decided to use the restroom and found a naked bearded vagrant when they flipped on the light switch.

I slowly cracked open the bathroom door and peeked outside to make sure no one caught me in the act. When I saw no one, I quickly shoved the gear out the door and snuck out unseen. *Success*, I thought. Well, almost. Before launching I went back for one last use of the restroom.

"Eh, how'd you get the combination for the commercial fishing bathroom?" said a man wearing green fishing bibs as he ambushed me on the way out.

"Well, hmm ..."

"Did Dan give it to you?"

"Yes! Dan gave it to me," I answered without even thinking.

"Oh, God damn Dead-Beat Dan. I'll have a word with him when he's in and crack the whip on his ass. I told him not to give away the combination. Word gets out and in a day everyone as far as Powell River finds out. We changed it just last week."

I was happy the fisherman said he would be cracking the whip on "his ass" rather than "hers." Dan was obviously some random guy and not the waitress who'd been so kind to me. Hopefully, Dan's ass went unscathed.

I put the boat on the water and was anxious to paddle out quickly before I had to answer any more questions.

The crossing to Quadra Island 25 miles to the west was done in two hops. The first, a five-and-a-half-mile open water crossing to Hernando Island, followed by 10 miles of mostly protected bay and passages between the Hernando, Cortes, and Marina islands, before ending with a seven-and-a-half-mile crossing to Heriot Bay on Quadra Island. Had the hotel been open I would have taken a rest day in Lund. The previous night I had checked the forecast on my phone. It showed a powerful low-pressure system barreling in from the Pacific Ocean that would be slamming into Vancouver Island sometime in the early afternoon with 25 to 30 mile-per-hour winds and at least an inch of rain. The choice was to go, or have an awkward meeting with Dead-Beat Dan. I chose to go.

The crosswinds were already blowing hard on the Hernando crossing with every other wave washing over the boat deck. Strangely, the wind and the waves misaligned, with the wind at a 45-degree reach, and the swells hitting me almost at the perpendicular, which made it very difficult to hold my heading without constant stroke adjustments.

On the back of Hernando Island I had a chance to catch my breath and then turned north into the passage between Cortes and Marina islands where for about two miles, I had the wind on my back, but the rain intensified and visibility became very poor. My prescription goggles made visibility especially difficult with their constant fogging and I spent more time wiping them than paddling until I gave up on them entirely. In the gray haze they hardly made a difference.

In the blurriness and dealing with the nuisance of the goggles I must have become a bit distracted. I noticed something brown directly in front of me which I thought was the back of a huge sea lion before realizing I was deadheaded for a boulder with breaking shoals. I leaned hard to the right and narrowly missed it, only to find that the boulder was actually two rocks and then I had to brace in the opposite direction with my body almost in the water. I felt a gentle scrape of the rudder against the rock and held my breath expecting something worse which fortunately never came. Those were close calls. Two exposed boulders in the middle of dark deep water was a prank of nature which I was not at all amused by.

I considered camping on the sand spit on the north of the island and then attempting the crossing to Heriot Bay. There had been enough drama already and the weather would be much better the next day. However, at that moment, the rain eased, there was a hint that sunshine might break through the clouds, and I felt that there was a window to make the crossing. I could even see Quadra Island across the channel.

Unfortunately, that was a fleeting tease and halfway in, the rain came down again in curtains, and Quadra Island was quickly shrouded from view. The only thing to guide me roughly in the right direction was the Cortes-to-Quadra ferry sailing in front of me and which I knew was headed the same way. Once I was close enough to see the shoreline again, I noticed the ferry on its way back to Cortes Island, but it had taken a more southerly route. It was deadheaded right for me.

"Really? You have the whole channel and you want to come this way?" I quipped at the ferry.

I made a sharp tack to the north and downwind to jet out of its way as fast as I could. At some point the ferry bow wave must have merged with the prevailing swell as it caught up to me and I was sideswiped into a bongo slide and my paddle plowed into the foam pile. The wave vanished as quickly as it appeared.

The weather only released its grip on me after I cleared the long skinny sandbank called Rebecca Spit that shelters Heriot Bay from the rest of the Georgia Strait. Suddenly there was an eerie sense of quiet, the towering pines along the spit seemed not to care about the wind, and the line of drift logs along the shore might as well have been made of stone. I wondered how the spit got its name and who the famous Rebecca might be – perhaps some protectress of mariners seeking to escape the rough seas.

I landed on the shore directly in front of the Heriot Bay Inn, whose placard was visible from the kayak while I navigated through the harbor. Straddling a craggy bay at the end of a pebble beach, the rambling white clapboard inn, backed by a pine forest, was the only hotel in town.

After carrying my kayak and gear above the high tide mark, I walked into the hotel reception still wearing my damp dry suit with water dripping off my wide-brim hat from the horrible weather just outside the door.

"Please tell me you have a room for tonight," I whimpered to the front-desk lady.

"Goodness me! Where did you arrive from? Were you swimming in your clothes or something? You're soaking the carpet."

"Oh. I'm sorry. I just paddled in from Lund across the channel."

"Have you? Anyone else crazy enough to be out in a whiteout? I can barely see the pier. Well, let's see, yes, we do have one room left, but it is right above the pub, and tonight is karaoke night. You'll have to pardon the noise; they stay kind of loud until about 2 a.m. The singing on most nights is ... how to describe it ... amateurish, but after everyone's had a pint or two it doesn't sound so bad, eh."

"It will be just fine," I said, relieved.

She handed me the room key. "If you need to call the front desk, my name is Rebecca. I am the one staffing the night-shift tonight until 10 p.m."

"Oh, like the –"

"No, the spit is not named after me, and no I do not spit there either. Every guest asks me that and it drives me nuts."

BRITISH COLUMBIA
VANCOUVER ISLAND
CAPE MUDGE
HERIOT BAY
CAMBPELL RIVER
SONORA ISLAND
QUADRA ISLAND
OKISOLLO RAPIDS
HOLE IN THE WALL
SURGE NARROWS
RIPPLE ROCK
EAST THURLOW ISLAND
SEYMOUR NARROWS
CHATHAM POINT
WEST THURLOW Is.
HARDWICKE ISLAND
SAYWARD
CHATHAM POINT
NAKA CREEK
GILFORD ISLAND
CRAFORD ISLAND
JOHNSTONE STRAIT
HARBLEDOWN Is.
BLACKNEY PASSAGE
BIG CEDAR
HANDSON Is.
TELEGRAPH COVE
MALCOLM ISLAND
ALERT BAY
NIMPKISH LAKE
SOINTULA
PORT MCNEILL
PULTENEY POINT
QUEEN CHARLOTTE STRAIT
ALICE LAKE
VICTORIA LAKE
FORT RUPERT
PORT HARDY
N

PART 3 - NAVIGATING THE JOHNSTONE STRAIT

June 10 – Day 12

If the karaoke bar at the Heriot Bay Inn was packed with drunken Mounties and lumberjacks whaling away to Celine Dion songs I probably wouldn't have noticed as I had the heaviest sleep I can remember. At one point I thought someone might have been trying very hard to do a Chad Kroeger impression for a Nickelback song, but that could also have been the creaking floorboards from someone dragging luggage down the hallway, or water flowing down the pipes. The Heriot Bay Inn was an old building, built in 1912 after the original logging camp from 1895 had burned down in a fire, and the walls were paper thin.

In eight days of paddling I covered 250 miles. *Not bad for someone for whom lifting weights means loading the printer with paper*, I thought. I inspected my naked self in the bathroom mirror and tried to flex my arms to see if I noticed any difference. *You need to do sit-ups to get rid of that belly*, I heard my mother's voice in my head. Perhaps paddling another 750 miles would do the trick. For today, however, I decided to take the day off.

Two days prior, a fellow kayaker spending the summer in Heriot Bay contacted me through Facebook and invited me for a drink. We met at a café next to the local supermarket and after priming with a morning coffee, he told me his story. Steve had come to Heriot Bay to work on his father-in-law's property. He'd been at it from dawn to dusk seven days a week for the past month and only now had found an excuse to sneak out for a break.

"Man, I'll tell you, it's heavy work. I cut the grass, nail the floorboards, and paint the walls. If the weather permits, this week I'll start replacing the roof. I'm kind of an indentured servant to my father-in-law," he said laughing.

"Well, I hope she was worth it all," I said.

"Oh, she is definitely worth it. Though she doesn't always act like it," he said laughing. "Do you have any tips, tricks, and advice that you've picked up in your kayaking adventures around Florida and Puerto Rico? I would love to know."

I wasn't sure how to respond. I had never considered myself an authority on the sport. Sure, I have paddled a lot of miles, but paddling around Florida wasn't very technically challenging; along the Atlantic there's an intracoastal waterway where you can hide during a storm, and unless there's a hurricane in the Gulf of Mexico, it's fairly calm. In Puerto Rico there were big swells and breakers along the north coast, but I was careful where I landed, kept an eye on the weather, and did my utmost to avoid any angry confrontations with the sea. Pretty basic common-sense kind of things.

"You know, one thing I like to do with my bilge pump and water bottles is to wrap them in waterproof Velcro," I said, struggling to come up with something smart to say, "I put the furry part around the bottles and the pump, and the rough part I stick it on the floor of the cockpit. You do away with having to fiberglass in eye plates for bungies. It'll last for a few months before you have to redo it, but I can roll with my kayak, even do a wet exit, and everything stays sort of in place."

"That's brilliant. You'll have to show me."

"Oh, you know something else I've learned? Don't get an electric bilge pump. They are so much more trouble than they're worth. It's hard to install them properly, and sooner or later, the saltwater finds its way to the copper wire and burns the motor. You're better off having a strong roll. If the conditions are ever so bad that you have to exit the kayak and swim, chances are you're not going to get back in before the next wave gets you."

In the afternoon I met a couple that had been paddling the Johnstone Strait for a week and had just arrived at the Heriot Bay Inn at almost the same put-out point I had landed at the previous day. I struck up a conversation with George and Marla who were very excited to tell me about their adventure over dinner.

"We saw one black bear on Sonora Island just north of Quadra," Marla said. "He was right on the campsite we were planning to stay at looking very focused on something, and ran into the bush when we landed. I swear he kept eyeing us for a good ten minutes. George said he was fine camping there, but I didn't want to find out if the bear was planning to come back for dessert. We kept going to Francisco Island; that's a neat place to camp, you're right on the mouth of the Hole in the Wall and you see these huge dancing whirlpools from the current. Speaking of that, do you have a good way to know the exact tide times in this area? You're going to need it."

"Well, I usually look at the tide table on my phone for the closest station. There is one here on Heriot Bay," I answered.

Marla gazed at me with a look that spoke of disapproval.

"Yeah, that probably works on the west coast of Vancouver where the change isn't as dramatic, but in the sounds, that's going to get you into trouble. The turn of the tide doesn't always coincide with the high or the low tide. Yes, it might be the celestial high or low tide, but the narrow passageways between the sounds can mess up the timing by a lot. You might get to one passage thinking it's slack tide, and you'll be waiting there for an additional hour before the current will let you through, or worse, your time to cross through has already passed."

She reached into her purse and pulled out a few sheets of letter-sized paper that she had carefully folded into two ziplock bags.

"Let me give you something that will be useful to you," she whispered.

I watched intrigued as she unfolded the paper, like a treasure map, that had a long spreadsheet table.

"These are the current tables for all the passageways in the Discovery Islands. It gives you the time and speed of the peak flood and ebb currents, and the time of the turns. There are only a few passageways for which there is raw data on the Canadian Hydrological Services website. So for a few of the others like the Hole in the Wall, the Surge Narrows, and Okissolo, I extrapolated the times and speeds based on the distances from the closest gauges. It's worked remarkably well for us during the past week. The tables go until June 15 which will cover you. You see here you have the times for the Surge Narrows where you'll be going through."

"Thank you so much for this. I wish there was a way I could repay this kind of generosity."

"No worries. You can put me in the story of your great adventure if you want," she said with a smile. "Keep me posted on your progress. Not many people have circumnavigated Vancouver Island. It's a small group you'll be joining. But be careful on the west coast. It can get very rough on the ocean side. I certainly wouldn't paddle there by myself. Oh, and by the way, if you decide to go to Sonora Island, don't bother stopping at the Sonora Resort. The place has nothing but rich snobbish people paying a thousand dollars a night or more. The staff wouldn't even let us land to stretch our legs."

June 11 – Day 13

I've noticed that there are a lot of place names in the Pacific Northwest that have Spanish origins. Cortes Island, Juan de Fuca Strait, San Juan Islands, Laredo Sound, Port Angeles, and many others. I asked Rebecca, the front-desk lady at the Heriot Bay Inn, if she knew why.

"Well, the Spanish were the first Europeans to explore the Pacific Northwest, in the 1700s if I remember my high school history class, or maybe it was the Russians sailing down from the coast of Alaska. There's even some legends that say it might've even been the Chinese who first saw the coast a thousand years before after their ship was blown off course in a storm and they called the island Fousang. So yes, everybody who came here exploring was keen to put their name on something, that's what everyone did back then. The British arrived when Captain Cook sailed through on his voyages around the Pacific. The British and the Spanish feuded a lot over who was going to own what, so they put their names on the same bays and islands. Sometimes the Spanish name stuck, but most times it was the British version. In fact, Quadra Island you might've guessed is named after a Spanish sea captain. His full name was Juan Francisco de la Bodega y Quadra, quite the mouthful. He was a friend of George Vancouver, yes, that Vancouver."

"Oh really, and how do you know that?"

"Well, funny, no one's asked me that. I actually learned it from a statue on the harbor in Victoria next to the Parliament Building. It says they had a meeting in Nootka Island on the west coast, in fact, you might pass by there on your way around the island. The two were fond of each other even though neither spoke the other's language. Their translators must have been very polite because usually in those days it was all cannon talk, and they agreed to name the whole island after themselves, though since Quadra was older, his name went first and it was called Quadra and Vancouver's Island

"But then of course, once the British got control, the name became Vancouver and Quadra Island, because your guy's name goes first, and because that was too long it became just Vancouver Island.

"Haha, I guess that Vancouver must have spoken from the grave, 'Hey, he was a friend of mine. Can he get a consolation prize?' And so that's how he got Quadra Island named after him?"

"Ha, that would make sense, eh. He didn't come out too badly. There's a Bodega Point, a Francisco Island, and Sonora Island is named after one of his ships. Juan de Fuca, however, is a different Juan but I don't know which one, there are too many different Juans."

We then talked about what I should buy at the supermarket. "You like Chef Boyardee? Yeah, they have that there, but it's so gross! Who eats pasta from a can? Then again, you're paddling around the whole island, I guess you know what works better than me.

I asked if I could stay one more day. She checked the availability and said the room was free for one more night, but I had to be gone the next day because a group of Chinese tourists on a tour had the entire hotel booked.

With the opportunity to stay another day, I looked at my map to get a sense of the journey ahead. North of Heriot Bay the tides have a strange quirk. When Captain Vancouver and his expedition reached the end of Georgia Strait they entered another maze of islands, passages, and dead ends up sounds that sometimes stretched for more than 50 miles in their search of the fabled Northwest Passage into the interior. It was with one of the advanced survey teams led by a certain James Johnstone that something peculiar was noticed. The flooding tide rising through a narrow channel came from the north instead of the south. That could only mean one thing: the vast landmass to their west which they presumed rimmed the shore of a great seaway across North America was in fact an island. Johnstone concluded that if he waited for the tide to ebb and then sailed down this narrow channel he should eventually find open water, which he did, emerging at what is now Queen Charlotte Sound which separates the north of Vancouver Island. The channel he discovered bears his name and is now called the Johnstone Strait. However, he must have had a very rough time sailing back to meet with the rest of the Vancouver fleet in the Strait of Georgia, if he came back the way he went against the tide and rough winds.

There are two main pathways north from Heriot Bay and into the Johnstone Strait. The main path runs between Quadra and Vancouver islands and is called the Discovery Passage (named after the *Discovery* which was the ship captained by George Vancouver), and it begins on the southern tip of Quadra Island in a place called Cape Mudge where a lighthouse marks the entrance to the passage. From there Quadra Island progressively hugs ever closer to Vancouver Island, and the channel becomes ever narrower over a stretch of about 13 miles. Here the water speeds up because of the venturi effect (there is a device called a Venturi Meter which calculates flow by measuring the drop in pressure in the pipe before and after an induced constriction). Water is an incompressible liquid so the only way to pass the same amount of fluid through an increasingly narrower opening is for the flow velocity to increase. The throat, and the most dreaded part of the passage, is called the Seymour Narrows. It lies just north of Campbell River and my kayaking friend Lee from Victoria told me harrowing stories about the place.

"At peak flow the Seymour Narrows are like a horizontal waterfall. You'll see white foam everywhere, the ferries get tossed around like rubber ducks in a bathtub, and the whirlpools swirl like galaxies. Save for the most brave or foolish, everybody wanting to go across waits for the slack tide. I think that something like a hundred ships have sunk there over the years until the Ripple Rock Explosion.

"What was that?" I asked.

"Oh, it's a famous event in Canadian history. Ripple Rock was a huge underwater rock right on the mouth of the Seymour Narrows; it made the biggest standing wave in the world. When the current was ebbing, half the channel was a mini Niagara Falls, and when it was flooding it made a gigantic upwell. You could only sail up or down the passage at slack tide. Boat traffic piled up on either side waiting for the brief ten-minute window twice a day."

"And so they blew up the rock?

"Yes, that's right. In 1958 the Canadian government decided they would get rid of the rock by blowing it up. They had to drill an underwater tunnel to get under the dome of Ripple Rock, filled it up with a ton of explosives like the Coyote and the Roadrunner, and then blew it all up. You ask anyone here in BC and they'll tell you it's the biggest non-nuclear explosion in the world, ever.

"So, can you paddle through there now?

"I've heard of people paddling through but it's really treacherous. If you have a big powerful motorboat you can try to skip the wait and punch through the current. Otherwise you have to wait for the slack tide at Maud Island on the mouth of the narrows with everybody else who are going to want to go at the same time as you. I certainly wouldn't do it on a kayak loaded with gear.

I ruled out paddling through the Seymour Narrows.

The other path north is through the Surge Narrows and the Okisollo Channel along the opposite side of Quadra Island. It's a finger of the Johnstone Strait before it turns into the Discovery Passage. The current there is not quite as ominous but easily flows above 10 knots with foaming overfalls, rapids, and whirlpools which any kayaker will dread to be caught in.

At the throat of the Narrows there are three rock islets poking above the water. They are Goepel, Sturt, and Peck. Peck Island is a special place. Not only does it have a submerged shelf that creates a perfect silky smooth standing wave where kayak surfers can glide on almost indefinitely, the island is also called Proposal Rock for being the place where Lee asked his long-time girlfriend to marry him.

I set off in the late morning for a day paddle to the Surge Narrows to get a feel for how my 18-foot kayak would perform in the twisted and shifting tidal currents.

Almost immediately after taking off, I felt an incredible sense of lightness and agility just from not having some 30 pounds of gear in the hulls. I could accelerate on a whim and turn on a dime as though I had flipped a button to turn on sport mode.

I quickly covered the 10 miles to the narrows with a brief stop at Discovery Islands Lodge half hidden by the pine forest. Lee had tipped me that the third-floor balcony of the lodge would be the last place to get a phone signal until the Queen Charlotte Sound some 80 miles farther.

There was a couple at the lodge who, to my astonishment, were happily swimming next to the boat pier wearing nothing more than a bikini and Speedos. I removed my neoprene gloves, and after dipping my hands, was surprised by the mellowness of the water. *What kind of witchcraft is going on here? Has everyone decided to drain the bathwater into the ocean at the same time?* I did not know it at the time but I had stumbled on a quirk of BC geography that produces the warmest water in the Pacific coast north of Mexico. From Desolation Sound near Cortes Island to the eastern shore of Quadra Island lies the tidal convergence from the north and south of Vancouver Island, which is too far inland for the water to normally mix with the ocean. In the long days of summer, the sea surface basks in the sun and the water temperature peaks at 75°F. Perhaps not quite a Miami kind of water, but had the sun been out, and perhaps I a little braver, I might have dipped in for a swim.

I paddled the remaining mile to the Surge Narrows by hopping between eddies formed by the flooding tide's embrace of several small rocky islets until I reached a sheltered ledge on Proposal Rock, at the mouth of the Narrows.

This was as far as I could go against the tide; beyond that was the standing wave formed by a three-foot drop from the calm flat water above, teasingly close, but which would've taken herculean levels of strength to paddle through the 10-knot current to get to. A hydraulic engineer would have been delighted to observe this natural hydraulic jump and note how the flow looked exactly like a faucet splashing a flat disk of water over a sink or the thin slick smoke rising from a burning log that suddenly scrambles into confusing curls. For a moment, the water accelerating down the ledge became knee deep and smooth as silk before rising into a ringing white foam pile a few feet downstream.

I had been here once before with Lee on a five-day course to practice kayak surfing on the standing wave. Lee spent a good deal of time explaining the technique to launch the kayak onto the sweet spot of the wave and the paddle strokes needed to maintain control. His demonstration had made it look much easier than it was, and at the time I was quickly overpowered and capsized.

Today, however, there'd be no one to ask for help if something happened, but also no one to be embarrassed in front of either. With a couple of backstrokes I gave myself some runway in the back eddy formed by the edge of the current, pointed the kayak to within 20 degrees from deadheading into the current, and then paddled with all the vigor I could muster. It is a strange experience – and one to appreciate – the moment your kayak drops into the front trough of a standing wave. The speed decelerates from maximum to almost zero and the frantic paddle strokes you had been putting in suddenly become unnecessary; the kayak is in a state of freefall, falling down the face of the wave as fast as the wave is pushing it back up. I rested the paddle across the kayak while the smooth water rushed on either side and the rocks below shimmered with sunlight.

Unfortunately, the peaceful free-fall condition is also an unstable equilibrium, and any slight deviation to the side will send the kayak into a broach. When I last tried surfing the standing wave with Lee, I had been paddling a 15-foot P&H Delphin which was considerably more responsive and maneuverable than the 18-foot Rockpool I now had with me. The longer length combined with the steepness of the wave meant that at the first loss of balance I had the bow plowed, capsized, and was sent rolling downstream.

At least the water isn't cold, I thought to myself after rolling back up. *I'll try a few more.*

None of my next five attempts were any better. After a few more swims I was out of steam and decided to do the more leisurely exercise of zigzagging on the current by ferrying from one eddy to another.

East of the three islands on the throat of the Narrows the channel was somewhat wider and the current a good deal slower, so I took this route paddling against the flow to reach the southern shore of Maurelle Island. From there I hugged the shore past a thundering waterfall until I reached the bifurcation point of the current, where I would then paddle back through the Narrows. It was now close to midafternoon. I pulled the tide tables Marla had given me from a ziplock bag and confirmed that the turn would be in less than an hour. I began to head back rather than risk being caught on the wrong side of the Narrows.

I made a strenuous ferry crossing from the southernmost point of Maurelle Island back to Proposal Rock, in which I had to paddle almost perpendicular to the direction I was moving; it took nearly 15 minutes to cover just 200 yards until finally, the current released its grip.

Once across I could paddle through the Narrows with ease and rode over the waves like a bumpy waterslide. I didn't stop to catch my breath and continued at full speed back to Heriot Bay. Once the tide turn happens, the current quickly speeds up the other way like a wave sliding back into the sea after running up a steep beach. To further complicate things, the rain began coming down in curtains. I arrived back very much relieved but in need of a hot chocolate and a bath. *At least I didn't have to carry all the gear with me,* I thought. In the next few days that wouldn't be the case.

June 12 – Day 14

There was one very important thing to do while I was still at the Heriot Bay Inn. Laundry. I was down to my last clean shirt. Clean, of course, was a relative term. The shirt had already been worn for two days, and only the dry talcum powder kept the smell bearable.

When I gathered the dirty laundry I was disappointed to find out that both my gear bags had huge rips in them. I had bought them for my journey around Florida two years earlier and they had always been an essential part of my expeditions. Every kayaker quickly learns that making numerous trips carrying gear to and from the kayak is both laborious and an especially good way to lose something. That's why I normally have at least two large gear bags, one for the front hatch and one for the stern and day hatches, cutting down the number of back-and-forth trips to a maximum of three. Without them I'd be doing a lot more walking, or worse, I'd possibly lose something small but important like a wallet or the GPS tracker.

While I carried the laundry down two flights of stairs wondering how to deal with the damaged bags, a solution appeared in front of me as if the God of Lottery Tickets had picked my numbers out of his hat. Right there on top of one of the dryers was a hefty blue Ikea bag. There were no dryers or washers running and no clothes left to be picked up. I looked at the bag with its sturdy fabric, double stitched handles, and sand-proof zipper.

"My goodness me! Am I lucky or what? It's like someone deliberately forgot it here for me," I said aloud.

I was about to grab it and carry it back to my room when I felt some hesitation as if there was a voice whispering in my ear: *You remember that time at work you forgot your iPhone in the public bathroom on the second floor. You left it on top of the paper box after watching some video on YouTube. You pulled up your pants, flushed, and forgot to put it back in your pocket. You went back to work, sat back at your desk, and immediately realized it wasn't there with you. You ran back to get it but it was gone in less than five minutes. What did you say you would do if you found the guy who stole your phone? You told me you would stab the son of a bitch. Don't be the son of a bitch.*

Then another voice spoke: *Oh nonsense. Why do you give yourself bad advice? You're scorning a gift from the gods. Who do you know that has more luck than you? Treat Lady Luck with disdain, and she will throw the disdain back in your face.*

I struggled over what to do. I really wanted the bag, but I would hate to label myself a thief. I settled on a Solomonic compromise to split the baby down the middle. I took the bag and placed it in the drawer under the laundry sink and left the drawer open. In the morning I would come by and check if it was still there. If it was, then that would mean that it was left behind and forgotten and I would keep it. If it was gone, it would mean that the owner had come back and clearly made the effort to look for it.

The next morning I felt a bit disappointed; the bag was gone. *You should have taken it when you could. No one would have blamed you for taking it, and no one will give you praise for having left it.*

The flooding tide allowed me to have a very late start. At Surge Narrows, the slack current wouldn't be until 4 p.m., so I arrived there five minutes before and had to tip my hat to Marla and her meticulous calculations. She was spot on. For a brief 10-minute window the water was calm like a pond, and the foaming rapids and standing waves were dormant without even a hint of their existence. Soon, all that would begin to change and very quickly the tide would begin ebbing in the opposite direction to carry me northward.

I paddled six miles north of Surge Narrows to a place called Octopus Islands Provincial Park. The park supposedly gets its name from the shape of the many passages between the islets which from above resemble the tentacles of an octopus. However, after staring at the map of the islands spilled like ink blots in a Rorschach test, I struggled to see any semblance of an octopus. My best interpretation was that two islands resembled two amoebas devouring each other.

On the largest island of the group was a sailboat anchored in a sheltered bay, three tents amidst the trees, and a small dinghy tied to a boulder.

"Would there be room for one more in your island kingdom?" I asked the young man resting comfortably on his folding chair, soaking in the afternoon sun with his bare feet in the water.

"We saw you paddling in and battling the headwind. I'm sure we can sell you a plot of land for you to call your own, provided of course that you pony up the royal fifth to her majesty the Queen, eh," he answered with a smirk.

"I'll pay your majesty with a can of beef ravioli from Chef Boyardee. Got lots of those with me," I said.

He was there with four college friends from Toronto on their summer break taking a two-week tour through the island maze on a 30-foot Catalina called *Vancouver Princess.*

"We went as far as Port Hardy on the north of the Island and are now heading back to Vancouver."

"What's it like on the Johnstone Strait? I'll be paddling through there in a day or two."

"Oh, very windy!" he said with a slight gasp. "We cheated on that part and motored our way with the sails down. Would have taken us forever to tack our way against the wind and the current."

That didn't sound at all encouraging given I had no motor to fall back on.

"I've never been to Toronto," I said. "I don't know much about it except that you guys once had a very funny mayor. Wasn't he the guy who was accused of offering oral sex to one of his employees, and his deadpan response to the crowd of reporters was, 'They said I wanted to eat her pussy. I never said that in my life. I am happily married, and I have more than enough to eat at home. Thank you very much.' It was the headline story for late night comedy for a whole week.

"Yup! That's Rob Ford. And that was just one of the crazy things he said. He also admitted on TV that he'd smoked crack cocaine, or at least he thought he did because he couldn't recall the details because he was in a drunken stupor. Yeah, he made Toronto famous. And his brother is just as sleazy, and he's the premier of Ontario. But at least he knows how to run the province. It's better to have politicians who are bad actors than bad actors who think they can be politicians, like Donald Trump.

"I agree, but not all actors turn into bad politicians. Zelensky was a comedian, he played the president in a movie, and now he's president. Imagine if Harrison Ford after starring in *Air Force One* had gone on to become president. He definitely looked the part. You might not know that movie if you're in college right now. It came out in 1997, but it was pretty good. He played the president too."

The Heriot Bay Inn, Quadra Island

A shingle beach landing on an island in the Georgia Strait

[ABOVE] *Starfish near the Surge Narrows. The normally frigid waters felt like balmy South Florida.* [BELOW] *Waterfall in the Okisollo Channel.*

[ABOVE] *Johnstone Strait near Chatham Point.*
[BOTTOM LEFT] *The Author, enjoying the afternoon sun and the low tide in the Johnstone Strait ... but caught unaware by the flood tide that same night.* [BOTTOM RIGHT]

Big Cedar on Hanson Island,
Johnstone Strait. The tree is
almost a thousand years old.

[ABOVE] *Finding a safe place to park the kayak for the night can sometimes be the can be the hardest task of the day, Alert Bay.* [BELOW] *Packed harbor on Port Hardy.*

[ABOVE] *Fellow kayakers caught in the storm near Hanson Island, Johnstone Strait.*
[BELOW] *A rare easterly tailwind on the Johnstone Strait gives the opportunity to use the kayak sail.*

June 13 – Day 15

A few miles north of the Octopus Islands are the Okisollo Rapids where the northern shore of Quadra Island pushes up against Sonora Island, and the channel makes a sharp west turn before merging with the Johnstone Strait. My guidebook did not mince words about this treacherous stretch of water, and I felt the author was wagging his finger at me lest I underestimate what lay ahead. "Exercise extreme caution when crossing the rapids. You may run into violent rips, foaming overfalls, and gigantic whirlpools. Be aware of the tides and the winds and be especially careful with the Hole in the Wall gap to the northeast between Maurelle and Sonora islands."

I unfolded the tide tables and looked for the Okisollo Channel. The tide would start ebbing in the morning, reaching peak flow at 11 a.m. The Hole in the Wall channel had a similar timetable, but a note from Marla on the margin caught my attention. It read: "The tide floods to the northeast and ebbs to the southwest." This was good. It meant the water would be flowing into the Okisollo Channel, and there would be no risk of being sucked into a maelstrom with a current that flows above 12 knots.

Looking at the map of northeast Vancouver Island, I thought the maze of interconnecting channels and passages reminded me of the pipe network in a water distribution system. Every channel had a different length and unique cross section that was like a pipe segment, and every point where two or more channels meet was like a node in the network. When the tide moves the water through the labyrinth, the same family of hydraulic formulas can be used to solve the flow volume and direction through the system. In hydraulics class, we used an approach called the Hardy-Cross. My college hydraulics professor at the University of Florida loved putting the Hardy-Cross into the midterm and final exams to see who had been paying attention in class and who had been slacking all semester. It was a difficult exercise requiring several rounds of laborious iterative calculations to eventually arrive at the answer, and any small oversight, typo, or wrongly pressed button in the calculator would send your work astray. "Think of it as a fancy magic trick you practice over and over so when you're at the bar you'll impress the girls," he would say in class. "When you do the magic trick flawlessly you get laid. If you solve a Hardy-Cross on your job interview, you'll get the job.

You would need to be a hydraulic savant to work out a hydraulics problem the size of the Pacific Northwest all by hand, but modern computational fluid dynamics software can certainly do it.

I checked the time while I lay inside my warm sleeping bag. It was 5:30 a.m. *I better get moving or I'll be crossing the rapids in the peak of the current*, I thought. Loud snoring from one of the other tents indicated that my Toronto mates were sleeping like rocks.

After a breakfast of canned tuna and a few spoonfuls of Nutella, I packed up camp and tediously carried all the gear down to the kayak. Without my gear bags I had to be especially careful not to leave anything behind as there would be no way to paddle back against the tide. I counted the number of dry bags at the campsite, and then again as I put them inside each hatch. As if I had some kind of compulsive mania, I carefully walked the path between the campsite and the kayak with my head bent to the ground to make sure nothing had fallen on the way, and looked twice inside the front day hatch to visually confirm and then reconfirm that the GPS, phone, and wallet were indeed there. Only then did I feel comfortable to launch and be on my way.

The ebbing tide quickly carried me to the head of the Okisollo Rapids. At first everything seemed calm, the water was flat, and there was no sound from the churning rapids. Even so, when I glanced at my GPS, it indicated that I was moving at seven miles per hour – without paddling.

No way, this thing has to be malfunctioning.

I decided to run a test. I turned around and began paddling against the current and soon enough, the speed began dropping the harder I paddled, but never below three miles per hour.

The rapids didn't disappoint. Beyond the entrance to the Hole in the Wall the channel formed the largest whirlpool I had ever seen. The width was at least twice the length of my kayak, the eye dropped more than two feet, and it made ominous gurgling sounds like a drunkard at a bar chugging down a pint of beer. I steered clear of it by a good distance, not wanting to provoke it into a fight.

Beyond the whirlpool the conditions were not so treacherous. The current hadn't yet sped up enough to steepen the standing waves into a foam pile, and I rolled over them like a gentle slide. In another half hour, however, things would be very different, and I wouldn't want to be testing my surfing skills in a boat laden with gear, lacking both maneuverability and acceleration.

The Okisollo Channel emptied into Discovery Passage which, as it flows north from of the Seymour Narrows, becomes Johnstone Strait. It all provided a momentous feeling as the landscape widened revealing a snow-topped mountain range on Vancouver Island with verdant slopes rolling into the dark-blue waters.

These would have been the same waters sailed by Captain Vancouver on his circumnavigation of the island with the *Discovery* and the *Chatham* around July of 1792 when he spent a whole month surveying the channels. Unlucky for Captain Vancouver, during his passage he had terrible weather with rain and fog obscuring nearly every feature of the landscape, leaving him at the mercy of the treacherous tides and currents. Both ships managed to run aground in shallow water at least once where they were left nearly completely exposed during low tide. That would not be a problem for a kayak like mine, but I would still need to keep an eye on the tides if I did not want my boat to wander on its own.

A little farther north I made a stop at the Chatham Point Lighthouse where the Johnstone Strait makes a sharp west bend. Captain Vancouver stopped at this same place as well on his way north through the Seymour Narrows and waited for favorable tides so he could continue on to Queen Charlotte Sound. He noted that the rocky outcrop extending from the island shore was at the confluence of three channels and had a bay on either side with good anchorage points and a few small islets.

I would certainly have agreed with him as I pulled my kayak on the boat ramp next to the pier, possibly on the same bay he anchored in. I walked up a steep boardwalk and arrived on a grassy field with three white houses with bright red roofs and a helicopter pad. The lighthouse keeper was nowhere to be seen, though I could tell from his manicured garden that he took pride in his lupin flowers which were in full bloom. Beyond the houses the grass field gave way to a gravel road from which it would be at least a 25-mile drive along winding mountain paths to Highway 19. There was also an enormous foghorn with a sign that read: "Stay at least 50 feet away. Risk of hearing loss." Ironically, the sign wasn't very big, and you might need to be closer than 50 feet to read it. The foghorn was definitely a necessity. Even on a cloudless day like today, it would be impossible to see a ship sailing around the blind corner in the opposite direction.

I had already had the tide sneak up on me once at the beginning of the journey and wasn't hoping to let it happen a second time. One glance at the rocky islets just beyond the shore was enough for me to clearly see that the tide had turned and that I should quickly get back to the kayak, which already had the water slapping at the rudder. Another five minutes and I would have been swimming after it.

While continuing west against the now flooding tide, I was further hampered by a strong headwind and it soon felt like I was paddling on a treadmill. I edged closer to the north shore of the Johnstone channel where a chain of islands and swirling eddies allowed me to hop along slowly but steadily. On reaching the last island on the chain, however, there was nowhere else to go. I pulled out my phone and looked for the closest place to camp, and like Captain Vancouver, waited for a favorable tide.

June 14 – Day 16

Last night I must have done something to garner Poseidon's wrath.

NAVIGATING THE JOHNSTONE STRAIT

Where's that sacrificial horse I'm supposed to get in exchange for the fair weather and calm seas I've been giving you? You haven't even tossed me a single Chef Boyardee meatball so far this trip. Tonight I'm going to teach you a lesson you won't soon forget.

I picked a campsite beyond the last island on the daisy chain of eddies I had been hopping through. The area had a pebbled beach on the foot of a small escarpment with overgrown bushes and cedar trees. The beach was narrow, but a line of seaweed marking the extent of the previous high tide seemed to leave plenty of room for the tent and a kayak. *Well, I hope it doesn't climb much higher than this,* I thought. I looked at my phone to confirm when the next high tide would be. The table indicated it would be around 1 a.m.

Unfortunately, I should have looked at the table a bit more carefully and checked how high the next high tide would be. The answer was right there for me to see; four feet higher than the previous afternoon's high. But I glossed over it. Being from Florida, I had never contemplated that two subsequent back-to-back high or low tides could be so different. I knew that the full and new moons make bigger tides than the waxing and waning moons because in those conditions, the sun and the moon pull together in the same direction. But the transition happens slowly, and the next tide is only a little higher or lower than the previous ones. However, here in the mid-latitudes between about 45 and 60 degrees, the tilt of the Earth, the orbital plane of the moon, and the moon phase create conditions where four different types of tides can occur in a single day. They could colloquially be called the *sort of low, sort of high, very low, and very high* tides.

Unbeknownst to me, the last high tide had been of the *sort of high* variety and a *very high* tide was about to follow.

Like a mouse checking out a mouse trap, I had a feeling something wasn't quite right. The foot of the escarpment had huge driftwood logs piled over each other as if a giant had tossed them, but I attributed that to a storm, which wasn't in the forecast for the night. Nonetheless, I placed four large boulders between the previous high tide mark and my tent. *Sometime at night I'll check on the tide and if it's past these rocks, I'll move the tent farther up the beach,* I thought. However, I didn't think it would be necessary; the falling tide was now incredibly far away. The narrow beach I had landed on had grown to nearly 100 feet in width. If anything, I'd be carrying the kayak to the edge of the water the next morning.

At 11 p.m., some three hours before the high tide peak, I peeked out of the tent with my headlamp and saw that the waterline was already past the rocks.

Oh, I better get up and move things up the beach.

I dragged the tent and everything inside to the base edge of the escarpment next to the kayak and the driftwood.

That should be fine now. How much higher could it get?

Much higher still it seemed. After 30 minutes I peeked out again, the water was even closer than before, and the situation was starting to look worrisome. There was still plenty of time for the tide to continue rising and rather than insist on denial in the face of overwhelming evidence, I assumed that the worst might well happen. The beach wasn't going to be around for much longer.

The water kept rising. There wouldn't be enough time to pack the kayak, so I started tossing all the gear into the bushes above the embankment and eventually I tossed the tent up there as well. I would've tossed the kayak too, but it was far too heavy. The best I could do was put it on top of the driftwood logs.

And still, the water kept rising.

I got dressed in my dry suit. *I hope the water isn't too cold.*

Fifteen minutes later I was in permanent ankle-deep water, the waves started breaking over the driftwood I had put the kayak on, and it was twitching with every wave.

And still, the water kept rising. Soon, it was knee deep.

It won't be long before the driftwood floats away with the kayak. I'd better get this thing down and hold on to it.

Now the water was waist deep.

In the middle of getting the kayak down, a bigger wave set rolled in and the whole thing came undone like a house of cards. I lost my footing, plunged into the water, the kayak slid upside down, and the cockpit filled with water.

Uh-oh, how much worse will it get?

I grabbed the boat before it could float away, lifted the bow to empty the water, and shone the headlamp onto the bushes above the escarpment to locate where I had tossed the paddles and spray skirt. *Better I wait this thing out sitting in the kayak than in the water.*

Having found them, I realized I would have to let go of the kayak to grab the stuff in the bushes and waited for a lull in the waves.

"Don't go anywhere. I'll be back in a second or two," I said to the kayak.

I quickly got hold of the paddle and the spray skirt and climbed on the back of the kayak for a cowboy-style entry. When I clipped the spray skirt around the comb, I felt a great sense of relief and could now afford to finally breathe and relax a little. *This wasn't so bad*, I thought. I even had a silvery view of the full moon silhouetting the mountains across the Johnstone Strait. The moonshine was illuminating the clear night so there was no need to keep the headlamp on. All I had to do was float in place for a few hours and wait.

While bobbing in my kayak I noticed a strange round object drifting on the dark water. When I realized it was one of my cart wheels, I desperately reached for it with the paddle until it was close enough to grab and toss into the cockpit under the spray skirt.

I hope nothing else fell off the bushes into the water because I'm definitely never going to find it.

Only when the tide finally receded and there was enough land to set foot on again did the exhaustion from the previous night's effort finally settle in. I grabbed the folding chair out of the bushes and tried to snuggle into a comfortable position to get a few hours of sleep. The thought that my carelessness could have been far more consequential didn't register in my head at the time, but I had nearly lost the kayak.

I'll figure out where I tossed everything and what I'll do next when there's daylight.

I slept for a couple hours until a chilly breeze picked up with the sunrise.

I might as well get an early start on the water. I'm definitely not spending another night here.

The breeze soon turned into a strong and persistent headwind from the west. The mountains along Johnstone Strait form a wind tunnel that shepherds air currents with tremendous force along the entire length of the strait. If the regional forecast calls for 5 to 10 mile per hour winds in the strait, it will actually be more like 15 to 20, and I soon realized that even though I had the tide helping me along, I wasn't making much progress. I hugged the southern edge of West Thurlow Island along the north shore of the channel as far as I could go. Then I had to decide whether to stay on the north side, hopping across open channels from island to island, or make one crossing of the Johnstone channel to paddle along Vancouver Island until Kelsey Bay where I hoped the small village would have an inn with a comfortable bed. After the previous night, I would very much be happy to pay top dollar for it.

I rested for a while on a back eddy while I waited for two cruise ships bound for Alaska to pass by. I assumed that the ships had left from Vancouver the previous afternoon and had been sailing through the night. While not quite as big as some of the cruise liners I regularly see in my paddles around the Port of Miami, they were still the largest vessels I had seen thus far in the journey, likely carrying hundreds of passengers who would hardly have been able to discern me in the water.

I hesitated if I should cross the strait. The guidebook gave a warning loud and clear: "Do not attempt to cross the Johnstone Strait when the wind is blowing against the current. It can be very rough and very dangerous." The exact conditions I found myself in.

"Oh seriously, it doesn't look so bad," I scolded the author as though he could hear me. "You're making my life difficult. The channel is only about a mile wide here, I can clearly see the trees on the opposite shore, and the water there doesn't look so rough. I'm sure you must mean at peak current and with a lot more wind than today. I'll be fine.

I pointed the kayak at an oblique bearing to the southwest and after checking to make sure there wasn't a third cruise liner on the way, put my muscle into the wing paddle at full strength.

Up until three-quarters of the way things were not bad; then came the part the author of the guidebook tried to warn me about. Somewhere on the channel bottom there must have been a large shallow boulder like the Ripple Rock at Seymour Narrows, and I soon saw that I was about to cross through several rows of chirping whirlpools.

I contemplated changing my mind and going back, but the window for that decision was already behind me and I rode with the flow along the edge of the whirlpools hopping from one spinning waterwheel to the other.

This, of course, was easier said than done. Each whirlpool was separated by a ridge of water that always flowed counter to my direction. I entered the first whirlpool with a clockwise flow and immediately picked up a tangential speed. As I followed the flowline, I found myself paddling east, counter to the tide, but with the wind on my back which momentarily felt stagnant. This was the moment to put as much power as possible into every stroke. The boat began to turn south along the edge of the whirlpool and I had to slingshot myself over the water ridge into the next whirlpool before facing the headwind. I knew I had succeeded only when the boat suddenly stopped pulling to the right and I had to throw a sharp low-brace turn to the left and bank away from the westerly headwind. I repeated this technique two more times from one whirlpool to the next until I was close enough to the Vancouver Island shore to overpower the current.

As I continued along the southern shore of Johnstone Strait, the water became progressively smoother, but the ebbing tide aiding my progress against the wind began losing strength.

Already? I thought with some disappointment. *Now I have to paddle against the wind with only my own strength.*

Kelsey Bay was still five miles away and I already felt exhausted.

I landed on the corner of a cratered boat ramp in the harbor and started to unload.

I was greeted by the marina master who walked down to see what I was doing there.

"So, what are you, eh? Where'd you come from? Oh, sorry, but I must tell you. This is a private marina. So you can't just land here, eh."

"Oh I am so sorry. I'm coming all the way from Seattle. Well, not today of course, it's been about two weeks. I was hoping to stop here and then walk into town and maybe stay at the campsite. I'm happy to pay the boat landing fee for the ramp, if there is one.

"From Seattle, eh? So you're on the Race to Alaska, eh? Wuz a pretty bad day not too long ago, eh?"

The Race to Alaska (R2AK for short) is an adventure competition that takes place every summer where sailboats and kayaks race from Port Townsend in Washington to Ketchikan in Alaska. It's a grueling 750-mile endeavor. There are only two checkpoints. One in Victoria, which is the prequalification stage that must be completed in a day and a half, and another in a town called Bella Bella roughly halfway. The rest of the route is up to the racers. There are no vessel categories. Kayaks and sailboats compete against each other, which might seem unfair, until you remember that the wind isn't always blowing, and a kayak can take shortcuts through the sounds that might be too tight or shallow for a larger sailboat. That said, no kayak has won the competition since the first edition of the challenge in 2015.

"No. I'm paddling around Vancouver Island. What happened?"

"Oh, wuz on the TV, eh. Big storm rolled in through the Juan de Fuca Strait. Caught some folks by surprise. Seven boats sank. The American and Canadian coast guards were working overtime to fetch everybody outta the water, eh. Some of the guys were shivering like pins in a bowling alley, eh.

I thought back about when the incident might have happened and concluded it must have been on the day I had crossed from Lund to Heriot Bay. That had been the roughest day so far.

"So, you think you're walking to town with your boat, eh? It's a bit far, eh. Why not stay here, eh? We own the marina RV park, but there's a motel as well. There's a room. It's forty bucks but you have to pay cash. Go talk to my wife Christine. She's at the mobile trailer tending the garden. Oh, m'name is Moore! Come for happy hour, eh?"

I was more than happy to accept the invitation. The motel room in the marina was a real bargain. It had a comfortable king bed, a spotless bathroom, kitchenette, living room with TV, and a million-dollar balcony view facing the blue waters of the Johnstone Strait and the cloud-ringed mountains beyond. Mr. Moore was sitting on a goldmine of a location, but didn't seem to know it.

"How about we start happy hour a little early, eh? I'm heading into town to swing by the liquor store.

"If you don't mind, I'll go with you, and I'll buy the wine," I offered

I jumped in Mr. Moore's truck and we drove off. On the way we passed a multitude of log piles neatly stacked on the side of the road.

"A lot of logs, eh," Mr. Moore remarked. "You'll see plenty more on the water. One of the barges had a mishap and now they're floating all over, eh.

We arrived at the liquor store at the junction with Highway 19 that runs the length of Vancouver Island until Port Hardy.

I must admit that I have next to no knowledge of fine wines or liquors of any kind. Drinking has never been a form of entertainment for me and I was unsure of what to get. I looked through the wooden wine racks on the store aisle until I found a bottle with a pretty label. A cabernet sauvignon from Alexander Valley. It was called The Silver Oak and had a picture of a wooden hut shaded by a twisted oak in a rolling field of lavenders.

"Oh, we are drinking the fancy stuff, eh?" Mr. Moore remarked with a laugh

Back at the marina and after a few glasses, Mr. Moore started telling me the story of his life.

"Oh, he's a talker," his wife said, "if you keep giving him rope, he will keep pulling.

He was born in Manitoba, had worked for the oil and gas industry in the tar sands of Alberta as bulldozer driver, and had met his wife in a place called the Gopher Hole Museum.

"You make good money working the sands, but it's backbreaking shift work, eh. Twelve-hour days, fourteen days on, seven days off. The mine is a bleak place like the surface of the moon and it smells like an inferno from all the sulfur in the air

"At least you had something to look forward to on those seven days off," his wife said with a smirk.

"It's what kept me going and from going mad, eh!

"Oh, look at who's nearly gone. I think you're boring him."

I was dozing off in my chair and struggling to keep my eyes open.

"Must be the fine wine, eh?"

At that moment I was jolted awake by my phone ringing which was a surprise because I'd not had reception since leaving Heriot Bay. It was my mother wanting to check in with me. I told her that everything had been fine the previous two days, conveniently not mentioning that I had nearly lost the kayak the night before.

"Was that French you were speaking? You from Quebec?

"Oh, no. It was Portuguese. My family is from Brazil.

"I could never tell the difference. The only French I know are the curse words, you know, *putain, merde, and tabarnac,* just in case you need them."

"I speak some French from the time I lived in Geneva. I never heard the word *tabarnac.* What does that mean?"

"Oh, nevermind. You better turn in for the night. Got another long day tomorrow, eh?"

June 15 – Day 17

I had another weird dream about my kayak. I was paddling when suddenly an enormous hole opened under the hull like a wooden floor being ripped by a saw. The cockpit filled up with water, but the water was warm as if I was in a bathtub. Suddenly I woke up from the dream, and I knew exactly what it meant. I had to urgently go pee. The alcohol was working its way out of my system. Just in case, I also went to check up on the kayak sitting on the balcony. The hull looked fine.

From Kelsey Bay there were only 80 more miles along the Queen Charlotte Sound until Port Hardy, the last major settlement on the north of the island where I would reset a few days, plan the route around Cape Scott, and coordinate the eventual meet up with JF and the Skils kayak group. The forecast called for calm weather with a slight tail breeze to push me along for at least the next three days, and I would have an ebbing tide in the early mornings for the remainder of the Johnstone Strait.

"You better get moving to make the most of this while it lasts, eh?" said Mr. Moore while splitting logs on a stump. "And keep an eye for the floating logs."

He wasn't kidding; the sea was littered with driftwood like road debris. None had barnacles so they mustn't have been floating for long.

There were many logging boats transiting the channel. They were of two types: tugboats that dragged huge rafts of logs tied together like cattle in a corral; and barges that carried a comical quantity of logs piled on their decks. If a big wave tossed the barge too far to one side or the other, all the logs would roll away like pencil sticks. Perhaps that's how so many logs were lost on the water.

There was a noticeable change along the shore of Vancouver Island since entering the Johnstone Strait. The forest is evidently not a natural forest, but a managed plantation of the lumber industry. Every fir and cedar has a nearly identical height and grows in evenly spaced, orderly columns on the hillsides, interspaced with a checkerboard of clearcuts and knee-tall saplings. It is not a pleasing sight to behold, and no doubt all the wasted floating logs came from one of these many tree plantations.

Late afternoon I arrived at the mouth of a small estuary called Naka Creek on the Vancouver Island shore, next to a lumber boom where logs are processed and tied together in rafts. There were no facilities nearby, but a clear stream emptying into the estuary proved to be an excellent place to wash the dry suit clean from the encrusted salt.

On the patch of grass next to the pebbled beach exposed by the tide was the only vehicle in the camp, a trailer with a fleur-de-lis license plate. The passengers were a girl and her boyfriend on a summer trip, and their three over-the-top friendly Labradors.

"Gosh, how do you feed them every day? You must go through sacks of dog food.

"We do. About a 10-pound bag every week, and having them in the trailer with us every day is like a sleepover party every night. Sometimes I wake up with a dog's butt on my face.

"Are you French?" I asked, noticing that she had an accent.

"We are from Quebec," said her boyfriend.

I switched to French which really delighted them. When I was ready to turn in for the night, the boyfriend handed me a can of Molson beer and said, "Thank you for speaking French!"

June 16 – Day 18

I had a text conversation with my friend Lee from Victoria.

"Hey, how's the progress going?

"I got to Naka Creek camp today."

"Oh, I know that place! I've been there. Guess what? I'm in Heriot Bay. Heard from some locals you came through here. The front-desk lady at the Heriot Bay Inn mentioned you. Have you seen any whales yet?

"No, not yet.

"Really? That's a surprise. Try going through the Blackney Passage between Hanson and Harbledown Island. I guarantee you'll see some there. I've done a few tours with clients there and we always see whales."

The Johnstone Strait and Queen Charlotte Sound are a favorite haunting ground for all kinds of whales. Humpbacks and gray whales make a side trip to the strait during their summer migration to Alaska to eat krill, and orcas are keen on catching chinook salmon during the yearly runs. The orcas of the strait are also especially fond of pebble beaches, much like the one exposed by the low tide on the

Naka Creek where they give themselves belly rubs. Apparently, like humans, orcas also get itchy in places that are difficult to scratch.

After paddling for 10 miles I turned north to cross the Johnstone Strait toward Hanson Island. Although there was no wind, the weather deteriorated considerably, a dense fog set in, and the rain poured heavily like an afternoon shower in the tropics.

When I entered the Blackney Passage I heard a puff of exhalation louder and deeper than any sigh I had ever heard from a human. I looked in the direction of the sound but couldn't see anything other than thousands of raindrops stirring the flat water. A little later I heard it again from a different direction, and this time I caught sight of the moisture cloud from the animal's breath but the whale had already submerged. On the third time hearing the powerful exhalation I saw the stumpy dorsal fin of a humpback whale breach the surface. I tried to paddle a bit closer to where I had seen the breath cloud and maybe get a better look, but it quickly moved around, unseen under the water like a mole through its tunnels. By the time I saw it take another breath it was already in a different place.

As I paddled around trying to catch up with the whale, I sighted what I thought was a flock of birds in the distance waiting out the rain and fog on the water. When I got closer, however, I realized they were not a flock of birds at all, but a flock of 15 paddlers.

"Wow! It's incredible how in this mist and rain, even the deck color on your boats takes a tone of gray. From a distance, I thought that you were a bunch of cormorants.

"Oh, not quite or we would have been flying," said Silka, a lady in the group who seemed to be in charge of the flock. "My fellow guide and I are leading a group for six days around the islands north of Johnstone Strait. We put in at Telegraph Cove. Got another two days to go before we go back. We heard there's a guy from Seattle kayaking around Vancouver on a yellow kayak. Is that you.

"Yes, that's me! My reputation travels faster than I can paddle, though I guess at four miles per hour that's not too difficult," I said.

"Well, for an average, from Seattle, and with gear, it's not bad."

Silka told me she had been running tours with a local kayak company at Telegraph Cove for the last four years.

"After a while you get to know the circuit like the back of your paddle and it feels like you're on autopilot. So long as you're paying attention, nothing too crazy happens, though I did once have a client who flipped his boat in the water. His stern hatch must not have been closed properly and all the gear started floating away. We recovered most things but the tent poles went down to the bottom of the sea. Four people had to spend a night in a tent made for only two. Come tag along with us for a little bit. We are going to see a thousand-year-old cedar."

I paddled with the group for the next hour. We landed on a pebbled beach on the western shore of Hanson Island.

"Let's not stick around for too long here." Silka told us. "The tide is going to turn and start rising soon.

As everyone got off their boats and carried them up the beach, I couldn't help but notice that I was the only one wearing a dry suit. Even the two guides in charge wore shorts and wet neoprene shoes.

"You don't wear dry suits?" I asked surprised.

"No, not for these trips, we are always in calm water and the clients are not required to have them. Our company's boss thinks it would look bad if the guides are warm and dry but the clients are wet and cold, so everybody gets to be wet and cold together."

"Oh, that sucks. Don't you guys have something like an occupational safety and health act here in Canada? I would complain. Seems like you are working in a cold sweat shop.

"We do. It's called Canadian Occupational Safety and Health. But good luck working with them. I've never heard of anyone filing a complaint and heard back. Besides, getting wet is part of being a kayak guide.

"Yeah, just like getting skin burns is part of the job of being a firefighter. I bet that's what your boss told you," I said. "What you guys really need, even more than a dry suit, is a union."

She didn't respond and I concluded it must be a touchy subject not to be discussed.

"You know, the tree is five minutes up the trail; you will see it on the left. I need to give a talk to the group but you can go ahead.

So I did. The woodland was thick with undergrowth and shrubs and it was difficult to see very far, let alone a tree that wasn't much different from any other. After what felt like more than five minutes, I saw one very large tree that had toppled and its roots had ripped up a hole in the ground. Mushroom ears were growing on the bark like the steps of a staircase.

"I think your tree fell over," I told the guide as she was wrapping up her talk. A look of fear abruptly appeared on her face.

We all walked together up the trail and I pointed out the fallen tree.

"Oh no, it's not that one! Thank God! You didn't go far enough," she said and gave me a little slap on the shoulder. "You scared the loonies out of me. That tree better be around long after I'm gone!'

"You said it was five minutes."

"Well, you know, five minutes-ISH."

We walked a little farther past a small stream after which the trail made a slight bend to the left. Then in between the foliage of the undergrowth appeared the trunk of an enormous cedar wide enough that 10 people holding hands would not have been enough to encircle it.

"You should have said go beyond the stream," I teased, but she ignored me.

"This tree has an interesting story. The whole island had its old-growth forest logged, except for this lone cedar. Its trunk is a little crooked and the inside has some rot, so it wasn't high-quality wood. It's interesting to see what we value as society changes. A hundred years ago these trees weren't worth more than what their wood could be turned into. Today, how much more money than that would we pay to have them back? We're fortunate that one ancient cedar escaped the axe. This tree has been here so long that it was already ancient when the two hemlocks next to it were little saplings, and they are big 200-year-old trees."

The tide was rising quickly. Soon it reached the kayaks and mine, which was closest to the water, was almost floating. I said goodbye to the group and continued westward along the north coast of Hanson Island while they went east to Harbledown Island across the passage.

Hanson Island fractured into a crumble of islets between which the rising tide gushed with swirling whirlpools and eddies. Further west were the Pearse Islands, an archipelago of potato-shaped islands separated by long, winding narrow channels that flowed with crystal water and foaming rapids like mountain streams. Occasionally, there was even a half-fallen tree in the water blocking the way after the tidal stream had eroded the shore into a steep bank. I tried my best to paddle against this marine river but was eventually overpowered and forced to take the long way around the islands.

I reached Cormorant Island which was the day's destination and home to a settlement of 'Namgis people in Kwakwaka'wakw territory. The village, called Alert Bay, was nestled in a bean-shaped bay rimmed with a boardwalk and wood stilt houses that merged with a marina packed with boats down to the last slip.

"Look at that, how lucky can I be?" I said to myself as I navigated through the marina until I found a concrete boat ramp. Immediately across the street was the

Pass'n Thyme Inn. *I won't have to portage my kayak to find a bed,* I thought. I walked through the hotel bar to find the reception desk.

"Oh, you picked the busiest day of the year to arrive in town without a reservation. It's high school graduation day. And this year we are hosting the Indigenous soccer tournament. All the rival schools from BC are here too. I doubt you'd even find a place to pitch a tent."

"You sure? The bar is empty and there's hardly a person or car on the street."

"That's because everyone, and I really mean almost everyone, is at the Big House. They are having the potlatch right now."

"What's a potlatch?"

"It's the graduation ceremony."

I later learned at the local museum that a potlatch is much more than just a graduation ceremony. In Native cultures of the Pacific Northwest, it's common for big events like births, weddings, coming-of-ages, and memorials to be commemorated with a big party where on top of the usual big feast and performances, the host of the potlatch would also give away a substantial portion of their wealth. The more that was given the greater the prestige bestowed on the host and some would give to the point of being left with nothing but the clothes on their backs. It was a way to say that material possessions were of temporary importance, at least until someone hosted the next potlatch when hopefully there would be equal reciprocity for past generosity.

I could see how early European settlers and administrators in the Pacific Northwest, versed in the principles of Adam Smith's *Wealth of Nations,* would have had issues with an economic system based on the extreme redistribution of wealth. That's why they were quick to ban it once they could exert control over Native land. *Who is going to put in the work to make a new canoe, weave a basket, or skin an otter if everyone is waiting until the next potlatch to get all those things? Nothing will ever get done. What would Adam Smith say? Become an expert canoe carver, make lots of fine canoes, and then sell them to those who want to be fine fishermen. Then you can buy fish from fishermen, pelts from the hunters, baskets from the weavers, and everyone can have more of everything by doing more of what they do best.*

If, however, you engage in some abstract thought, the two systems aren't wholly dissimilar if you identify the real product that is being traded. If reverence and respect from your tight-knit community can only be obtained through great generosity, and there is a deficit of good canoes, then surely an enterprising individual in the group will see the opportunity for an easy climb of the rungs on the social-status ladder and arrange a canoe giveaway at the next potlatch.

At the moment, though, I was hoping that the potlatch taking place in town included either a hotel bed or a patch of grass not too far away to pitch my tent.

Things weren't looking promising. Every hostel door I knocked on told me they were booked and I was left walking aimlessly while pulling my kayak behind me.

Then an intervention from heaven happened. I was approached by a bystander on the street.

"You look like you're looking for a place to stay," said a smiling unassuming lady.

"Indeed I am."

"Well, try the Seine Boat Inn which you just passed . They are probably full, but I am friends with the owner. His name is Edward. His brother was coming for the weekend, but he had an emergency in Port McNeill and is only coming the day after tomorrow. He might rent the room for you. Tell him Jane sent you."

I thanked this mysterious lady for her generous advice and for the fortunate meeting. It seemed so convenient in both time and place that our encounter reminded me of stories about the Greek gods who disguise themselves to speak with the mortal hero and steer him in the right direction.

I was all the more suspicious of the nature of our encounter when the innkeeper's wife said, "Yes indeed, my husband's brother isn't coming until Saturday, so yes, I do have a room available. But who is this Jane? I don't think I know a Jane."

Her husband wasn't there but on hearing that, I concluded it was best not to mention Jane again. There are some things the passing traveler should not go digging into.

I walked along the boardwalk by the bay until I heard the sound of beating drums from one of the side streets up a short hill and found my way to the Big House where the high school potlatch was in full swing. The building had the appearance of a large wooden warehouse with a shallow gabled roof and an elongated chimney. The front facade was painted with the image of a gaping killer whale with the front door hanging between its teeth. On the corner of the building was the tallest totem pole that I had ever seen, which at first I had mistaken for a radio tower with guide cables to stop it from toppling in the wind.

The drumming bangs were loud and flowing out of the Big House through the door gaps like a steaming pressure cooker. The front door, however, was locked.

No late arrivals were allowed, I guessed.

I strode around the building where I found a back door. This door was unlocked and I opened a small crack to take a peek.

There was a large white tapestry at least 20 feet wide and 15 feet tall with the image of two killer whales. It was hung between two girthed totem poles topped with spread eagles. In front I saw a fire pit at least six feet round with a roaring cauldron of tall shimmering flames. Three dancers dressed in colorful tapestries trod barefoot around the fire with their arms spread wide. They each wore a white-feathered headdress with small prickly feathers, perhaps from a goose or duck, and every time a dancer made a sudden shake with his head, the feathers dislodged and flew in all directions as if they had been blown by a fan. A little worryingly, some feathers ended up in the burning fire pit and quickly shot up in flames in the updraft through the chimney hole above. The room was packed to capacity. There were two sets of bleachers along the lengths of the building some 10 rows deep where all the spectators sat attentively watching the dancers while seemingly hypnotized by the beating drums.

For what must have been at least 15 minutes, I stayed hidden next to the door behind the large tapestry, perhaps also hypnotized by the drumbeats and the rhythmic movement of the dancers and the jumping fire. Then suddenly, the drumming stopped, the dancing ceased, and the room was momentarily quiet. I was snapped out my trance and not wanting to be caught, snuck out the door before anyone found out.

June 17 – Day 19

It was a short six-mile paddle from Alert Bay to Port McNeill. The forecast called for a northwesterly breeze in the afternoon , and I concluded that I'd rather do the remaining 25 miles to Port Hardy without having to plow into the wind for the next six to seven hours. I would cover that distance the next morning when dead calm conditions were expected.

Nonetheless, it felt strange to be done before midday, and so after confirming that there was room at the hotel marina, I backed out into the water just beyond the harbor entrance to firm up my rolls with the Euro blade. For good measure, I practiced a few wet reentry rolls as well, which involves getting out of the kayak and then inserting yourself back into the upside-down cockpit before completing the roll back up. That exercise drew concerned looks from bystanders onshore who I assumed must have thought I was in some kind of distress. When I paddled back into the marina, however, I was the one who was startled by their questions.

"Did you see the orca?" said a man walking his dachshund on the pontoon pier as I paddled in.

"Orca? Really? No, I didn't. Where was it?"

"Oh, it was right where you were, eh. A big bull with a dorsal fin as big as a man. I think you had your back to it when you were doing your flippy thing with the kayak, eh. He sure was looking at you doing all that splashing and kicking. Poked his head out of the water to check you out two times. Probably thought you were a seal in distress or something. An easy lunch. Lizzie here was barking like crazy."

"I must not have heard it sneak up on me because of the ear plugs."

I have never seen a wild orca. The only orca I ever saw was the mighty Shamu at SeaWorld. It's an enormous creature, bigger than the largest African elephant, but can swim and turn with the agility of a leopard. You have to go back to the Cretaceous period and meet a dinosaur to find an equivalent land predator. Although there has never been a recorded incident of a wild orca attacking a human, captive orcas have over the years given their handlers a dose of reality about what can happen if you swim with an animal that occasionally hunts great white sharks. The last incident happened in 2010 at SeaWorld Orlando when Shamu grabbed a female trainer outside the pool tank by the hair and drowned her in front of a crowd of tourists. That evening show called, "Dine With Shamu," took on a different meaning that day.

Fortunately, orcas are usually very fussy eaters and don't like switching up their diet. The resident orcas in North Vancouver Island only eat salmon, and different pods even stick to specific species. Some transient pods eat sea lions but shun salmon, and others are specialist whale hunters who eat only the tongues of gray and humpback whales. Hopefully, none of the orcas ever decides to experiment and see if a plumpy human on a kayak, fed on a rich diet of canned fish, pasta, and Nutella, would be worth the indigestion.

June 18 – Day 20

The morning brought dead calm conditions. The tide was falling and that helped make fast progress early on, perhaps a little too fast.

I covered the first six miles to the western tip of Malcolm Island in a little over an hour. Here a lighthouse marked the end of Johnstone Strait and the beginning of Queen Charlotte Sound. The beach under the lighthouse would have been an excellent place to stop and take a pee break, but I didn't feel that I needed to at the time and kept on going. That was a big mistake. The first time I put on a dry suit Lee warned me that pee breaks should be taken when you can, and not when you have to. Port Hardy was 18 miles of open water away.

Three hours later, the urge to go had me folding into a pretzel. Peeing in a bottle in the kayak felt a little too difficult because opening the pee zipper in a dry suit is a very risky thing to do in the water, even in relatively calm conditions. In the warm Florida waters, taking a pee break in the kayak is easy. You just pee in the kayak and then splash in some water to dilute the urine and make enough volume to pump it out. Here, however, if I capsized with the zipper open, the onset of shrinkage would be the least of my problems. Perhaps if I had someone else next to me to hold on to my boat, weeing would not be so daunting. Alone, however, it was too hard to get in the right position and relax.

I spotted a humpback whale far in the distance hitting its pectoral fin on the water. The whale was already gone by the time I heard the sound, which was loud like the wind slamming a door. The beating fins are a form of communication between whales; the sound of the splashes carries through the water much farther and faster than in air, and it's possible the whale was having a conversation with a friend more than a hundred miles away. What it was saying is a mystery, but may have been something like, "Hey, you won't believe the faces this guy on the kayak is making trying not to whiz himself."

I pulled into the Port Hardy marina south of the main town early afternoon, stood up on the boat ramp, and took one of the longest leaks I've ever done, not caring one bit if anyone was looking.

There were two hotels adjacent to the marina but both were full.

"Come back tomorrow and we will have a room. For tonight, however, you'll have to try and see what you find in town."

Ever since I made a 25-mile portage on my kayak journey around Florida, I have been convinced that it is always worth it to pay not to walk. I had been paddling up the St. Mary's River on the border between Georgia and Florida for three days when I reached the put-out point where I had planned for a short walk to a boat ramp on the eastern edge of a swamp called the Okefenokee. The swamp was a vast alligator-ridden marsh drained by the Suwannee River which I had planned to then follow for 250 miles before reaching the Gulf of Mexico. Unfortunately, I had not accounted for the possibility that the swamp would be mostly devoid of water in the dry season.

"You're definitely not going to make it across, I guarantee it," the park ranger warned me. That meant I would have to walk nearly 55 miles around the swamp to reach the put-in point. A three-day walk.

I tried not to feel beaten down but that first day was brutal. The road was narrow and constantly traversed by 50-foot-long logging trucks that had me and my kayak squeezed into the narrow gravel shoulder whenever they rumbled by with a bow wave of air that had my hat flying off my head. As bad as that was, the most harrowing parts happened whenever I had to climb a hill - not from the effort of pulling an 18-

foot kayak with gear, or the kayak bow handle that snapped halfway through the day, or the beach sandals I was wearing that would soon snap as well - but from the fact that I could not see the oncoming traffic and had to rely on my ears to decide when it was time to jump off the road.

After walking for 10 hours I arrived at a Florida hamlet called St. George where I camped in the town park and spent a shivering sleepless night from a winter cold front that dropped temperatures to 25°F.

"You want me to pick you up and drive you the rest of the way?" read a text message the next morning from my mother. She had been following the ordeal through my GPS tracker.

If it weren't for personal pride, or shame about having my mom drive more than 400 miles on short notice for a bailout, I would have said yes right away. The put-in point on the Suwannee River was still at least 30 miles away, farther than the distance I had walked already.

"Thanks Mom, but let me first see if I can find someone here who can help me. There's got to be at least one good Samaritan in this town who also owns a pickup."

I walked into a breakfast joint next to the town gas station where I found three elderly Southern gentlemen having fried eggs and bacon, pancakes, and coffee.

"Good morning friends! Lovely day, isn't it?" I said in the most jovial voice I could muster. "I'm the guy camped in the park. No, I'm not a passing sea hobo. I need to get to Fargo on the Suwannee River with my kayak so I can continue my journey. I'm going around Florida. Can anyone drive me and my kayak there?"

No response.

"I'll give a full tank of gas and one hundred dollars."

"I can definitely get you there," said one of the men. "My brother Wayne here has a truck; we'll take care of you. I'm Bud by the way."

Mr. Benjamin can always be relied on as a trusted friend to resolve a bind. Within the hour my kayak and I were on our way with Bud and Wayne, and what would have been a two-day walk became a 40-minute drive.

Except for one steep hill on the way, the portage to downtown Port Hardy was nowhere near as long or demanding. I even stopped at the gas station and had a welcome ice-cream break.

I called ahead to a hotel called Kwa'lilas which had a room available. As usual, I didn't let them know ahead of time that my 18-foot kayak would be a guest with special needs, and only sprung the situation on the receptionist once I had already checked in.

"What's your vehicle?" he asked.

"An eighteen-foot kayak."

"Like on the roof of the car?"

"No, that is the vehicle. It's on a cart. Any chance you have a place for me to park it?"

He looked outside through the lobby door.

"Oh ... hmm ... Let me call the manager."

The manager arrived after a few minutes. He was an indigenous man with a very round face and a shiny, broad forehead. His hair was pulled back tightly and braided into a long silky ponytail. He had an imposing frame and wore a suit that looked chiseled from a lump of black obsidian stone. A sharp contrast to my ragged beard and loose dry suit.

"So, you're kayaking around the island, eh?"

"Yes, that's right."

"Ah, we can help with that. We can put it in the back courtyard, that way it's not out in the street."

We walked past the lobby, down a corridor, and through a dining hall. On every wall were paintings and carvings of Native art which I found hard not to pause at and appreciate. There were images of bears, eagles, killer whales, and wolves with radiant shades of red and black and geometric forms that fit together like a puzzle. I especially liked one carving of a school of salmon appearing to frantically swim up a river, and I imagined how stylish something like that would look on the deck of my kayak.

"Yes, it was done by one of our locals. He has a gallery downtown. If you have the time you should go see it."

"Yes, they're beautiful works."

"We also sell many carvings and paintings in the hotel gift shop. You should look and see if you want to take something home with you."

"Oh, I wish I could. I don't think a delicate wooden sculpture would survive a whole month inside my kayak. And I would hate to fold one of the paintings down the middle like a napkin."

"Ah yes, you can keep your kayak here." He pointed at a wooden bleacher next to a large flat deck in the back courtyard. "This is where we had our grand opening potlatch six years ago. The first native funded, constructed, operated, and owned hotel in BC. The whole news media from Canada came to see the chiefs bless the building and watch the kids from the high school perform. It was a big deal, eh. I think the blessings worked. We survived the pandemic and the tourists are back in droves. We're the fanciest place in town and the business is booming."

"That is such good news!"

"There's a water hose too if you want to wash your kayak."

It was as if he could read my mind. After nearly three weeks of paddling, all three hatches in the kayak were starting to get encrusted with salt crystals and a freshwater rinse was certainly in order.

My arrival in Port Hardy marked the completion of a major milestone. The first third of the journey was now behind me, and with the exception of almost losing the kayak one night, the journey had thus far been incident free. However, the east coast of Vancouver Island, with its devious tidal currents, unpredictable whirlpools, and the occasional BC ferry scare, had been the easy part. Onward from here lay 400 remote miles of open coast. Barreling swells, raging storms, rugged capes, and whatever else the temperamental Pacific Ocean could conjure up – these were all very real possibilities in the days and weeks to come.

ALICE LAKE
FORT RUPERT
PORT HARDY
COAL HARBOR
QUEEN CHARLOTTE SOUND
STAPLES ISLANDS
BALAKLAVA Is.
NIGEI ISLAND
HOPE ISLAND
SHUSHARTIE
NAHWITTI RIVER
CAPE SUTIL
QUATSINO SOUND
WINTER HARBOR
KAINS Is.
GRANT BAY
STRANBY RIVER
WILLIAM LAKE
CAPE SCOTT PROVINCIAL PARK
SAN JOSEF BAY
SHUTTLEWORTH BIGHT
NAHWITTI CONE
Mt. St. PATRICK
NISSEN BEACH
NELLS BEACH
RAFT COVE
EXPERIMENT BIGHT
SEA OTTER COVE
CAPE SCOTT
GUISE BAY
STRANGE ROCK
PACIFIC OCEAN
CAPE SCOTT ISLANDS
N

PART 4 - ROUNDING CAPE SCOTT

June 19 and 20 – Days 21 and 22 – Port Hardy and Around

My main priority while in Port Hardy was to coordinate my arrival at San Josef Bay with the Skils kayak group with whom I would paddle for two weeks around the Brooks Peninsula. This was an appointment that I could not afford to miss. I was depending on them to be resupplied. Rain or shine, I had to be at San Josef Bay on the morning of June 26, and it was crucial to make the most of the favorable weather windows in the next seven days when they came and cover the 70 miles to get there.

"Hi Mom! I'm going to need you to update me on the forecast through the satellite phone. At least until I confirm with you that I'm with the Skils group. As soon as I leave Port Hardy, I'm going to be out of cell service for the next three weeks."

"Yes, no worries. Let me know when you leave Port Hardy and I'll send you an update at least once a day."

I concluded from the current extended forecast that the best time to set off would be in three days when I would have a falling morning tide, coupled with a light breeze from the southeast to push me along the last narrow stretch of Johnstone Strait between Vancouver Island and the Nigei and Hope islands, after which I would camp on one of the north-facing beaches. From there I would wait for the best weather window to paddle around Cape Scott, and hopefully in one go, make it all the way to San Josef Bay.

"When you round Cape Scott you must have the currents and the wind with you," JF from Skils advised. He and his partner Justine would be our guides for the subsequent section around the Brooks Peninsula. "Otherwise it will get very choppy. Mornings are usually calmer. That's when I would aim to go if I was taking a group with me."

"Okay, and what about the swells? I saw that the prevailing swell is from the southwest."

"If you have light winds, the swell won't be an issue. But a strong northwest wind with opposing currents will make for some crazy conditions. You'll have clear weather, but you'll be riding the back of a dragon. That's why you should go early when the winds are usually weak."

We coordinated a few other logistical items, including the meet-up location, picking up some of my gear in Port Hardy, including my kayak cart, which though essential for portages when paddling solo, wouldn't be needed while I was with the group. That freed up a huge amount of space in the stern hatch which I filled with 20 bottles of Perrier.

Port Hardy is the last town in Vancouver Island along Highway 19. North of it there are no settlements and no people save for the odd park ranger at one of the few official campsites on the Cape Scott Trail. And lighthouse keepers. The town had a sleepy deserted atmosphere with hardly a soul to be seen as I walked down the market street past empty coffee shops, restaurants, and a Ford dealership. The only place of activity was a liquor store where five cars were parked in front.

At the waterfront was a wide green lawn facing the calm waters of Queen Charlotte Sound with faraway mountains rimmed by a dissipating mist. The lawn had several monuments. One was a quirky statue of a giant carrot with a bite mark and a plaque noting that it marked the northern end of the island highway. A little way from the carrot was the conjunction of a white stone obelisk next to a short totem pole with a plaque inscription honoring the Canadian war dead from WWI, WWII, Korea, and even Vietnam.

While looking at both the obelisk and the totem pole I had what I felt was an epiphany. The totem poles must be kind of like an Egyptian obelisk. They are meant to be read. If the reader knows which clan carved the pole and is versed on the meanings of the figures and how their positions relative to each other should be interpreted, then they should be able to decipher what it all means. Sadly, I had no guide to advise me on how to read this particular pole, though I think it must have said something similar to what was written on the obelisk: "Brothers in Life, Forever Together in Death."

I rested on one of the park benches facing the bay where I noticed a strange scene. A bald eagle swooped up and down from a tree chased by a murder of some 10 crows. The eagle flew close to the ground before rising up high and then made another dive as though it were riding an invisible rollercoaster in the air. The crows tailed the eagle, screaming like hounds chasing a fox, almost nipping one of the eagle's tail feathers. The eagle, however, seemed to be having fun and even slowed down a little to let the crows catch up before slipping from their grasp. I pointed this out to a local man walking by and he gave out a loud laugh.

"Ah yes, it happens all the time. He's taunting them. The eagles fly right next to the crows' nests and it drives them insane. They're like kids in the neighborhood running away after ringing your doorbell; always making mischief ..."

When I later walked beyond the park to the north of town I caught a whiff of a smell I found to be oddly familiar.

There must be a wastewater plant somewhere nearby.

Sure enough, after the bend on the road there was a dirt path leading to a wall of trees strategically planted to hide the concrete and metal behind it which I immediately recognized as a package wastewater plant. These compact plants are normally used in small communities where a centralized sewage system would be cost prohibitive, but existing septic tanks are causing issues with groundwater pollution. In Miami, there are three enormous wastewater plants, each treating more than 100 million gallons per day, so I had never seen a small-scale system like this that treats perhaps a few thousand gallons per day. They are equipped with a bar screen, equalization tank, aeration system, clarifier, sludge tank, tertiary filter, and disinfection, all jigsawed together to fit on two or three truck beds. I concluded that Port Hardy must be growing if it's investing in this type of infrastructure. Any property that switches from a septic tank to a sewer network would immediately shoot up in value.

Walking back to the center of town I found myself in the mood for a good meal, and spotted a pizzeria on Market Street downtown. I ordered a large pepperoni pizza forgetting about my regrettable experience back in Port Sidney, and again, the pepperoni slices were almost a quarter-inch thick and soggy.

"Why is food in Canada so nasty?" I moaned again while picking out the pepperoni slices and tossing them in the trash. I came to the somewhat pejorative conclusion that it must have something to do with their British heritage. Good food isn't one of the first associations a person makes with English-speaking cultures like one would with Italian or French. An English friend once joked that if you want to eat good "English" in London, you should go dine at an Indian restaurant.

I read on Google that there was a curling club at the Fort Rupert settlement adjacent to Port Hardy. During my days in college my flatmates and I enjoyed watching the women's curling during the Winter Olympics on TV and I thought it would be interesting to see a curling match in person.

I called up a cab and said to the driver, "I'd like to go see the curling rink in Fort Rupert."

"Are you sure?"

"Yes," I said without even thinking why he would ask. We drove the six miles and he dropped me off in front of a prefab metal building with a sign that read, "Fort Rupert Curling Club, G.E. Wilson Memorial Arena."

"You want me to wait?"

"No worries, I'll be here for a while," I said, and he drove off.

I walked across the dirt parking lot to the building entrance and promptly discovered that it was locked.

"When do they open?" I asked a bystander walking his dog along the street.

"In winter," he replied.

The rest of the afternoon was spent walking the six miles back to Port Hardy. This did at least give me the opportunity to exercise my legs a little. If there is a downside to kayaking for days on end it's the atrophy of the muscles in the lower body.

June 21 – Day 23

The morning conditions were exactly as the forecast predicted, and I got on the water as soon as there was daylight to catch the falling tide and the tail breeze. While I paddled through the channel between Vancouver Island and Nigei and Hope islands, the air became saturated in a gray haze extending down almost to the water's edge and it was nearly impossible to see the horizon. Some ways up the channel I came across another kayaker heading to Port Hardy and we stopped to exchange information. He was from Victoria and had been on a six-day trip around the northern islands of Queen Charlotte Sound.

"The last few days have been very warm; I'd be sweating if I was wearing that dry suit you have."

"Have you seen any bears?" I asked.

"Yes! I got a great shot of a black bear sitting on a rock watching me on the kayak. I was the day's attraction for him, and he even kept walking along the shoreline to keep up with me. I think he was one of those bears that lost his fear of people. You have to be especially careful with those bears."

"Any advice about the road ahead?"

"Yeah, don't stop at the indigenous village on Hope Island. They don't like outsiders. Had to get some water there and folks were giving me the 'you're not from around here' kind of look."

That last warning seemed a bit strange given that nearly everyone I had met so far had been extremely accommodating to the passing traveler. After looking up the place on Google, their website noted in bold capitalized red letters that the entire Tlatlasikwala First Nation territory was closed to the public and: "Absolutely nobody is permitted to come to shore at this time. To do so will be considered trespassing." There was no explanation for the reason, but I would venture to guess it had something to do with the Covid pandemic.

We continued our separate ways after our chance encounter on the water. The haze continued through the morning with visibility extremely limited, but after reaching Shushartie Point and the side channel that separates Nigei and Hope islands, I noticed the first signs of ocean swells as the lonely waves rolled through the flat water under my kayak. The swell period was very long, maybe 15 seconds, but it had a tall amplitude, and when I was at the crest, several islets became visible far in the distance.

At Cape Sutil I made a rest stop to stretch my legs on a shingled beach just beyond the Nahwitti River estuary. This was a significant geographic marker for the journey; it was the northernmost point on Vancouver Island. I checked the GPS unit to get the latitude reading which was 50.52 degrees north.

Interesting, I thought. *This isn't even as far north as London.* They are at about 51 degrees. The moderating influence of the Gulf Stream on the Atlantic coast of Europe shifts the climate zones some 10 degrees higher than the equivalent latitudes on the Pacific coast of North America where the current brings frigid waters from the Bering Sea and Alaska. The coastal climate along Vancouver Island is more like what you'd experience on the coast of Norway.

My guidebook gave me a stern warning about Cape Sutil and the river estuary where I was currently taking my leisure break in the bush. "Beware of the Nahwitti bar when the west wind blows against the ebbing tide. It will form dangerous rips and overfalls. Only attempt to cross it in ideal conditions."

I looked around and the water was flat like a mirror, but the afternoon forecast I had checked before leaving had called for westerly winds. The time was now 2 p.m. If the forecast was right, the winds would be waiting just around the next headland.

I better pull my pants up and get out of here.

The forecast was bang on the money. Immediately after clearing islets on the Cape Sutil headland, the west wind hit like a brick wall, and I was forced to headbutt a path through the waves before deciding to put-out after just six miles at a place called Shuttleworth Bight, the first of the north-facing beaches rimming the last stretch of coast before Cape Scott.

June 22 – Day 24

The west wind blew with force the entire day. Back at Port Hardy I had been fiddling with the VHF radio to find the channel with the marine weather forecast. I finally found the robotic voice of the Continuous Marine Broadcast on channels 09 and 21A, but was disappointed with the information as their reporting regions are so broad they're near meaninglessness. The North Vancouver Island region encompasses everything from Port McNeill on the Johnstone Strait to Nootka Island in the Pacific

Ocean. It could be a bright sunny day on Port McNeill, and just as easily feel like the end of the world paddling in a storm around the Brooks Peninsula 50 miles away as the bird flies.

I looked at the inReach messages on the GPS unit to see if Mom had sent me anything. There was a series of texts.

From here onward there is very little to no phone reception. My weather forecasts would come by VHS radio and most importantly, my mom who would be sending me the updates through the inReach GPS messenger. However, we should have trained on how we would communicate, before I left Port Hardy.

"It's going to blow from the west all day today," she wrote.

Then, "Lots of wind and rain."

And, "But things look better for tomorrow."

"Mom," I wrote back to her, "that doesn't mean much to me. Tomorrow, what time? From which direction is the wind coming, and how strong? You need to tell me the wind forecast strength and direction for the next day from 5 a.m. to 8 p.m. every three hours which is what the phone app gives. That way I can decide if I go out on the water and when I need to get back onshore."

When I set up the monthly billing plan, I went for the cheaper option with 30 free text messages which I thought was more than sufficient. Those 30 messages were quickly exhausted.

"Okay," she texted back, followed by another message saying, "No Problem."

"Mom, please try to keep everything in one text message as much as possible. I'm paying fifty cents per message. It adds up."

"Fifty cents is nothing for the peace of mind to check up on you, and make sure you're okay."

"Okay. No Problem."

"Sending you the forecast every three hours right now."

She sent me 12 messages, one for each of the forecast intervals for the rest of the day and the next which I was more than happy to pay the $6 it cost me. I decided to stay on shore for the day.

The falling tide at Shuttleworth Bight exposed a wide stretch of sand resembling the sickle of a crescent moon. At the far eastern end of the beach I saw two people fishing and walked over to meet them.

Larry and John were two lifelong buddies from Nanaimo taking a weeklong trip to hike and fish along the length of the Cape Scott Trail, a hiking route that runs about 16 miles along the north shore of Vancouver Island. They had started in San Josef Bay where they had been dropped off, and after having completed the section to the Cape, were headed north to Shushartie Bay from where they had scheduled a water taxi to ferry them back to Port Hardy. Larry worked as a freelance software engineer who did work for Google and Facebook, while John had recently retired from the BC Forestry Service.

"Those are very different professions," I noted. "How did you two come to meet each other?"

"We get that question sometimes," said Larry with a chuckle. "Both of our wives are nurses at the Nanaimo Regional General Hospital. We met at the hospital Christmas party and discovered that we both liked going fishing as a way to get a break from the wife nagging."

"Yes, camping and fishing, so here we are," John added. "You won't believe what happened yesterday. We were fishing from the headland and I caught three good-sized lingcods which we were going to roast for dinner over a fire. While I was cleaning the fish, I noticed a raven on the tree watching me. I finished cleaning two of the fish, and put the filets in a ziplock bag and hid it under a rock in a tidal pool so the smell wouldn't attract bears. Didn't think much of the raven, and went to take care of business in the bush. When I came back for the fish, I couldn't believe it. The bag was out of the water and the fish I had just cleaned were gone. The son of a bitch robbed me blind when I had my pants down."

"You were working for the raven," I said laughing. "He was probably looking at you cleaning the fish and thinking, *I'll let him get all the spines out so it's easier for me.* You're not the first and won't be the last person to get outwitted by a clever raven. Have you guys seen any bears on the trail? I met a kayaker yesterday who said he saw one on Hope Island."

"Not on this trip, but I can tell you a story about a bear from my years with the Forestry Service. I was clearing a trail one spring when a female black bear came out of the bush right in front of me. Usually if you're loud and talk directly to the bear they get the point and go on their way. But for some reason I really upset her. She walked toward me with her head low and the ears pointed back. Right there I knew she meant business and I made a run for it up the closest tree. She had me pinned up the tree for a good ten minutes before I noticed her cub hiding in the bush. I didn't come down till they were both long gone. It was the kind of experience you don't forget."

June 23 – Day 25

Although Cape Scott (the Cape) was only about 15 miles from my campsite on Shuttleworth Bight, the tide there was forecast to start rising around 8 a.m. which meant that unless I had a predawn start, I would be paddling against the flow by the time I got there. With that in mind, I decided to inch a little closer and paddle as far as Nels Bight. That would place me just three and half miles from the Cape to make an early morning attempt the next day. It would also coincide with the slack tide when the conditions should be calmest.

The Author, portaging the kayak, Port Hardy.

[TOP] *Camping mates on Shuttleworth Bight.* [MIDDLE] *The Cape Scott Lighthouse. Scott Islands seen in the distance.* [BOTTOM] *Arrival on San Josef Bay.*

[ABOVE] *The Author, rounding Cape Scott. Thick fog had reduced visibility to less than 50 feet.*
[BELOW] *Approach to San Josef Bay, one hour after passing Cape Scott, the fog had cleared.*

[ABOVE] Campsite on San Josef Bay. [BELOW] A deer and her fawn stroll across Nels Bight. The fawn would make a welcome meal for a bear or wolf.

While packing the kayak, I saw the remnant of a strange encounter that happened during the night while I slept. There were deer footprints on the gray sand. One set was from an adult, and another, much smaller in size, was made by a fawn. They had been walking side by side along the pine-fringed beach when suddenly the footprints became a tangled mess with skid marks in all directions as though the deer had been spooked into skipping and jumping. Intermixed with the deer prints were the pawprints of a wolf, not a very big one, but it had claws that left deep grooves in the sand. Whatever happened in the night, the wolf did not get the meal it was after. A short walk away I found the fawn gracefully skipping around its mother, elated to spend the morning on the beach like an excited toddler.

It was a quick hop to Nels Bight where I arrived before 10 a.m. The beach was flat and the waves were breaking gently.I tried to glide in as far as I could to minimize the walk to the campsite where several tents from hikers on the Cape Scott Trail were set up underneath a wall of pine trees rimming the sand.

The tents belonged to two families of friends from Winnipeg on holiday. They were a group of about sixteen.

"We saw you coming from a mile away," one of them said, "when you appeared suddenly around the headland. We were wondering what you were. We could see you paddling but were a little confused by the sail. Then just as you were coming in for the landing you dropped it down and for a while we thought you were in trouble."

I was then happy to demonstrate the workings of the kayak sail and the unique three-piece kayak setup which they were delighted to see.

They were all very friendly; I spent a good chunk of the next hour telling them about my kayak adventure from Seattle to the present spot, but all the while I noticed one man in their group about my age who gave me a silent but fixated and uncomfortable look. When he finally spoke to me, I was setting up my tent. His tone of voice suggested that he was annoyed by my existence.

"Why did you choose to camp right next to us?" he asked me twice.

"From the water, the place with all the tents looked like the campsite marked on the map," I answered nonchalantly. He didn't reply.

True, I could have packed and camped anywhere else on the beach, but I didn't feel like getting everything back into the kayak and paddling 300 feet just to please someone acting like I was a gerbil up their ass. My plan that afternoon was to hike the remaining six miles of the Cape Scott Trail leading to the lighthouse at the Cape, and try to catch a glimpse of the sea conditions through which I would be paddling the next day.

From Nels Bight the trail climbed steeply through an interminable number of switchbacks over a forested hill that had me sweating profusely (and a little disheartened that I'd be retiring my first clean T-shirt after just three days) in the midday heat. The trail gave way to another wide, north-facing, windswept flat sandy beach called Experiment Bight that was shielded by the Cape headland. A long time ago, this would have been an island separated from the mainland by a narrow channel. Over time, the tides filled in the channel and it had become a sand dune covered in tall, stalky grasses.

A sign marking the trail section over the dune noted that Experiment Bight had been part of the homeland of the Kwakiutl people who were renowned for their craftsmanship in building canoes and for being skilled open-ocean hunters of whales, seals, and sea lions. However, even they treated the storms around Cape Scott with due deference. When the weather was particularly bad, they would land on Experiment Bight, pull their canoes over the sand dune, and continue their journey through the well-sheltered southward-facing Guise Bay, rather than brave their way around the Cape. Imagining the back-breaking effort it must have taken to drag a massive wooden canoe up a 50-foot-high dune I concluded that they must have either been well aware of the fury that the Pacific Ocean could hurl at the Cape, or the sand dune was much smaller 200 years ago. I prayed that dragging my kayak up such a sandy hill wouldn't be something I would have to do.

At the top of the dune I felt refreshed by a northern breeze rolling down into the calm dark waters of Guise Bay. The tall grasses on the dune faded into a rolling prairie scattered with dandelions and buttercups rimming the sickle-shaped beach. At the edge of the prairie where the grasses gave way to forest were the stakes of a half-buried fence with broken and rusty barbed wire. I asked a hiker camped on the beach if he knew what it was.

"Probably a remnant of the old Cape Scott settlement," he said. "You'll see a lot more ruins around the meadow by the Hansen Lagoon. Stoves, farm tools, and even an old rusty tractor hidden in the forest. It's kind of spooky, like walking through an abandoned cemetery."

My guidebook noted that there was once a village here in the late 19th century. A group of Danish migrants set up a colony after the Canadian government promised homesteads for anyone of European descent who settled and farmed the land, but the environment was rougher than what many people were prepared to endure. All the nearby bays and coves were ill-suited for safe harbor, and ships bringing in supplies had a habit of getting wrecked in the shallow reefs and strong tides. The Canadian government had promised to build a road from Port Hardy but never did. Goods had to be brought through the Cape Scott Trail from San Josef Bay, but the path was too steep for horses, so everything had to be carried in by foot. The settlers eventually gave up eking out an existence in the unforgiving environment. The last settler, a man named Alfred Spencer who lived in Cape Scott for just over 40 years, abandoned the colony in the 1950s after he could no longer make the trek for supplies.

The trail turned west into the forest and climbed up the Cape Scott headland for another two miles to the lighthouse. The forest was thick with underbrush and the trail was like a green tunnel. Back in Port Hardy at the Kwa'lilas Hotel, the manager gave me some bear advice should I ever decide to hike the trail I now found myself on.

"There's a lot of bears in Cape Scott," he'd said. "If you don't want to run into one, make lots of noise while you walk so the bear hears you before he sees you."

In the green whiteout of the forest trail, I certainly hoped that none of the bears around were hard of hearing. What noises I should make I wasn't too sure, so I walked along talking loudly to myself.

That strategy didn't work out as well as I'd hoped. When I turned a U-bend on the trail, I suddenly saw a large black mass in the middle of the path staring back at me.

Oh crap. The bear had glossy black fur, a cookie brown snout, and was about four feet tall on all fours. He was big and looked quite strong, fit, and well fed.

The bear stopped almost as soon as I did about 30 feet away, taking up the whole width of the trail. Like me, he found it much easier to walk on the trail than in the thick bush. For a moment I thought he had a look of confusion, perplexed as I was about what to do next.

"What do you want me to do?" I talked to the bear as if he could understand what I was saying.

Since he didn't move, I started walking back slowly, but then he began pacing forward.

"Oh come on," I shouted. "We're not going on like this all the way to the beach. If you close the distance anymore, you're not going to like what I brought for you," I shouted while at the same time pulling the safety trigger from the can of bear spray I was carrying.

Back in Miami when I purchased a set of three bear spray cans at my mother's insistence, I took one can to the beach for a trial to see how it worked. (I didn't want to later risk screwing up at a moment when decisive action was needed.) Bear spray is nothing like a deodorant spray can that slowly releases a mist while you press down on a button. The can head has a trigger like a revolver, and when you engage it, the entire concoction in the one-pound can is immediately blasted out in a narrow orange jet like a pressure hose wherever you are pointing it. The recoil caught me unprepared and bent my elbow backward, sending some of the spray sideways and into my left eye. It was a tiny amount, but it left me squinting for 15 minutes.

"Don't get any closer," I shouted at the bear one more time.

I had to stop walking backward when I got to a fallen log across the trail that would have forced me to crouch on my knees to pass underneath. The bear also stopped.

"You can see my problem, right? I'm not moving anymore. You have to go around in the bush."

We stood in this awkward Mexican standoff looking at each other for what felt like an eternity, but eventually the bear managed to put himself in my shoes.

He is stuck, he must have thought.

He veered off the trail, walked about 10 feet away through the bush, scraping his way through the foliage like a tractor but completely hidden in the undergrowth, climbed back on the trail behind me and continued on with his day.

"That's right, you keep going your way, you don't want to tangle with me again," I shouted at the bear with some fake bravado, which he completely ignored.

After the adrenaline of the moment had passed, the sweat on my back felt cold and chilled in the breeze. I just had a faceoff with a bear!

When I reached the lighthouse, I spoke with the keeper about the experience.

"Ah yes," he said. "That's the big bull. He makes the rounds on the trail nearly every day to visit his females. At low tide he goes down to Guise Beach to look for shellfish. He's probably there right now. Sometimes he comes up here to the lighthouse too. I think he likes to make my dog go crazy. When little Pompey here suddenly erupts into a barking frenzy, I know what's up. If you stick around until late afternoon, you might see him again heading back up the trail."

John Campbell, the lighthouse keeper, had a smooth shaved face as though he had never grown a beard, and eyes buried deep in their sockets like gems hidden in the earth. He had been working as the Cape Scott lighthouse keeper since 2004, keeping an eye on the weather conditions and greeting hikers ecstatic at having reached the end of the Cape Scott Trail.

"I won't stay too long then," I said. "What's it like working here?"

"On a sunny day like today it's bliss. You can't complain about being able to look out at the ocean every day and watch the swells and the birds. Good steady job with eight weeks of paid vacation, if you can find someone to cover for you when you want to take time off. Most days it's calm, but if someone shows up with an emergency, it gets hectic very quickly. I had a guy once who was suffering a heart attack and we couldn't land the helicopter on the helipad because of the fog. He landed on the beach, and we had to get the guy down the trail on a stretcher. He lived, but it took almost three hours to get him to the hospital in Port Hardy."

"I guess no bears that day," I said. "Is there a place where we can see the channel?"

He pointed me to the lighthouse tower which had a steep ladder leading to a metal scaffold platform around the light beam panels. The view was not what I had hoped for. I would've liked to have seen down the cliff face to the water and perhaps catch a glimpse of the rocks, kelp beds, and swirling eddy currents I would need to keep an eye on when paddling through in my kayak. Instead, the forest stretched on for at least another hundred feet west and I could only catch a sliver of the ocean and the first two Scott Islands six miles away, well beyond where I would want to be paddling to round the cape. There was a lot of chop on the sea, and I observed a churning swell fixed in the middle of the channel by the rising tide running north and the 15-knot wind pushing against it.

"Yeah, not too good right now with the wind against the tide," John said after I came down from the platform. "The worst part is right on the northern tip of the Cape headland which you can't see from here. That's where the tide wraps around the Cape and runs along the northeast coast. The waves can get nasty there. In the morning, however, it will probably be fine."

"I certainly hope so. I have to be in San Josef Bay in two days. If tomorrow morning looks good, then it's tomorrow I'll be paddling around the Cape."

June 24 – Day 26

A thick fog barreled in during the night and the view of the sea from Nels Bight the next morning was a whiteout. I could hear the waves breaking a little off shore, but they were hidden behind the mist. The tide was more than halfway out and falling. In another hour or two it would be slack tide by which time I hoped to be rounding the Cape.

My campsite neighbors were already awake and warming up an oatmeal breakfast. I ate my five-minute breakfast of canned tuna, Chef Boyardee, and a few scoops of Nutella, and after packing my gear, I asked if anyone could give me a hand carrying the kayak to the water's edge. The volunteer was the individual who'd given me the unappreciative look the day before.

We carried the kayak in silence and after putting it down by the water he felt that he had to make his feelings known. "So I have to ask this. Out of the whole fucking beach, why the fuck did you have to camp right next to us?"

"I told you already. I paddled in from the water, I saw the tents, and concluded that was the campsite, so that's where I went."

"You Americans are just so brash! Can't you see I'm here with my family? How dare you just bust in like you own the place."

My experiences with other kayakers and campers everywhere had always been marked by comradery and cordiality, people who were always willing to lend a helping hand or share advice or knowledge. I took a moment to think how to answer. My mind had been focused on the Cape. *How rough would the waves be? Would there be wind and current? Would there be churning standing waves like the ones I saw from the lighthouse?* I was also frustrated with my headlamp which had moisture problems and was turning on and off on its own.

And now to top it all, I was also extremely irritated with this man's overinflated opinion of himself and his disrespect. I considered answering with a snarky comment – that he was a rare type, a Canadian douche bag, or that I hadn't realized he was from the House of Windsor and giving him a sarcastic bow. Instead, I went in for the kill, shoving a sharp dagger of truth into his gut.

"You know, it's obvious you're not like the rest of your family. I know it, you know it, they know it. It's not a secret. It's the first thing everybody notices about you when they meet you; it's nakedly obvious that people call you a weirdo behind your back. You know what happens to people like you with that kind of attitude? They die alone in the woods. I don't have to tell you how, you already know how it ends."

His face drooped and I immediately went from feeling angry to feeling guilty. He walked back to his camp and didn't speak another word to me or anyone else and I regretted that I hadn't just ignored him.

Although the fog was dense, the lack of wind meant the air felt warm and sticky, and the effort of carrying the gear down to the kayak quickly had me sweating and wiping the mist off my goggles. I powered over the few waves crashing on the beach and then pointed my kayak due west to the faint outline of the Cape headland. Unfortunately, the closer I seemed to get to the Cape, the worse the fog became and soon it became disorienting. When I heard the sound of breaking waves I worried that when I made the turn south, I might not have gone far enough west to clear the headland and might instead find myself paddling into Experiment Bight.

Then suddenly the sea changed from smooth rolling swells to a confused washing machine with short waves buffeting me from all directions, and I had to throw a low brace or two to stay upright.

This must be the point the lighthouse keeper spoke about where the tide loops around the headland and changes direction. If I go on a bit more, I will have the Cape cleared.

That seemed to be the right assessment as the sea flattened again which indicated that I had entered a different current and was now moving with the flow. In which direction, however, it was hard to know since there was no land for reference, but the north wind slacked suddenly, which probably meant that I was drifting south and had cleared the Cape. I looked at my compass, took a due south bearing, and started paddling.

While I paddled through the fog the sound of the swells breaking on the cliffs hidden in the fog became ever more remote. Picturing the map of the Cape in my head, I remembered that the coast ran slightly to the southeast, and concluded that I was progressively farther away from blundering into adverse conditions where a breaking wave might catch me by surprise. At least that's what I thought.

Through the haze there materialized a dark smudge at least 10 feet tall above the water and elongated like a submarine rapidly closing the gap between us. Had it breathed out a waterspout I would have sworn that it was a gigantic whale, but it was a large islet randomly tossed in the midst of the sea, and likely the culprit of many unfortunate shipwrecks in the fog. When I later checked the GPS track through this section, I was surprised to see that I had been moving at over seven miles per hour with almost no effort, and that the islet was a big enough hazard to deserve a name, Strange Rock.

I would have called it Widow Rock, I thought. It would have been the last piece of land many a sailor would have seen before being sent to the bottom of the sea. Some eight miles south of the fog I began getting glimpses of the landscape. The summits of green cliffs were illuminated with pockets of sunshine before precipitously tumbling into a haze that hid the scattered boulders and swells below. The roar of the swells again got louder, and eventually, the fog cleared enough to expose the commotion at the base of the cliff. I didn't know whether to feel relief or disappointment; the breaking swells were more thunder and bluster than thrash and foam. How could such little waves make so much noise? I thought. There was nothing to fear here. This was a calm day on the Cape.

I paused while letting the waves roll underneath me before tantruming on the rocks.

I paddled around Cape Scott, I thought. *Few people can say that, and fewer still have done it alone.*

And yet, with all the worries and warnings, I couldn't say it had been hard. It was easy. Not quite the feeling of achievement I was hoping for, I thought.

Oh, come on, don't be so humble. Give yourself the credit, said the voice in my head. You picked the day with the right weather, you picked the time with the right tide, and you paddled it. Oh, and you had to deal with an asshole this morning. That's enough to fill a day for anyone.

Eh, I guess you're right, I thought in return. I was hoping that I would feel like a more skilled paddler for having done it. Instead, I feel like I'm a lucky paddler. Luck is luck; it's not skill. You don't get better by being lucky.

Ah, but what is skill, and what is luck? If you survive paddling through a terrible storm because you didn't check on the weather, would that be a demonstration of skill or imprudence? If you had an eventless passage around one of the stormiest capes in the Pacific Northwest because you planned for the wind and the tide, is that skill or luck? And if a whale had gaped its mouth and swallowed you, would that have been poor judgment? An archer aims the arrow, but he can't tell it how to fly. Sometimes the arrow hits the mark, sometimes a sudden wind blows it off course, and sometimes the bow snaps. When you survive poor judgment, be thankful. When you reap the fruits of your efforts, be happy. And if you fail despite doing all that could have been done, then be at peace. Today, you enjoyed an easy success so feel free to feel happy. At the end of the journey, well, no one can predict how it will turn out...

VANCOUVER ISLAND
Mt. MCKELVIE
TAHSIS
NOOTKA ISLAND
RUGGED MOUNTAIN
THE WATERFALL
THE TAHSIS NARROWS
ZEBALLOS INLET
ZEBALLOS
ESPERANZA INLET
BOSTON 1805
QUEEN CHARLOTTE SOUND
NUCHATLITZ Is.
CATALA Is.
TATCHU POINT
PORT MCNEILL
UNION Is.
RUGGED POINT
KYUQUOT
SPRING Is.
CHECLESET BAY
FORT RUPERT
JACKOBSON POINT
PORT HARDY
PORT ALICE
THE BUNSBY Is.
COAL HARBOR
QUATSINO SOUND
THE BROOKS PENINSULA
RESTLESS MOUNTAIN
CRABAPPLE BEACH
CAPE CLARK
SOLANDER Is. & CAPE COOK
LAWN POINT
GOODING COVE
THOMAS FOSTER 1895
JANE GREY 1893
DORA II 1922
ATOMIC 1946
KAINS Is.
GRANT BAY
SAN JOSEF BAY
RAFT COVE
PACIFIC OCEAN
N

PART 5 - PADDLING WITH FRIENDS - THE BROOKS CHALLENGE

June 25 – Day 27

The coastline south of Cape Scott is verdant with pine trees pressed tightly to the cliff's edge as if someone had cut a slice from a mint-crusted chocolate cake. The almost vertical walls seemed foreboding as if inscribed with a warning to any passing kayaker, "Don't even think to land here."

I continued on, trusting the GPS map which showed that nine miles south of the Cape I would encounter a gap in the impenetrable wall leading into a bay gouged deep into the shoreline. Soon enough, after rounding a few islets, the bay appeared. The headland behind me blocked off the wind letting me roll gently with the swells until I landed on a beach nearly a thousand feet wide. Here the sand had been canvased into a never-ending myriad of colorful troughs and ridges by the receding tide that even the most skilled abstract painter would find hard to match the detail.

Above the beach was a grove of tall cedars and pines where the canopy blocked off nearly all the light reaching to the floor. The undergrowth was sparse and short, and the forest seemed almost transparent, with the thick cedar trunks reminding me of the columns of a great temple.

San Josef Bay must be the most beautiful beach in all of Vancouver Island, I thought.

After setting camp and notifying JF that I had made it to our rendezvous point with a day to spare, I went on a walk in the coastal landscape. The low tide had revealed all sorts of interesting things to discover.

Several sea stacks – 50-foot-high monoliths sculpted by the sea – had become connected to the beach and one could walk between them like they were great statues in an art gallery.

In the tidal pools I was fascinated by how the marine creatures organized themselves in a precise hierarchy. At the very bottom where the rocks were wet even at low tide were the mollusks and starfish. Then the shellfish, which always have the larger individuals at the bottom and smaller ones on the top as those bigger ones at the bottom get more time to feed in the water. After them, the barnacles which can survive longest when exposed to air. The final layer, before the point where the rock is permanently exposed in all but the highest tides, we have the scrawny little algae called rockweed which is the kayaker's most feared plant. If you blunder with your kayak over a patch of rockweed, you know you're about to hit the bottom of your boat.

While I was meandering my way through the sea stacks I found a deep cave gouged into the rock cliff ringing the beach. The cave must have been at least 200 feet deep as my eyes needed a moment to adjust to the low light, and when I turned to stare at the entrance, the landscape outside was a white glare. The cave roof, covered with a thin moss layer, dripped constantly like drizzle which made the air moist and cool, and the water percolating through the rocks and tree roots above was fresh like a mountain stream. At the deepest point in the cave, I found an interesting artifact from the sea; a large piece of driftwood that had been tossed and mangled in between the rocks which was proof that in a storm, this cave would be no safe refuge to hide in.

The walk from the trees to the water was like a book about the work the sea had done on the coast. At first, you see an imposing cliff that stands against the sea. The sea, however, isn't intimidated nor pressed for time. The swells pound the cliff walls tirelessly like ants stripping a carcass; each wave chipping a tiny sliver off the wall until one day a cave is gouged, and it is made ever deeper until the roof caves in. When the debris is wiped away all that is left is a stack watching over the tides, but even the stack doesn't live forever. The base is constantly worn down by sand slushed back and forth with the tide like a saw. When the stack topples like a tower under siege, mollusks and barnacles finish off crunching the rock until all that's left is the sea.

In the afternoon, I hiked part of the Cape Scott Trail inland as I was told by a fellow camper, who had just completed the multi-day trek back from the Cape, that he had seen an immense spruce tree.

"It's definitely worth the walk, it's about a mile beyond Eric Lake on the way to Nels Bight."

Looking at the map, Eric Lake was definitely walkable in a few hours, so I put on my boots and wide-brim hat, holstered the bear spray on my shorts, grabbed two Perriers from my treasure stash, and fitted them to the back pockets on my shirt.

The walk wasn't very eventful and there wasn't much to see. The trail was buried in the forest, there were no viewpoints, and the canopy was thick with only a few shafts of light landing on the forest floor. After so many days of kayaking and lack of lower body work, my legs started to feel wobbly like spaghetti straws. As the distance from the sea increased, the moderating effect of the ocean on the temperature became less pronounced and the humidity felt like a spring day in Florida.

When I arrived at Eric Lake I found a pebbled beach where I could catch a glimpse of the sunny blue sky. I stretched my neck to look as far down each side of the trail as I could, and when I was reasonably sure there wasn't anyone nearby, took a skinny dip in the refreshingly cool water.

After passing the lake, I was on the lookout for the big spruce. *It can't be much farther*, I thought.

The trail began a steep climb and my thighs felt like they were on fire when called to march up the winding switchbacks. I eventually caught up with a couple on their way to Cape Scott.

"Oh, we passed it a while ago," they said to my chagrin.

I turned around and began walking but soon was back at the lake without finding the tree. I concluded that my expectations must have been too high after seeing the big cedar on Hansen Island. I had seen a few large spruce trees on the trail but none whose height and girth exclaimed, *Yes, I'm the big tree everyone writes home about.* I must have passed the tree and failed to be impressed enough to notice it.

Walking back, and somewhat disappointed, I reached a fork on the trail I hadn't noticed at first. It led to a cul-de-sac at the end of a winding logging road with a gravel parking lot with far more cars than people. *This is one of the access points for the Cape Scott Trail*, I thought.

Three girls of college age were unloading bagfuls of gear from their minivan onto a wheelbarrow. Given the scarcity of space in a kayak, and how every item needs to be vetted for its essentialness, I wondered what superfluous things they might be carrying.

"Ah! Those fancy Hawaiian shorts sure go with this wheelbarrow," one of them said while pointing at my colorful attire.

"Even if they'd fit, I couldn't give them to you. It's the only pair I got, " I said, deliberately pretending to misunderstand her. They laughed and she gave the obvious clarification.

"We are asking if you would be a gentleman and push the wheelbarrow for us."

"You mean the two miles to the beach?"

"Yes."

"With all that stuff?"

"Yes."

I thought about how I could diplomatically decline the somewhat entitled-sounding request.

"Sorry. But I have to go take a massive dump. Seriously, it cannot wait," I said, trying to ignore their look of indignation as I walked back to the trail. Mom would certainly have frowned at my lack of chivalry. I would argue, however, that this being their first day, it would be best for them to make the hard choices now about what items to abandon, rather than kill themselves carrying it all. A few hills, mud puddles, and slipups would teach them everything they'd need to know.

June 26 – Day 28

I woke at 5 a.m. to a horrible discomfort in my bowels.

Oh god, this one definitely can't wait, I thought while wondering what caused the whirl of commotion in my stomach. It must have been the energy bars with extra fiber.

I walked barefoot out of the tent in the early light and down a sand path to the nearest outhouse shed. When I flipped open the lid on the latrine pit, I found a huge yellow slug on the seat rim. *Ugh. How am I going to get rid of this bad boy?*

I cringed and grabbed him with a piece of toilet paper, but he was heavy and slippery and he slid from my hand and fell inside the latrine pit. He hit the bottom with a thump.

What a horrible way to go, I thought. *So sorry but now I must also add some horrible insult on top of your injury.* I marked his demise with a thunderous salute.

This wasn't my first encounter with these nasty slugs. These buggers live everywhere in these forests. Two days earlier I had found a huge one nearly as big as my hand crawling halfway into my booties. If I hadn't immediately noticed him, I might have buried my foot in him and his slimy body would have squeezed between my toes. The slugs appeared seemingly out of nowhere. You'd leave something on the ground unattended for five minutes and suddenly there'd be two or three of them crawling on top of your stuff. I hoped I'd never have to deal with one inside my dry suit.

I paddled up the San Josef River that empties into an estuary at the end of the beach to a boat ramp and campsite where JF from the Skils kayak group and I would be meeting. The tide was low and I had to dismount and walk sections of the river to avoid scraping over the river boulders.

I arrived a little early and the only person at the camp was the site's keeper.

Henry was the closest person I've met who I would consider a hermit. He'd lived in a little wooden shack on the campground for almost 40 years. His beard was full and silvery, his hair was long, wavy, and white as sea foam, and his eyes were buried deep inside wrinkly sockets. He was a plump fellow, and I imagined him working as a mall Santa in Nanaimo or Port Hardy during the holidays. Perhaps that was the only time in the year he ever went into town.

He sat on a folding chair with a plumpy orange tabby cat on his lap. "I adopted him some years ago. Someone dumped him in the forest one night. The little thing feared everything and everyone. Took him a month to trust me. I'd put food outside and for a long time he wouldn't even touch it. But we're best friends now, aren't we Garfield?" The cat purred in agreement.

"He must be in good company. Do you know when the folks from Skils Sea Kayak are coming? They should be here soon I think."

"Is someone supposed to be coming here? Nobody told me. I don't have a phone though, so no one could've called to tell me they're coming. But folks do come by from time to time and show up unannounced, eh."

Fortunately, I didn't have to worry or wonder for too long if I was at the right location. A white van with a trailer carrying several kayaks drove down the one-way dirt road into the campsite and stopped at the wooden shack. The slide-side door opened.

"Good to see you again," said a man in a French accent. "Hey Felipe! Congrats on making it around Cape Scott! We'll park by the ramp, and I'll introduce you to the group."

"I've no clue who he is," Henry whispered to me with deadpan. "But more folks know me than I know them, so maybe I am a friend of his."

For some reason, for all the times I had spoken to JF over the phone I had assumed that his accent was Chinese. It kind of made sense that he might be of Asian descent as there is a large population of Asian Canadians and Americans in the Pacific Northwest. I attribute this mistake to the Yanny/Laurel effect where if you're primed to hear something a certain way, your brain hears it that way. For sure, I was surprised on our first in-person meeting to discover that he was very European looking, and in fact, French Canadian.

We were supposed to be a party of 10 but after counting everyone present, I noticed there were only nine of us.

"Yes, unfortunately one of our friends got Covid two days before the trip. It's a shame, but it also means everyone will have to make an effort and eat more of the food. In fact, everyone's boat will be very heavy going out today."

JF's partner was a British lady named Justine. I had spoken with her over the phone as well, but now meeting her in person I could not help but think that I had seen her before somewhere. "Were you in that series of kayaking films called *This Is The Sea?*" I asked.

"I was the one who made the series." She smiled like someone who's just received recognition for their work.

There wasn't much time for me to get to know everyone else save for brief introductions. There would be plenty of get-to-know-you time in our landbound weather days to come. We did, however, briefly go over the 120-mile route we would be covering over the next two weeks. This would take us along the coast, past Quatsino Sound, before reaching the base of the Brooks Peninsula where we would wait for a favorable weather window. After that, we would continue through several small archipelagoes rimming the mainland, make a resupply stop near the Indigenous village of Kyuquot, and then continue to Esperanza Inlet where the same white van would pick up everyone just outside the village of Zeballos. JF and Justine organize both skills and training and expedition courses through Skils and this was to be their longest trip of the year so far in BC, and had previously led a 30 day trip in Antarctica a few months prior. "Time is a little bit late. We should eat lunch, get all the kit packed up, and get going," said JF.

The lunch was simple but surprisingly good. For someone accustomed to eating nothing but canned fish, canned pasta, and Nutella every day, my two ham with salami and Swiss cheese sandwiches with hummus was simple but delicious. The banana and Fuji apple for dessert were also great treats.

We launched a little after midday. The tide had risen and squeezing the kayak over the river boulders without dismounting was just about doable, even with all the additional gear.

I don't think my kayak had ever felt so heavy. In addition to all the food, we were each carrying a 10-liter water bag inside the cockpit. They were positioned underneath our legs, squeezed up against the thigh braces. Getting out of the kayak on a steep landing when speed is of the essence proved nearly impossible for me. After three embarrassing capsizes, I concluded that I first had to remove the bag and strap it onto the deck under the bungees. That did not always work, and at times I had to fetch the water bag out of the surf and hope it hadn't banged itself open.

Almost immediately out of San Josef Bay, our flotilla ran into its first incident. The wind had whipped up considerably by the afternoon and waves bashing against the cliffs reflected into the incoming swells, shaking us up and down like a roller coaster. One of our kayaking mates developed debilitating sea sickness and his stomach nearly forced his lunch overboard. He looked like he was seeing stars. One of us made a brace with their kayak to give him some stability and tied a towline to JF's boat, who then pulled two kayaks plus his own.

After an hour of furious paddling, he announced what we could already see. "Guys, I am spent. We have to pause for a break."

Fortunately, the northwest wind was pushing us all along, so resting in the water did not mean that we would be losing ground, and after a few breaks in between paddled we landed in a sheltered cove at a beach 10 miles south of San Josef Bay. Only when we were again safely on land and called in the day did our seasick mate improve.

June 27 – Day 29

Our beach camp had one of the steepest landings I have ever made. The slope was a bed of boulders that rolled and crackled with the waves washing back to sea. After tossing the water bag to one of the mates onshore, I waited for a lull in the waves. When the lull came I quickly dismounted in knee-deep water and then ran up the beach pulling the boat behind me to try and climb as high as possible with the waves for help. Nonetheless, I was irked by the scraping sounds against the rocks, and I dreaded to find out how many new scratches I had just put on my hull.

"Hopefully the paint-protection tape is doing its job," I said to myself after noticing it had several rips. If there is one thing anyone who buys a new kayak from the factory can relate to, it's that when you scratch your boat, the gut-wrenching anguish is enough to make you convulse with pain. I would absolutely lick my entire kayak if it would wipe away the scars.

The beach had a narrow rocky ledge about 25 feet above the water just below the treeline. It was just wide enough to pitch our tents in a row. A line of driftwood logs lay immediately above us on the ledge which gave me chills to think that the waves could get that high. I checked the moon phase; it was a waning crescent. "No danger tonight," I said to myself, relieved.

I woke up at 2 a.m. when I heard a howling animal noise outside. After I came to my senses and was certain that it was not a bear, I became rather annoyed.

"God damn it. We have a snorer in the group." We were packed together so closely that it could have been anyone. However, when dawn came and I stepped outside, I found a set of wolf tracks crossing the beach by the water. The paw marks were as big as a human hand and judging from their depth on the coarse sand, it was a large and heavy animal.

"Looks like the morning beach patrol was doing the rounds," I said.

"Or the beach landlord came by looking for rent, that's why the food always needs to be in the kayaks, and the hatches closed tight," said JF.

This being our first full day together we began what would be a regimented routine necessary for living in a tight-knit group. Every morning we'd wake up a little after sunrise. JF and Justine were up earlier still to get the coffee boiling and prepare breakfast. We would then get dressed in our gear, pack our kits, and pack it into the kayak stern hatch (the bow hatch was reserved for food which JF and Justine could access for breakfast, lunch, or dinner). The time for us to get organized usually coincided with what became a familiar call from JF indicating that the meal was ready.

"Time to wash hands!"

On our first meal, JF set the campground ground rules.

"Folks, as I'm sure you're all aware, we won't have a meaningful chance for a shower for the whole two weeks we are together. It is, however, important that we keep a bare minimum of personal hygiene out of respect for each other and our health. That includes washing hands before every meal so we are not eating each other's poop. And speaking of which, please make sure you do yours below the high tide mark, and mark it with a wood stack or big rock on top so no one has the misfortune of digging into the same place. You should burn the used toilet paper whenever possible but be careful not to set the forest on fire."

After each meal, we designated one person to be the dishwasher. This was not a pleasant job, but it always had to be done or our dishes and wares encrusted with food scraps would begin attracting unwanted visitors. Depending on the type of food, the plates, pots, and pans sometimes got very greasy and needed vigorous scrubbing with biodegradable detergent (which is another term for not very effective detergent), and an ultra-heavy-duty sponge.

Not long after eating, we would push off into the water on our kayaks. If the tide had been receding, this invariably meant we needed to make a second round of carrying the kayaks to the water's edge, which now loaded with gear, were very heavy and required the combined efforts of four people. JF's and Justine's kayaks were especially heavy as they also carried all the kitchen gear, including the cooker, gas canisters, and the folding tables; their kayaks needed six carriers, and I was all the more impressed that they were for a while pulling three boats the day before.

I was very apprehensive about carrying my kayak loaded with gear as the hinges were not guaranteed to bear the full weight of the boat and gear without the buoyancy of the water. I had not brought any hinge replacements, and having my 18-foot sea kayak suddenly turned into a short puggy whitewater boat would be a problem.

"Folks, can I have six people to carry my three-piece baby as well? I'll do two rounds of dishes when it's my turn." The offer was judged to be a fair compromise.

A rising tide floods the sea stacks in San Josef Bay.

[ABOVE] *Sea cave at low tide, San Josef Bay.*
[BELOW] *Paddling up the tidal waters of the San Josef River.*

[ABOVE] Wood cabin near Godding Cove. The Author left a Perrier bottle for the next lucky occupant. [BELOW] Group campsite at Crabapple Beach near the Brooks Peninsula.

A hidden waterfall pours into an arm of the sea, Nutchatlitz Islands.

[TOP LEFT] *Campfire at Crabapple Beach.* [TOP RIGHT] *The SKILS Group paddling calm waters around Point Cook, Brooks Peninsula.* [MIDDLE LEFT] *Tidal channels on the Bunsby Islands. The paddler has to be constantly aware of the tide to not get left high and dry in the shallows during the ebbing flow.* [MIDDLE RIGHT] *The Author, Thinking about the challenges ahead, photograph by JF.* [BOTTOM] *Roasted Marshmallow evening at Rugged Point.*

[TOP] Fresh fish for lunch. [MIDDLE LEFT] JF inspecting the days dinner. [MIDDLE RIGHT] The infamous Banana Slug. These creatures love to find their way into a paddler's boot. [BOTTOM LEFT] JF providing Philip with bracing support while he tries to land a halibut. The 42 pound fish is visible just below the water near the kayak bow. Photograph by Gerry Molnar. [BOTTOM RIGHT] JF and Justine prepare a pop-up lunch on the Brooks Peninsula.

[ABOVE] Dense Canopy at the Rosa Island campsite.
[BELOW] The Author, three weeks after leaving Port Hardy.

[ABOVE] Justine explains the intricacies of a nine-way handshake. [BELOW] The SKILS Kayak Group after completing the Brooks Challenge. The Author is fourth from the right.

We only paddled 10 miles to a southward-facing beach called Grant Bay. The forecast called for the winds to begin blowing from the southwest which meant bad weather was on the way.

The weather follows a cyclical pattern on the west coast of Vancouver Island. When the wind blows from the northwest and west, it means that a high-pressure system is close by, and that makes the mornings begin with fog which then transitions into clear sunny afternoons. Over the course of a few days, the high-pressure system moves from west to east, and the wind shifts from northwest to northeast. Eventually, when the high pressure is past, the wind shifts to due east which can be particularly treacherous as it blows against the prevailing swells and steepens the waves which barrel onto the shore. Then about a day after that there's a sudden calmness. The wind dies down, and the water flattens, and you can even hear birds chirping in the forest.

That, however, is when you need to be most vigilant. It means there's a low-pressure trough somewhere out in the sea. You notice a slight breeze from the south which slowly turns southwest. At first, you think that's a refreshing waft, but after a few hours it starts to feel a little rough and uncomfortable, and by the time you see the cloud ridge over the ocean you better know where you're landing because the storm front will be rolling in soon.

When we rounded the headland into Grant Bay, I caught sight of the cloud ridge behind the Brooks Peninsula some 25 miles away. Thirty minutes later the peninsula became obscured, the temperature dropped, the wind picked up, and the rain began pouring. Fortunately, by then we were all on dry land waiting for what JF and Justine had planned for dinner.

June 28 – Day 30

On our third day together we watched from shore on Grant Bay as the wind and rain blew hard from the southwest.

"Folks, we're going to make today a rest day and wait out the storm. No worries though, we've budgeted for four rest days over the two weeks, so this fits the schedule just fine. Make yourselves at home. We'll make sure there is plenty of food."

JF and Justine were really good cooks. The day's lunch included spicy deer steak and mashed potatoes all cooked on-site with his portable camp kitchen. Cooking three fine meals a day for 14 days for nine very hungry people is a feat to be lauded.

"You know, I always thought that food in Canada was like food in the United States; bland and bad for your health. But I am eating better with you than I do at home. You've set the bar very high for the rest of the trip."

"Oh, as you might've guessed, I'm from the part of Canada with the French connection, so we take great pride in what we put in our bellies. The food definitely makes or breaks a trip. If the food is bad, that's the only thing that people will remember. By the way, the onions are separate from the mash potatoes; someone mentioned before the trip that they didn't like onions."

"Haha, that was me ... thanks! I'm the one who wrote, 'the more boring the food the better,' on the application. I'll admit I'm a picky eater. It's not that I don't like onions, it's more like I don't like seeing them in the food, so I like to cut them really small. I draw the line on pickles though. I really don't like those. Oh, and the tomato sauce I like is rich and creamy, not the chunky stuff. When I was little, my mother had to put me in front of the TV to watch cartoons and distract me enough to shovel the food I didn't like in my mouth."

"A few years ago on the trip around the Great Bear Forest up north, we had a guy who liked his onions cut small too," Justine chipped in. "What have you been eating on your trip?"

"Well, I'm kind of spartan when it comes to food and kayaking. I don't like to cook, so in the morning I have canned fish and a canned pasta. I like Chef Boyardee and the Bumble Bee tuna brands. During the day I only eat cereal bars, and in the evening I have the same thing as in the morning, tuna, pasta, and maybe some Nutella."

"So you don't even warm up the pasta?"

"No. I just add lots of grated cheese to give it some texture."

"That just sounds so awful ..."

"Haha. I don't disagree with you, but after you eat sardines for five straight days, canned ravioli becomes very palatable."

"Yes, hunger will do that to you. We are going to spoil you a bit with us! It might take you a while to get used to your Chef Boyardee again."

Being landbound the entire day, we had time to sit on the beach and watch the breakers roll onshore while sheltered from the downpour under a tarp JF had set up over the makeshift kitchen.

I got talking to one of our mates. John was a high school teacher in the Seattle Public School system.

"I teach high school civics," he said. "Used to be a criminal defense attorney before I decided there was more to life than money and sixty-hour work weeks, much to the chagrin of my wife. She thought she was dating a lawyer, but she married a high school teacher." He laughed.

"The rain isn't letting up anytime soon. Tell us some crazy cases you've had to defend."

"I've had a few interesting clients over the years. The one I most often talk about was a guy I represented who had robbed thirty-three banks in one year in the Seattle area. He was probably putting in more hours per week robbing banks than I was at my law firm. That was his full-time job, and he was very good at it. Then he made a mistake and got caught. He tried to rob the same bank twice in the same week. I think I did a pretty good job representing him. I got most of the charges dismissed. During a seven-hour interrogation, the cops extracted a confession from him by threatening his mother. Confession under duress is a big no-no; that's an easy way to get a case thrown out. The best friend of a criminal defense attorney, after the Fifth Amendment, is a cop who's bad at his job."

"That must be useful when you teach your students about civil rights."

"It is. I teach in a poor neighborhood, so the kids and their families there have all kinds of problems. I tell them that if the cops want to talk to you, and you know you're not a choir boy, it's never a good sign. Invoke the Fifth Amendment and then stay mute. Your mouth is your worst enemy. And it's very important that you orally invoke the Fifth. Otherwise, your silence might not count, and the cops can use your silence as evidence of guilt. That's from the *Salinas v Texas* case."

"And what's teaching high school like?"

"Tough but rewarding. Tough because you don't have the resources. The school district budget comes from property taxes. If you're from a poor neighborhood, the properties are worth less, the district collects less money, so the schools have less money and lack enough of everything. Heck, in some of the really poor neighborhoods, the schools have to ration writing paper. In contrast, if you're from a rich neighborhood, then it's the opposite. They have resources my students wouldn't even think to ask for. The rewarding part comes from me feeling like I'm making a difference, even if it is small. There are a few kids I teach for whom I'm not just a teacher, I'm kind of a dad figure too, and that's rewarding to me."

The onshore wind picked up a few gusts, and we huddled in the middle of the tarp to avoid getting soaked by the side rain.

"Seems like the education system is a factory for inequality," I said to John, squeezed into the huddle.

"Yes. The irony isn't lost on anyone who has ever heard the expression 'school-to-prison pipeline' or knows anything about the Veil of Ignorance."

"What's the Veil of Ignorance?"

"It's a thought experiment made by a philosopher called John Rawls to make you think outside of your own head. If you could shape the society you will be born into, but with no way to know what position in that society you would be born to, how would you want to change that society? And how close is the society that you live in now to that? If a person really thinks through the exercise honestly, then something clicks in their head and they can see the world through someone else's perspective. People don't realize how much of their lot in life boils down to what zip code they're born in."

June 29 – Day 31

We woke up to dead calm conditions and a thick low fog, the prelude to a radiantly sunny day, tempered with a coffee aroma wafting around in the air.

"Time to wash hands!" JF announced.

Soon after breakfast the fog lifted, and we were in our kayaks making our way to the headland marking the north shore of Quatsino Sound which is the most extensive of the fjord systems on the Vancouver Island west coast. The sound was carved by a glacier during the last ice age that extended to the Pacific Ocean that left a deep valley flooded by the sea. From the sound mouth, which is wide like the estuary of a great river, it splits into three fjords with the longest reaching 45 miles inland, and it almost slices through the north of the island into Queen Charlotte Sound near Port Hardy.

At the headland point was a small rocky islet called Kains Island, crowned with a mohawk of cedars and Douglas firs and a bright, red-roofed lighthouse rising some 100 feet above the water. There is no good harbor on the island save for a narrow pebble beach on the north side only accessible in good weather and high tide, when a kayaker can slip over a bed of sharp boulders covered in barnacles and rockweeds. Fortunately for us, the conditions allowed us to stop and pay a visit to the lighthouse keeper.

"Let's not be here too long or we will be stuck with having to carry our heavy boats to the water," said JF.

After climbing up a steep trail fitted with hand holds, we reached a fenced grassy field with a few scattered buildings perched precariously at the cliff's edge. There was a hanging boardwalk leading to an exposed wood-plank helipad facing the sound where a single false step would send you falling into the sea a hundred feet below.

"So sorry but I can't let visitors walk on the helipad," said the lighthouse keeper who came over to greet us. Dale was a man in his late 60s but stood straight as a pedestal, and wore a fluorescent safety jacket over his broad shoulders. "One of the previous keepers had a son who came to visit, slipped, fell down the cliff and drowned. He is buried just beside our dwelling."

Dale and his wife had been working as keepers on Kains Island for nearly six years. "We found the job through a Facebook ad, and thought, 'Hey, why not?' We're both retired. The job has good benefits, and we could rent out our house on the mainland. And whether the weather is good or bad, being able to wake up and work at a place with a 360-degree view of the ocean and the mountains, hear the song birds, and see deer out your window is just unbeatable."

"How do the deer get to this tiny island?" I asked, surprised.

"They swim and climb the same trail you came up, and then hang out in the woodland just beyond the buildings. Sometimes they walk around the grass and the boardwalk too. They're so used to seeing me, they're hardly bothered."

He was right. Just below the boardwalk walking along the grassy edge by the cliff face was a young buck with short antlers barely fazed by our presence.

Dale told us about what daily life here was like and I was convinced this line of work can be a good deal for the right person. In fact, I think that there would be a long line of applicants if the job was more widely advertised. The pay is decent, about $50,000 Canadian if you are the head keeper (as opposed to the assistant keeper who fills in when the head keeper is on holiday), and the accommodation and utilities are all included. The duties involve some light maintenance on the buildings and boardwalk such as painting and general upkeep, recording the weather and the sea conditions four times a day which takes about an hour, maintaining the weather instruments, and uploading the data to the Meteorological Service of Canada. If someone shows up to the lighthouse in distress, you are expected to provide first aid, and call in emergency services if needed. Other than that, it seemed to me like there was a fair amount of free time on most days, and now that there exists fast satellite internet and the pandemic made remote work socially acceptable, there aren't many impediments to being a lighthouse keeper and having a second full-time office job.

Heck, I wouldn't mind doing my engineering job from here for a year or two, I thought. If I could choose between working alone in an empty windowless office in the middle of town like I currently do, and a place where I could see the waves breaking onshore, the clouds rolling over the cliffs, and the bald eagles hovering in the wind, it wouldn't be a hard sell.

"Ever since Amazon struck a partnership with the Canadian Coast Guard we can pretty much order anything we need," Dale added. "The mail arrives every two weeks with the chopper. My wife even ordered a treadmill and some weights to get some exercise when the weather has us stuck indoors, so now we have our own personal gym as well."

With the tide falling, we hurried back to the kayaks lest we be trapped in the boulders. Crossing the mouth of Quatsino Sound to the south shore took us almost an hour. There was a slight north breeze, folks asked me for a little showboating with the kayak sail, and I happily indulged them. "Would love a few photos please. I mostly paddle alone. Every shot I have of myself is from the viewpoint of a rhinoceros," I joked.

On the opposite shore near Gooding Cove, past an archipelago of small islets, we came across a cabin nestled in the woods. It didn't look abandoned like others I had seen on the way to Nanaimo. The wooden deck and roof were varnished and in good condition, the door hinges swung without effort, and a 20-pound propane tank in the backyard was heavy with fuel.

"It's a communal house," Justine explained. "It works on a first-come-first-serve basis. Everyone who comes by brings something, takes the trash away, or does a little upkeep."

I walked inside through the kitchen door and noticed a variety of seasonings in the pantry, two metal pots by the oven, and two clean cast-iron pans on top of the cooker. The living room was homey; a drying clothesline hung from the ceiling over a wood furnace where a few logs had been left ready for the next arrival. I sat on a dusty futon pressed against the back wall and looked through a large glass window facing the sound as though it were a TV screen tuned to a nature documentary.

I could certainly rest here watching where the blue waves will break, I thought. If I stay long enough, perhaps a fishing boat will chug along from one side of the window to the other or maybe a whale will breach the surface and let off a spout, or a bald eagle will land on a tree branch with a catch. It felt blissful to be able to sit there for an hour or two and not think about anything other than what might be directly in front of you.

By the window on top of a round wooden table was a notebook closed over a pencil marking the last entry. It was a guestbook with the stories of previous occupants going back about three years. Most just noted their presence, but a few had curious and entertaining tales from their time at the cabin. I've copied a few of the most interesting anecdotes:

January 25-26, 2020

Hi Ellen,

What a nice weekend adventure we had with Shane, Hailey, and Ryland. We had some fireworks with us for the New Year's celebration at Restless Bight. Papa Walter is with Angela and Mom is visiting family in Thailand. We are thinking of you and dreaming up plans for the summer. I see that Lorian brought a new logbook too! We got to enjoy a calm day before a raging storm rolled through while we were beachcombing at night. The seas are very high now. Lots of logs moving around. We cut a little bit of wood, but the saw needs some attention. Shane and Ryland fixed the couch so please go easy when you sit on it. It's got to be from the 70s as it was Jary Olsen's. He helped my dad and Walter bring it here when his friends built the cabin.

July 5-9, 2020

Whoa man, we owe you guys one! My sister and brother-in-law stumbled across this cabin on a hike from Gooding Cove and thought it would be a great place for my three-year-old daughter and eight-month-old son for when we come down from Saskatchewan. We brought two tarps, but one is leaking and the other isn't very big. If we were stuck in our tents, the kids would be screaming mad. But we got to watch the rain out the window from the comfort of the couch.

My sister drew a sun in the sand yesterday, and the toddlers were running naked on the beach. You have to be careful though. In the morning we saw four wolf tracks on the sand. Then the next day we saw cougar tracks. They must have noticed the kids and were interested; the little ones would make a fine meal.

In the river there are lots of otters and even more fish. My sister is really good at catching them. I don't know how she does it. Seems like she just dips the line in the water and out come the fishes - red snapper, rockfish, greenlings, and black bass, she catches everything. I thought maybe there was something about the rod or the lure she was using that was lucky, but I had no luck with it. Witchcraft, I say.

We left a jolly jumper in the closet that we brought for little Sam. That gave him some bodily autonomy to get him standing, and after a little practice with it he finally took his first steps. At first, I felt very proud of my boy, but then I got worried; he moves around a lot now, and I have to keep an eye on him.

Not much evidence of mice. A few of the kitchen rags looked ripped, but that was it. By the way, who made the swing outside? The kids love it.

We chopped some wood and left the logs by the furnace for the next person that comes around. We would have left a few diaper wipes too, but my son bedeviled more *than we expected. Also, thank you to whomever it was that installed the rain barrel. I bathed my son in it before I realized what it was. He got in the muck and was filthy, so I emptied out all the water. Hopefully, the rain fills it up again soon. I left $40 in the book in case someone needs to buy supplies. Cheers! – Thomas*

July 26-29, 2020

I paddled across the sound from the lighthouse. The wind was really strong, and there is a gale warning for the next three days. What a surprise it was to find this little place in the woods with a million-dollar view.

I'm on an adventure that started in Campbell River. The first leg to Port Hardy I did it with friends. The second part rounding the Cape I did it solo. I'll be finishing in Coal Harbor, in Vancouver. I've spent a few days here in the cabin putting my head back in the right place before I head back (reluctantly) to civilization.

The weather is good now. Time to go around the Brooks! I noticed that there were two $20 bills inside the logbook. I've added a twenty toward the propane since I used some of it. Thank you for sharing this place. I am leaving with a sense of gratitude! – Drew Conway

September 13, 2020

Three guys from Victoria, spent two nights here at the end of a two-week kayak trip out of Winter Harbor, around the Brooks and back. Almost no wind and no rain the entire time! Thank you to the people who built this place. We split some wood for the next guest and cleaned out the rain barrel (it was kind of mucky on the bottom). Probably could use some bleach. Hope to come back sometime. – Rob, Alan, and David

November 12-14, 2020

The cabin looks great! The mice are out and about. I caught nine, and one in the pantry. The surf in the ocean is huge. The biggest I've seen in years. Thank you Rowley Reefs!

The storm washed up a lot of fish on the beach. The ravens are having a party! – Mike

PADDLING WITH FRIENDS - THE BROOKS CHALLENGE

December 17-20, 2020

My gosh, the bridge from Gooding Cove washed out in the storm from a few days ago. More rain is on the way it seems.

The cabin shook in the wind all night like an earthquake was going on. The rain came in sheets, and the sea is spraying close to the windows. The creek is a muddy torrent and there is no way we can cross it.

Storm has cleared, and we had a starry night. Thank you for this dry Oasis. Can't imagine what we would do without it. – Garry, Catherine, Frazer, Eva

May 15, 2021

We miss you, Ellen! Happy birthday! We thought maybe we would find you here. Instead, we only found your lone wolf. He's made it a habit to hang out by the cabin.

We spotted a lazy bear sleeping on the meadow. He didn't even notice us go by on our canoe.

There are wild strawberry flowers everywhere, which reminds me. I need to bring you some goodies for the garden.

P.S. Looks like the living-room couch is broken. We need to see what to do about it – Sarah & Kyle

May 27-30, 2021

This is our second trip to the cabin, but the first time we are spending the night. We just moved to Royston three months ago and are still getting to know the area. We are so grateful this place exists! We wanted to contribute to the upkeep, so we packed out a lot of the trash, including some Asian soy sauce from 2014! The hubby kept busy chopping some firewood to last the whole summer, while I paddled over to Lawn Point for a picnic.

There's a lazy bear hanging around down by the beach. I named him "Greg" for obvious reasons.

Oh, by the way, Brian engineered the living-room couch back to life, and the lucky mousetrap is working fabulously. The mice population is now down by two! – Juliet and Brian

Finally, after reading all the entries, I came to a blank page in the guest book where I wrote about my passage.

June 29, 2022

> *What a surprise to run into this place on my way around Vancouver Island! Sadly, I do not have the time to spend the night, as I and my group only stopped briefly to stretch our legs and lunch. The weather has been incredibly calm the past day with*
>
> *mirror-like conditions; not even a ripple to speak of. If this calm window lasts, we will have an easy time rounding the Brooks Peninsula.*
>
> *I see that everyone who passes through here contributes something so I will as well. I am leaving my last bottle of Perrier as a treat for the next lucky occupant. Enjoy! – Felipe Behrens, from Brazil!*

June 30 – Day 32

I finally retired the underpants I had been wearing since leaving Port Hardy. I was left with two more that would need to last a combined 10 days. It became obvious to me that three sets for three weeks were not close to being enough, even after spraying them with talcum powder.

After getting on the water, I struck up a conversation with another of my campmates. David was the only one in the group paddling with a Greenland paddle.

"How do you like the Greenland paddle?" I asked. "I've tried it before and did not like it much. It feels like you are pushing a stick through the water."

"Ah, that is because you must be using it like a Euro blade. The Greenland paddle is different. Here, let's switch paddles for a bit and let me see your stroke."

He handed me his paddle and I tried a few strokes while he observed.

"Yeah, I see," he said like a doctor making a diagnosis. "What you're doing is moving the paddle like you're pulling yourself with a stick; that's never going to work. It's like spinning your pedals on a bicycle; too much effort on too big a gear. You have to picture the Greenland paddle like a lever and pretend that you are going to swing yourself over a cliff with a long pole. The pole has to stay planted and you need to pivot your body around it. It's the same with the Greenland paddle, it doesn't move relative to the water and you have to *swing* your body and the kayak forward."

I pictured his instructions in my head, imagining that I was jamming the paddle into a crack in a rock and pivoting over a chasm. Somehow this mental image made the paddle feel different in my hand, and I sensed more resistance from the water through the entire stroke.

"Yes, yes!" he shouted enthusiastically. "You're looking better. I can see how your torso is more natural now. If you tilt the angle forward a little the fluttering will stop. Also try to push more with the upper hand rather than pulling with the lower. That will improve your movement even more."

"Thanks. Maybe I need to give it a second chance … sometime."

"There's a guy in Victoria who teaches a course called Secrets of the Greenland Paddle, kind of a corny name, I know, but once you master it, it's tough to ever want to go back to a Euro blade. I'm definitely not going back. The Greenland paddle is way kinder on the joints once you get older. If you observe, most old guys like me prefer the Greenland paddle. It's how you get to stay in this sport into your seventies, and even eighties."

After covering 15 miles we reached the base of the Brooks Peninsula which, until now, had loomed like a wall blocking the horizon. We ran into very thick kelp beds covering the water like cooked pasta in a watery bowl, and I observed that there are two very distinct types of this marine algae. One type resembles a weed with broad leaves and a textured pattern that reminded me of the folds on the human brain. It also has many tiny air sacs along the stems to sustain it, which allow it to grow from the seabed like an underwater tree. I would have named it brain kelp, but it already goes by the name giant kelp because of its enormous size. In summer, when the days are long, it can grow three feet in a day.

The other type has a more alien appearance and is called bull kelp. It grows out of a single hollow stem that rises from the seafloor like a street pole and terminates into a large round bulb as big as an orange. Both the bulb and the stem are very tough as though they were made of PVC pipe, and they make a woody sound if you knock the bulb against the kayak. From the bulb are strewn the bull kelp's leaves which flutter with the flow of the current, like long serpentines from a carnival parade. Paddling over a bed of bull kelp requires lots of effort; the leaves stick to your kayak like thousands of little hands holding onto you, and the floating bulbs congest the way forward like floating logs.

"Those are the kraken's tentacles," JF said.

"They definitely enthrall you like the giant sea squid about to pull you under," I said.

"You know, you can use bull kelp to pee in your kayak. You take the bulb, shave the leaves off, and then cut a round hole off the top of the bulb. You then just stick your willy into the hollow stem and whiz in it like a beer dispenser topping off a pint. Works really well."

"Is that what you've been doing at the back of the pack all day?"

"Perhaps … It's very convenient when you're on your own and there's no place to land."

"You'll have to demonstrate for us how it's done."

We camped about a third of the way along the north side of the Brooks Peninsula on a Beach called The Crabapple. I did not see any crabs or apples there, so it's a mystery why the place got the name. The beach is a popular staging spot for kayakers planning to round the peninsula from north to south, and it's not uncommon to stay put for a few days waiting on favorable conditions. JF got some updates on the VHF radio that there would be a southeast breeze building up through the night and the next day, so we decided on camping at The Crabapple for at least two nights.

Exactly as predicted, by evening, five miles to the southwest at the tip of the peninsula, the horizon had become a squiggly line from the rolling swells and we were all relieved to have towering mountains behind us for a shield against the wind. The beach in front of us was calm like a pond.

July 1 – Day 33

"Happy Canada Day!" JF exclaimed, followed by, "Time to wash hands!"

For obvious reasons, Canada doesn't have an Independence Day like the United States. Instead, it marks the day in 1867 when the colonies of Ontario, Quebec, Nova Scotia, and New Brunswick were combined into a single Confederation and granted Dominion status. British Columbia joined a little later in 1871 after it was promised a railway linking it to the Atlantic Provinces, though protection from invasion by the Americans and the unresolved Pig War probably also played a part in the decision.

What might have happened if the British had placated the rebellion in the American colonies with a reasonable proposal for Dominion status 91 years earlier? Perhaps people all the way down to Georgia would be finishing their questions with an "eh" at the end.

"I hear that Prime Minister Justin Trudeau isn't the rockstar we in the United States think he is," I said half joking.

"It's not just in the United States where you can win an election by coming in second in the popular vote," someone responded, noting that in the 2021 election, the Liberals came in 1 percent behind the Conservatives but won 51 more seats in Parliament.

"I think he's okay, but he's not very popular in Western Canada. If you walk around certain suburbs of Edmonton and Calgary, you might see a few 'Fuck Trudeau' yard signs made to resemble the blue-and-white Trump 2020 flag. Canadians aren't always so polite. There's also a running Conservative gag suggesting that Trudeau is the love-child of Fidel Castro."

I laughed at the ludicrous idea, but later couldn't help but check on Google for the origin of the rumor. Truth be told, he did have a curious resemblance to a young handsome Fidel Castro in military fatigues from his days fighting a guerilla war in the Sierra Madre Mountains. The source of the rumor, apparently, is that Justin Trudeau's father, Pierre Trudeau, was an admirer of Fidel Castro and visited Cuba in late January 1971 with his wife who later in June the same year, announced she was pregnant. Justin Trudeau was later born on December 25. Human biology, however, should have us quickly dismiss this conspiracy theory as it would be extremely improbable that Trudeau's mother had a pregnancy that lasted nearly 11 months.

The strong southwest wind kept us land bound for the weekend, but the sun pierced through the clouds and bore down on our heads, forcing us to take shelter under the tarp to avoid sunburn and our feet from being baked in the smoldering sand.

I spent some time talking to Justine who told me about her many kayaking adventures round the world. To date, she had kayaked around New Zealand's South Island, Tasmania, Ireland, the Ungava bay on the coast of Labrador and the Hudson Strait, and the Aleutian Islands in the Arctic Ocean.

"In the Arctic, one of the things you need to bring with you is an electric fence and rim it around your camp every night. Polar bears are nothing like black bears or even grizzly bears. They really do look at you and see their next meal."

"I've heard about that. Is it true that they hunt people the same way they hunt seals? Do they wait outside your tent waiting for you to stick your head out like a seal coming to a breathing hole in the ice?"

"I've never heard of that but wouldn't doubt it. In Churchill on Hudson Bay, they get landbound in the summer and walk into town almost every day. Only when the bay freezes can they go look for seals in the sea ice. Best not to walk alone."

"Oh, it's kind of like in Florida. If you leave your pet in the yard it can suddenly vanish into the belly of an alligator. In Canada, it's your neighbor, not your neighbor's dog, that suddenly isn't around anymore ..." I joked.

"On a kayaking trip in the Arctic, we heard the pack alarm off at night once. I opened the tent zipper and JF clambered out naked with a drawn revolver in hand. Luckily it was only a wolf that scuppered away."

"I remember that day," said JF with a laugh. "But it's not quite as good a story as one from our friend Jamie from when he was kayaking in Svalbard. He had no bear fence, a polar bear walked into the camp and sat on top of him and his tent while he was asleep."

"I know Jamie," I said surprised. "He was my kayak surfing instructor at a symposium in Oregon a few years ago. I'll need to ask him about the details next time I see him."

JF and I went to fetch water from a small stream he found in the forest just beyond the beach. The stream was barely a trickle but it created two small pools from where I could scoop the water with a cup and slowly fill up the bladders one by one.

"No need to rush it. We don't want to stir up any sediment," JF said.

After filling one of the water bladders, I went to place it on the ground by the other bags when I saw one of the nasty yellow slugs oozing its way over the rim.

"Oh God damn it. These nasty guys again. They're everywhere! I hope it didn't get into the bag or we're going to be drinking slug water."

JF had a laugh and gave me a lecture on the little slimy creature. "Oh, so I see you're familiar with the banana slug. Yeah, they are everywhere in the forest and eat everything that's dead, and along with the fungi are the main decomposers of the forest, when you see them around it's a sign of a healthy woodland."

"And nothing eats them?"

"Well yes, there is an animal that eats the slug, kind of. In British Columbia it's a hazing ritual for some high school sports teams that the newbies have to eat or lick a banana slug to join. It numbs the tongue like the anesthesia you get when they pull a wisdom tooth."

"Maybe that's how it was done back in the old days," I quipped.

July 2 – Day 34 – Rounding the Brooks

Last evening JF surprised us all with a fluffy chocolate cake topped with whip cream and blueberries he'd baked on the camping cooker.

"I think Skils needs to add a culinary class to its kayak guide training courses," I said. "Nobody should get their guide certification until they can bake a cake on the beach."

JF then started into that night's update on the upcoming paddle. "Guys, now that you've all been properly sugarcoated, I can give you an unsweetened pep talk on what is coming. So pay attention. Rounding the Brooks is a big deal. Not many people do it, and it's because it can be very dangerous if you get caught there in bad weather. Captain Cook who sailed through the Pacific Northwest didn't call it The Cape of Storms for nothing. Many big ships have been wrecked between the Cape and Solander Island, and as a little flotilla of kayaks in bad conditions, we'd be little more than driftwood. The stretch facing the Pacific Ocean is long, rocky, and there aren't many places to land if anyone gets into trouble. It's shallow and when the wind is blowing and the waves are breaking, the sea looks just like the cake you're eating now." He pointed at the white creamy icing splattered with dark chocolate Hershey's Kisses.

"Fortunately, tomorrow's conditions look like they will be ideal, but we have to start early to catch the ebbing tide and paddle with the flow. We want to be on the water by 6 a.m., so get a good night's sleep."

When I was preparing for this journey, I occasionally checked the weather patterns around Vancouver Island to get a sense of what I would be up against. The Brooks Peninsula always looked particularly menacing and was the reason I wanted to paddle this section with a group. The peninsula sticks out 12 miles into the Pacific Ocean and it catches the edge of storms out in the open sea. The color scale on the Windfinder app tells the story out here. At the base of the peninsula, the color will often be blue or light purple indicating the wind is blowing at 5 to 10 knots, while at Cape Cook it will be tinged yellow and orange which is 25 to 30 knots. That's the difference between a leisurely day on the water and struggling to stay upright. And if the wind is blowing against the tide, it could spawn monsters.

We were up and packed a little after sunrise. JF and Justine were up even earlier; they had to get breakfast ready and the coffee boiling for the rest of us. From the beach I looked north to the horizon. It was dead calm. I then looked to the southwest along the shore to Cape Cook just five miles away. Dead calm as well. It felt too easy, even a bit disappointing like at Cape Scott. *Could we have a little challenge please?* I almost said out loud before clapping my mouth shut, lest my hubris angered the sea gods.

We pushed off punctually at 6 a.m. over the flat water with our kayaks forming V-shaped ripples as we sliced through the quiet sea. We arrived at Cape Cook an hour later and the rocky outcrop of Solander Island appeared into view behind it.

As JF had described it, the six-mile stretch of shoreline along the peninsula facing the Pacific was littered with a boulder maze of hundreds of rocky islets that would have made navigation during a storm akin to running through a minefield. Today, however, the sea gods were distracted somewhere else, and we safely approached and even touched the rock outcrops, observed the cormorants and sea gulls sunning themselves, and posed for a group photo bobbing in our kayaks.

When we stopped for lunch at the only beach between Cape Cook and Cape Clark, JF felt like he owed us an explanation.

"Guys, I swear I wasn't crying wolf. I have never, ever seen this place so calm. Last time I paddled through here the northwest wind had us whizzing through at over six knots; and that was a good day. What we just did was crawl over the face of a sleeping giant. It gets ugly very fast when he wakes up."

Around Cape Clark at the opposite end of the peninsula the water was shallow and the swells crumbled with gentle foam starting at the wave crest. Had we not been loaded to the brim with gear I would have enjoyed some kayak surfing. We finished the day near Jacobson Point where we coasted gently to land on a wide flat beach. We had covered nearly 20 miles.

"Well, congratulations!" said JF while we coasted to a gentle landing on the beach. "You can all say that you have paddled the Brooks. Not many people can say that. Definitely gives you some bragging rights in the sea kayaking world."

"We just won't mention that Felipe slaughtered a sea otter last night so the gods would grant us safe passage," someone said.

"A baby sea otter, mind you. The cutest and cuddliest one I could find," I deadpanned back.

Still, I could not help feeling a little disappointed that the two major capes on the journey had been easier to paddle than an average outing on Biscayne Bay in Florida. I had hoped to use this journey to assess and build on my abilities to handle adverse conditions, but it did not seem like that would be happening.

July 3 – Day 35

Having rounded Brooks with time to spare, we took another rest day even though the conditions at sea were flatter than a hockey rink. For the first time in the trip I felt a little bored as there wasn't much to do except sit and pass the time. Justine offered a few books she carried in her makeshift kayak library for just such occasions. I picked one called *White Slaves of Maquinna*, a historical thriller about two English sailors held as slaves for two years at Nootka Island after the local tribe massacred the entire crew of a British vessel whose captain had disrespected the local chief.

JF left early before sunrise to fish for the day's lunch. He came back with three lingcods and a rockfish which he breaded and fried; it was enough for everyone to have four fish tacos. The lingcod, found all over the North Pacific, is a particularly hideous looking creature with a giant mouth filled with spiked teeth, a mean look in its eyes, and huge powerful pectoral fins that easily could have it crawling after you on a ship's deck. We ate until our stomachs grumbled that they could eat no more.

Near the campsite at the end of the beach was a shallow stream with crystal-clear water flowing over a wide bed of smooth rocks. The water was chilling and refreshing and looked so clean I had no qualms about drinking directly from the stream and filling my water bladder with it. I built a rock dam with boulders and a couple of driftwood logs and made a knee-deep pool, and then took off my clothes and savored my first bath since leaving Port Hardy. So much muck washed off me that my hair and beard fluffed up leaving me feeling that I needed to visit a barber shop.

The pool proved popular and everyone had a go. One of our mates, Jerry, was especially pleased. A couple of days earlier a tick bit him on the groin and left two large red blisters that seemed incredibly uncomfortable as they were likely rubbing against each other whenever he walked. He wasn't sure how he got bit; we hadn't walked through any bushes or tall grass where the buggers hide. The only time I recalled seeing any ticks on me was when I hiked through the meadow on the Cape Scott Trail and noticed one on my pants. I immediately slapped it dead and pulled my socks over my pants. Ticks are not very common in the Pacific Northwest, but they have been slowly making their way north with the changing climate and rising temperatures.

The worst thing about the ticks isn't the bite or the blister they leave behind, but getting infected with leishmaniasis, a terrible parasitic disease that lasts for years and causes recurring eruptions of slimy ulcers and patches of dead skin like leprosy. If it's not treated with antibiotics, it eventually attacks the spleen and the liver and can be fatal.

"There's a less than one-percent chance that the tick was a carrier, but it can happen," JF told Jerry. "It's much more common on the east coast of Canada. But I would still get a blood test and have a doctor check it out after we finish the trip."

In the afternoon I fetched the driftwood on the beach to make a campfire and burn the paper trash we had been accumulating. I had been assigned the position of trash carrier and the bag had been growing day after day, making it almost impossible to fit through my kayak hatch.

I made a two-foot-tall driftwood pyre, stuffed our trash in the middle, and for good measure added all the plastic bottles littering the beach. I noticed an interesting aspect on some of the bottles I picked up. They were nearly all stamped with Japanese labels. One water bottle even had a sealed cap. I opened it, took a sip, and to my surprise, it was perfectly good drinking water.

It's not unheard of that floating trash from Asia ends up on the west coast of North America. The North Pacific Gyre turns clockwise and any garbage tossed off a beach in Japan or China gets picked up by the current, swings around the Aleutian Islands, and eventually passes through British Columbia, sometimes going all the way to California. In 2011 when a 9.1 magnitude earthquake hit the east coast of Japan, the ensuing tsunami created millions of tons of garbage. Entire ghost ships and shipping containers ended up on the coast of North America.

While I combed the beach for more trash to put in the pyre, I found a Mickey Mouse bath toy with Japanese characters stamped under his foot. It had red pants with suspenders, and white gloved hands waving with a jolly smile. I wondered what story it would tell if it could talk.

Yes, many years ago I belonged to someone; a kid who lived in Japan. One day his family took him on a trip to the beach and brought me along. He buried me in the sand with a shovel as though I were treasure and then screamed when he saw a crab in his bucket. His mother picked him up, his dad packed the toys, and I was left behind and forgotten like so many countless playthings. Then one day a big wave came and washed me and the whole town out to sea and after drifting in the ocean landed here on this beach where I have been for many years and now you found me. What will you do with me?

I told Mickey he wasn't too heavy so I'd carry him along. "You're plastic," I said aloud, "so you'll probably be around longer than me."

July 4 – Day 36

We again had unbelievably calm conditions and paddled across Checleset Bay through a maze of sea stacks and boulders scattered like Lego pieces until we reached a rugged archipelago called the Bunsby Islands. Nearly every island was ringed in kelp and I was intrigued to see how the kelp forests dissipate the wave energy rolling through them. This was especially evident when a patch of kelp forest was adjacent to a boulder field and the swell thrashed and foamed over the boulders but was completely subdued through the tangled kelp. I mentioned this to JF who said that the kelp forests here were much sparser only a few decades ago. The fur trade in the 19th and early 20th centuries pushed sea otters to extinction in British Columbia; once gone, there was no predator to control the sea urchin population that fed on the kelp. Without the kelp to moderate the swells, many villages were flooded during storms and it was risky to build any structure close to the water.

"It's like the mangroves in Florida," I said. "Once they are gone from an area, you can bet the next hurricane that comes in with a high tide is certain to wipe out the town. It's a big problem in the Florida Keys. Everybody there builds their houses on pylons at least 20 feet high."

"I can imagine," said JF. "In winter, the west coast of Vancouver Island gets hit by monstrous storms. Nothing like what we're seeing today. The length of calm weather we've had is unusual even for the summer. The coastal erosion was part of the reason why the sea otters were reintroduced in the 1970s. Canada imported one family from Alaska. They took hold here in Checleset Bay and then spread all along the coast; wherever they went the kelp forests came back."

There used to be even more kelp along the Vancouver west coast a decade prior, but there was a considerable die off after two heatwaves in 2016 and 2021. The kelp struggles to survive if the water gets above 65°F, and during those years the temperature remained above that for several days at a time.

As we paddled through the kelp tangles, we caught sight of an otter that was extremely unhappy to see us. Encounters with otters usually follow a predictable pattern. It hears kayakers coming from a fair distance as the animal has an acute sense of hearing and it pokes its head out of the water as high as it can, making a puzzled face unsure about what you are. Once it is satisfied you're not some oddly colored killer whale, it loses interest and goes about its business catching more shellfish and sea urchins. This time, however, something really upset the otter. Even though we were a considerable distance away, it kept squeaking loudly long after we were gone.

"Very unusual," said JF. "Perhaps there was some other animal nearby that we did not see. Killer whales sometimes eat them."

Given my previous encounter with a killer whale that had snuck up on me like a cheetah stalking a gazelle, I wouldn't doubt that perhaps another one had snuck up on us and only the keen sea otter had noticed.

"I can't imagine that a sea otter tastes any good," I said. "The thing is almost all fur. It would be like the killer whale swallowed a hairball."

We made camp at the southern end of the Bunsby Islands where the narrow gaps between the islets created strong tidal currents. It was still early in the day, and JF went fishing along with three others while Justine took a group of three to explore the channel passages revealed by the rising water.

Later when we regrouped at the camp, JF was euphoric. "Phillip nearly caught a forty-two pound halibut!" he yelled as we paddled in.

The story went something like this; JF, Phillip, Geoff and Jerry had paddled to Cautious Point some 10 minutes from the campsite. Phillip was a newbie to kayak fishing so JF spent a few minutes explaining the technique.

"Find a reasonably calm spot, then put your paddle under the deck straps projecting out to one side for stability. Then, cast the lure in the water and keep giving it a few gentle tugs so it stays lively and entices the fish to bite. When you catch one, reel it in and then smack it with the wood club to stun it."

Phillip cast the lure 10 feet from the boat, gave it some line to sink, and started giving it a few tugs. Barely a minute later, he felt a powerful pull on the line and the fishing rod was bent into a U-shape.

"I think I got something!"

As he reeled in the line the kayak began drifting, slowly at first, and then with so much violence that Jerry braced his body across Phillip's kayak so he wouldn't tip. When the fish briefly broke the surface it became evident that they were dealing with something far too large to fit into the kayak let alone stun with a small wooden club no bigger than a lemon crusher. They would have to try and land the monster to overpower it. JF tied a tow rope to Jerry's kayak and began a tug-of-war with the fish who, motivated by its survival instinct, was putting up a tremendous fight.

After 20 minutes they made it to the beach. The beast was tiring faster than they were but only just. JF got off his boat and pulled on the line to tug the fish into shallow water where it could be manhandled. Suddenly, there was a loud thump and the line snapped.

"It got away!" Jerry shouted. The tension of the moment evaporated and all was eerily quiet.

"Did you at least get a picture?" I asked with some doubt. Forty-two pounds seemed suspiciously specific. Two days earlier, JF had said a twenty-pound salmon had gotten away as well.

"Yes, we did." He showed me a photograph of Phillip on his kayak holding the bent rod while Jerry braced the boat with his body. "You can't see the fish very well, but it's the white smudge on the water by the kayak. I swear to God, there was easily a thousand dollars' worth of flesh on that fish. The halibut is a fish that sports fishermen in the Pacific Northwest fantasize about."

Halibut is a fish served in high-end restaurants as it has an attractive marbled white flesh with a flaky texture and slightly sweet taste, but it's also a disturbingly odd-looking creature. It swims on its side to lay flat and camouflaged against the sandy sea bottom like a rug, and its weirdness comes from both its eyes being on the same side of its head. The seemingly utter lack of body symmetry makes them seem like an aberration of the natural order. Incredibly, depending on the species of halibut, all the fish are either right-eyed or left-eyed, just like shells of snails are all either left- or right-handed.

"Oh, it's a great photo!" I teased. "You can definitely tell it's something big. I'd up the size to a hundred pounds and say Phillip has a fishing tale for the ages."

July 5 and 6 – Days 37 and 38

We paddled through calm waters from the Bunsby Islands and arrived at the outskirts of a First Nation village called Kyuquot. It was so hidden in the tree-covered mountain folds between the remote headlands and bays that the small agglomeration of pastel-colored houses would have been easy to miss. There were no roads connecting Kyuquot to the rest of Vancouver Island on any map, and I think JF and Justine must have had our resupplies delivered by ferry from Zeballos or further afield.

"The indigenous lands are still closed to outsiders due to Covid," Justine explained. "So we'll be picking up our resupplies at Spring Island which is about two miles from the village. Our contact should be there for the rendezvous."

When I had been planning the journey and looking at possible resupply points on the map, I had Kyuquot marked as a crucial stop, especially if I had become stranded for a few days waiting on a favorable weather window to round the Brooks Peninsula, as food would have been tight, and I might've been on the last cans of tuna and Chef Boyardee. I hadn't envisioned, however, that I might not be allowed into town and been left scraping the bottom of the Nutella jar in search of calories to get me through the next 50 miles to Zeballos.

"You would've been an unwelcome malnourished apparition," JF teased. "The

First Nations can be a little wary of white men who show up unannounced in need of immediate favors. In Canada they are self-governing and each Nation has the same powers as a municipal government, so you need to know in advance what their rules are. But sometimes it's easier to ask for forgiveness than for permission. You'd have to use some of your Brazilian charm."

He was obviously joking, but from previous experience I have found that the lost Brazilian in need of assistance always receives a warm reception, especially in Latin America. The interaction starts with folks finding out I'm Brazilian, to which someone will make a rough attempt to demonstrate their command of Portuguese, which is greeted with general laughter, followed by questions about whether I am acquainted with famous soccer players like Ronaldinho, Pele, or Roberto Carlos. The camaraderie also happens in places where soccer is far down the list of popular sports, but whether this would happen in a remote corner of Canada where people likely have never seen a Brazilian, I don't know.

Fortunately, JF and Justine were on a first-name basis with everyone and we received a warm welcome.

"Nearly all the folks here were students of mine at some point. Skils trains and certifies about 200 kayak guides per year all over the world."

We didn't linger around for very long, and after picking up our resupplies we continued past Union Island to Rugged Point where we spent the next two days.

During the night I made the dire discovery that my air mattress was deflating from several pinprick punctures and a bad air valve. How it could have happened I have no idea. I had been extremely careful not to drag it in sand or rub it against anything rough, and I was really disappointed that a product made for the outdoors couldn't handle its most basic job. Sleeping on the hard ground became extremely uncomfortable and I was fuming with anger thinking about what I'd say to the president of the manufacturer.

The son of a bitch knows this thing is garbage but has no shame in selling it. I'm certain the five-star reviews on Amazon were either fake or paid for. Fuck 'em.

"How much did you pay for the mattress?" asked JF the next morning.

"About one hundred and thirty American."

"Ah. There's your problem right there. You went cheap. You should have spent something like three hundred. With camping mattresses, price and quality go hand in hand. If you spend less it's almost certain you'll get zero dollars' worth of value. When we have phone reception again, see if you can buy a new mattress and have it delivered to my address in Ucluelet and I'll hand it to you when you pass by. Money spent on a good night's sleep is always a good deal. That's why good mattresses cost so much. You find out very quickly when they're not good. Here, I have a spare foam mattress I can give you for now. It's a little thin, but it's better than the bare ground."

We camped on a flat beach on the north side of the Rugged Point Peninsula on the mouth of Kyuquot Sound which was protected from the ocean swells. Not that it would have mattered. The weather continued to be so calm that at times I wondered if nature was purposely lulling us into a false sense of security. Earlier that year someone posted an article on the Strictly Sea Kayaking Facebook group stating that the world's most extreme rogue wave had been recorded during a winter storm off the coast of Vancouver Island near Ucluelet. The wave was nearly 60 feet from trough to crest, and three times taller than the preceding and subsequent waves. It lasted only a few seconds, like a monster swimming to the surface to engulf an unsuspecting ship before diving back into the deep.

Rogue waves were for a long time thought to be nothing more than tall tales from mariners who'd gone crazy from spending too much time at sea. Today, however, with the availability of sonar buoys and other instruments providing a constant stream of data, we know that they are very much real. They appear seemingly out of nowhere and disappear without a trace. In the ocean, waves from distant storms travel at different speeds and directions. Sometimes a fast wave will catch up with a slow one. When that happens, if the trough of one wave overlaps with the crest of another, then the sea will for a moment be calmer than usual. But if wave crest meets wave crest, or if wave trough meets wave trough, then waves will briefly merge into a bigger wave that is the sum of the two.

When I paddled along the north coast of Puerto Rico which is exposed to the Atlantic swells, it was very common to sometimes be surprised by a sudden chasm opening in front of your kayak, or to be unexpectedly uplifted high above the immediate sea and see ships in the distance that had been hidden below the horizon. Two waves merging is a common event and happens many times a day. Three waves is much rarer, perhaps that happens once in a lifetime at sea, and four waves or more are the stuff of lore.

Today, however, the sea was so calm and the air so still that a boat wake would have counted for a rogue wave.

In the afternoon, JF again went out fishing to catch dinner and invited us to join him to bear witness to the next monster catch. Sadly, great fishing tales always seem to take place when you're not present. Phillip wasn't having any luck this time, and Jerry was the one with the hot hands. Over the course of just 10 minutes, he caught six lingcods.

"Okay, we're done fishing folks," said JF. "Any more cod and you'll start to think the food is boring."

"We can always invite a bear for dinner."

"Oh, they don't need an invitation to show up. In fact I'm surprised we haven't run into one yet."

That evening after we had eaten as much cod as we could gulp down, I made another fire pit on the beach. The wood was damp and there was no trash to burn or empty bottles littering the beach that I could use to start the fire. Seeing me struggle, JF gave some advice.

"You need to use cedar kindling; it burns really well," he said, pointing to a large log stored under the camp's pavilion. The log was covered in a gray dust, but once cut with a pocket knife along the wood grain, it peeled into thin springy sheets with a rich orange-red bark like the flesh of sockeye salmon.

The western red cedar is a special tree. This evergreen is sometimes called the Tree of Life and it is said to be nature's gift to Native peoples. From its soft flesh the First Nations of the Pacific Northwest carved totem poles in the images of their gods, and made immense canoes seaworthy enough to head out into the open ocean in pursuit of whales. Its bark is still used today to make baskets, matting, rope, even clothing. It also splits effortlessly along the grain into smooth boards for fine furniture. As I soon found out, a feathery pile of cedar kindling also burned with the fragrance of a fine Cuban cigar.

After stuffing the pyre with a few handfuls of kindling, I set the lit match to it and to my surprise, it caught on fire faster than a newspaper. Within minutes the entire pyre was engulfed in flames and burning brightly with little flying sparkles illuminating the night while we roasted a pack of marshmallows.

I was taken aback by how easily and quickly the cedar wood ignited. The forest behind us was a thick jungle of cedars and spruces, and there had not been any rain for several days. A carelessly tossed cigarette butt or even a single spark carried in the wind would be enough to set the forest ablaze. It was a chilling yet sobering thought, and I poured several buckets of seawater over the hot coals and covered the entire fire pit with wet sand before heading to bed.

July 7 – Day 39

It was another incredibly serene day with the sea looking like a blue serving tray filled with little stone islets. *How long can this last?* I thought. The west coast of Vancouver Island is littered with stories of shipwrecks which is in part the reason why lighthouses were built on almost every cape. One of the worst wrecks happened in 1906 to a 252-ton iron hull steamer called the SS *Valencia*. The ship was sailing from San Francisco to Seattle in January when fog, rain, and tempestuous seas caused it to miss the 12-mile-wide entrance to the Juan de Fuca Strait. It instead continued north until it blundered into a reef near Cape Beale about 120 miles south of us.

"It's close to our home in Ucluelet," said JF. "The wreck was the reason the lighthouses on Cape Beale and Pachena were built. When it ran aground, the storms were so fierce that no ship could approach to attempt a rescue and all except one of the lifeboats capsized and tossed everyone in the water. Bodies washed up onshore for weeks."

"It's almost hard to believe that can happen when it's so calm right now," I said. "The sea looks smoother than a flooded salt flat."

"Yes it does, but like I said, the sea is a sleeping giant. Any moment without much warning he can give out a snore and tussle around."

Our flock continued plodding south between the mainland and a string of islets which the long blue ocean swells licked with rumbling swooshes. I stretched my neck up to see how far the land extended before curling around a cape called Tatchu Point and into Esperanza Inlet that separated Vancouver Island and the north shore of Nootka Island. This cape didn't seem to have anything noteworthy about it. It was a long flat beach at the end of which a chain of evenly spaced islets barely poked above the horizon.

"Those are not islands," Justine said. "They are swells."

It became obvious as we got closer that she was right, and the little dark mounts were swells rolling to shore like moles digging just under the surface. The waves steepened just before the shore and then barreled onto the beach with thunderous white foam.

"Tachu Point is very shallow and you can imagine how rough it gets here in a storm." Justine explained. "Just offshore there's an underwater shelf with a steep drop, so the swells stay hidden right up until they break."

We steered wide of the breaking zone into Esperanza Sound toward Catala Island and pleasantly rode in with the swells until we landed on a shingle beach on the north of the island. The beach was steep, but the waters facing into the sound were so calm that we could just hop off as if we were in a bathtub.

From the shingle beach landing we had to pull our kayaks up a 12-foot-high slope to a flat grassy shelf stretching all the way to the treeline where we could pitch our tents. I was mesmerized to find huge driftwood logs, which were once trees nearly six feet across, tossed all over as if someone had spilled a jar of toothpicks. .

"You have to be kidding me that a storm can throw these logs all the way up here," I said to JF.

"I know it seems impossible right now, but the seas on the west coast of Vancouver Island can be the roughest in the world. You have to be humble and never let your guard down. The sea doesn't forgive hubris."

July 8 – Days 40

We had three days left together, but were already so close to the end point at Zeballos that we had to come up with a side adventure to fill the time. We decided to paddle into Nuchatlitz Sound, a 10-mile carving of the sea into Nootka Island immediately to our south. It was pocketed with small islets and kelp forests with a maze of passages and currents. We paddled along the north shore of the inlet and came across a series of caves carved by the sea into the sandstone cliffs. Some caves were wide enough to paddle into. However, that was sometimes an intricate endeavor as there was very little room to turn around, especially with an 18-foot kayak. Justine went to inspect one of the larger caves where a waterfall gushed into the sea through a light shaft. As she paddled past the mouth of the cave beyond the reach of the sunlight, she vanished in the contrast between light and shadow with the waves before reappearing after a couple of minutes.

"You can paddle in; there's a pocket at the very back where you can turn in place. But be careful. Do not paddle through the waterfall; there's a shallow rock below it, and you will get stuck on it unless you pass over the crest of a wave."

I went in beyond the reach of the sunlight and it took a moment for my eyes to adjust. The width between the walls was much narrower than the length of my kayak while the cave ceiling was about 15 feet above me and dripped with moisture from curtains of green moss and lichens. I continued until I reached the light shaft with the waterfall which I kept just to my right. When I passed it, I saw the shallow rock Justine had warned me about. It was barely visible in the splashing water and I wondered if Justine had tussled with it sometime before.

Two boat lengths beyond the waterfall was the turnaround pocket. For a while I considered whether I should paddle out backward rather than risk getting pinned. Justine's boat was a foot shorter than mine, so it would be tougher for me to spin in place. I decided against it and leaned into my strokes as much as possible. About a third of the way I brushed the rudder against a rock but only gently, and I followed through until the bow was pointing toward the white light at the cave's mouth.

"I'd hate to have been stuck back there," I said, emerging back into the open.

"Yeah, never go into a cave with your kayak without someone else around."

We continued paddling to the upper reaches of the sound and surprisingly came across another group of six kayakers who had paddled from Zeballos down the Esperanza Inlet.

"When you get to the next beach keep your wits about you. We saw two bears on the shore looking for clams and they had a curious look about them when they saw us," said a man in the group.

We didn't have to go much farther before catching sight of the first bear. The animal was sitting in the meadow above the water licking something which might have been a deer carcass; it didn't even raise an eye to look at us floating by. The second bear we saw after another three miles was right on the beach where we intended to camp. He looked at us with the same puzzled look as the bear on Cape Scott, trying to make sense of us. We floated on the water some distance away waiting to see what he might do. Eventually he understood that there were nine of us and one of him and took off into the bush.

Nevertheless, JF gave us a warning. "Folks, tonight if you hear something like a banging on the boats, we will have to scare away the animal, be it a bear, wolf, or cougar. And if it's persistent, be prepared to haze the animal. The beaches serve as corridors for wildlife and you never know if you're in a funnel where creatures pass through on their way up and down the coast."

That said, the bears, cougars, and wolves were the least of our worries. After pitching camp I walked bare legged through the grass above the beach to a waterfall for a shower. When I came back and sat on my chair, I noticed that a tick had buried its head in my calf and was plump like a red pimple. I slapped the bugger dead into a messy blood smudge but the consequences were now in the hands of fate. I'd have to monitor the bite for the next five days and hope the sore didn't develop into the tell-tale red ring of a leishmaniasis infection.

"It's unlikely, but yes, you never know," said JF. "Would have been better if you had picked off the tick and kept it in a ziplock bag, just in case."

"Too late now."

July 9 – Day 41

We left most of our gear on the campsite and paddled into the furthest reach of Nuchatlitz Sound where I heard the rumbling of a great waterfall followed by a cold breeze from cascading water. Soon we were paddling against a strong current and the water turned fresh and foamy. Beyond a rocky outcrop there appeared the thundering white torrent we had anticipated. It poured from a shelf 20 feet above the sea where a gentle river suddenly lost its stream bed.

This physical oddity reminded me of a lecture I had once attended at the University of Florida on the geologic formations of the Pacific Northwest. Some 30 miles off the coast is the remnant of a slice of oceanic crust called the Juan de Fuca Plate which is slowly being subducted under North America. Every few hundred years this oceanic plate gets jammed and causes the continental crust along the Pacific coast to buckle like a folding carpet, thereby forming the Cascade Mountains that run from northern California to the shores of British Columbia. When the plate unjams, it does so violently in the form of an enormous earthquake (possibly above 9 points on the Richter scale), and the unbuckling of the continent causes the entire coastline to plunge into the ocean in a gargantuan landslide. The last time this happened was January 26, 1700. Although there were no Europeans here at the time, Native people have many stories of a great flood that wiped away nearly all the coastal villages and in Japan there is a record of a strange tsunami that hit the island even though there was no preceding earthquake. *Perhaps that is what happened here*, I thought. Three hundred and twenty-two years ago the same earthquake sliced the river at this location and the part we were now paddling fell into the sea, while the remainder was left on the shelf. The waterfall hasn't yet had time to erode the rock down to the new sea level.

These megathrust earthquakes in the Pacific Northwest happen with some regularity about every 400 years, so the next big one could happen this century, and major urban centers like Seattle and Portland have been making contingency plans in the event they become isolated from the rest of the United States for several months.

I paddled in a back eddy along the edge of the stream right up to the ledge of the waterfall where I thrust the kayak into the current and made two rolls in the freshwater to wash away the salt which was extremely refreshing.

After packing camp we retraced our path out of Nuchatlitz Sound past the caves and the kelp beds to the mouth of Esperanza Inlet where we landed on a sparkling white sand beach on the north side of a tiny islet called Rosa Island. This was to be our last camp together. JF noted that we still had a lot of food and we should not be shy with the leftovers. I volunteered to make a clean sweep of the Nutella and blackberry jars along with any bread dough.

In the evening, the moment I had been dreading finally arrived - I ran out of toilet paper. I had tried being as frugal as possible over the last three days hoping that the remaining sheets would last until Tahsis. Unfortunately, JF and Justine's three generous meals a day had a few unwanted side effects. I contemplated what to do as I admired the sunset over the Pacific Ocean from a squatting position.

Those giant kelp leaves look sturdy enough that my fingers won't puncture through them, I thought.

I crab-walked to the water's edge, fetched a handful of the leaves, and polished off my work. A rinse in some fresh water would have been helpful, but that would have to do for now.

July 10 – Day 42

We were off to an early start to get to the rendezvous point and the group van outside Zeballos. The sky was overcast which cut down on the heat we had been experiencing the last three days. There was even a slight southwest breeze hinting that an afternoon shower might be in the cards. We paddled north up Esperanza Inlet in single file following the lay of the western shore where the ebbing tide was weakest.

Justine then caught up to me. "So, you have another adventure planned after this one?" she asked.

"I don't know. It takes a lot of pre-planning to carve out two months out of the ordinary world and answer the call to adventure. Maybe not next year, but the year after perhaps."

"You could go around Ireland or Britain. I've done Ireland. Takes about two months to do it calmly and sit out the storms. If you start thinking about it, I can put you in touch with a few friends I have there who can help you along the way."

"I don't know. Maybe. With enough time, I could go around Britain as well," I said with tongue- in-cheek.

"With all those journeys you've done, have you ever gotten a corporate sponsorship to do it?" I asked.

"Hmm. Mostly discounts on gear, things like that. Outside of the kayaking world you'd have to do a lot of digging; it would be difficult. Oh, I have an idea, there's this guy in Australia I've heard of who had a bean company sponsor an endeavor where he ate nothing but beans until he consumed his body weight worth of the stuff to prove its nutritional value. With a little determination you could do that with your canned pasta. Hopefully, Chef Boyardee doesn't give as much gas as beans do."

"When I left Florida I think I weighed around one hundred and eighty pounds," I said. "If each can is about a pound and I eat one can per day, that would take me six months. Perhaps that's doable. It would be a funny marketing campaign. 'What should you eat if you want to paddle around the UK and Ireland? Beef Ravioli, from a can!' Don't believe it? I'm pretty much there already!"

"Haha, I think you might be onto something. Give those ideas some thought."

After seven miles our flotilla reached a narrow tidal passage offshooting from the main sound into what would, in a couple of hours, become a tidal lake. We continued for another two miles until we arrived at a gravel road with a dirt ramp to the water. This was the first road we'd seen since San Josef. When a pickup truck rumbled by kicking up dust, the sound seemed alien and out of place. JF set up the food table for our last lunch together while we emptied the kayaks and piled the gear by the roadside to wait for the van that would take everyone back to Port Hardy.

"This is it guys," JF said cheerily, "we're done. Well, *we* are done. Felipe still has a ways to go."

I had been ruminating on our eventual breakup over the course of the morning. I had grown accustomed to our lively conversations over cups of hot chocolate over morning meals, and in our paddles where we talked about everything from Canadian politics to kelp reeds, to how we would fend off a bear attack to how the world might have changed since we'd been out of communication. The camaraderie added a social aspect to kayaking that I seldom experience, and now for the first time in the journey, I felt anguished that I might get lonely.

"Hey Felipe, do you want these?" someone asked while handing me a new roll of toilet paper.

"Oh, you're my best friend! I'll definitely think about you in a few hours!" I said, cracking with laughter.

When the van arrived, things happened quickly. Boats were loaded on the trailer, I picked up my kayak cart which I was happy had not gone missing, and the gear was thrown haphazardly into the back seats.

We asked the van driver to take a parting group photo to commemorate the occasion. Before leaving, Justine gave me a tidbit of advice, "When you get to Friendly Cove, look for Donna and Doug. They are friends of JF and mine and we've worked as their release lightkeepers before. Donna bakes great cookies, she might offer you some."

With that, everyone wished me a good rest of the trip and climbed in the van which gave a parting honk and disappeared around the bend in a cloud of dust.

I felt like a lost child, anxious with the dense quietude filling the air like a fog, and uncertain about what to do. For the last two weeks I had been coddled, fed, and taken care of. They hadn't been gone for more than five minutes and I already missed their company.

You're in charge of the journey again, said a voice in my head. *Tahsis is a long way still, and you should get paddling if you want to get there today.*

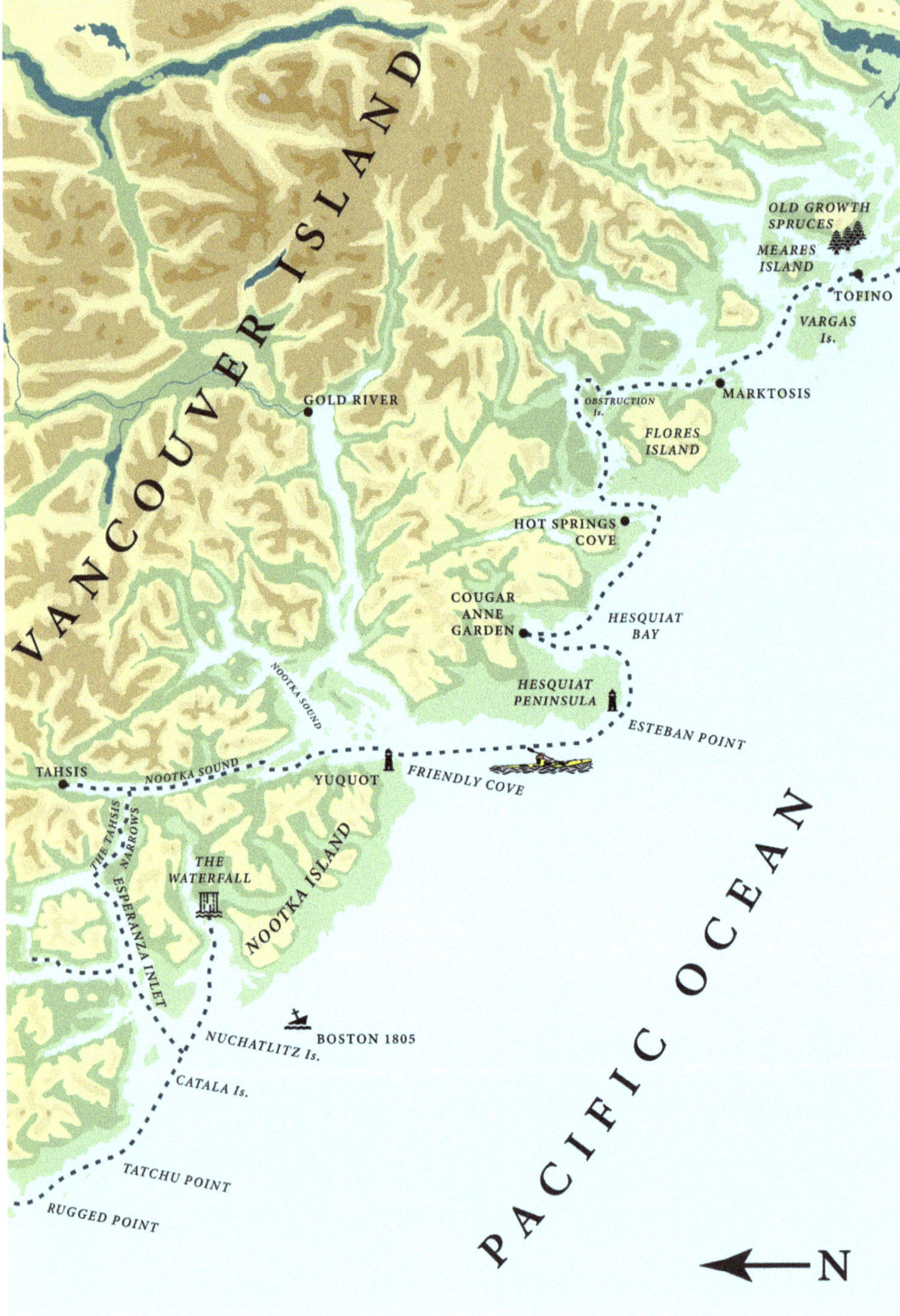

VANCOUVER ISLAND
PACIFIC OCEAN
OLD GROWTH SPRUCES
MEARES ISLAND
TOFINO
VARGAS Is.
MARKTOSIS
OBSTRUCTION Is.
FLORES ISLAND
GOLD RIVER
HOT SPRINGS COVE
COUGAR ANNE GARDEN
HESQUIAT BAY
HESQUIAT PENINSULA
ESTEBAN POINT
NOOTKA SOUND
NOOTKA SOUND
TAHSIS
YUQUOT
FRIENDLY COVE
THE TAHSIS NARROWS
ESPERANZA INLET
THE WATERFALL
NOOTKA ISLAND
NUCHATLITZ Is.
BOSTON 1805
CATALA Is.
TATCHU POINT
RUGGED POINT
N

PART 6 - TAHSIS TO TOFINO

July 10 – Day 42

The drizzly rain came suddenly as I backtracked through Esperanza Inlet. The mountain tops were hidden in the low clouds like an upside-down cream cake and my visibility was limited as I had to constantly wipe my lenses to see what lay ahead. Everything seemed gray and blurry and my progress became very slow. There were still another 22 miles to reach Tahsis and I was doubting whether I'd arrive there with daylight. *All are aspects of the journey you can't control,* I reminded myself.

At the branch with the Zeballos Sound there was a fork in the current. The falling tide had been against me, but when I entered the narrow channel connecting to the Nootka Sound, it became a following flow and I cruised past several fish hatcheries with little effort.

Justine had recommended I make a stop at the small backwater of Esperanza where I could buy supplies and if needed, get a bed for the night. "They're a Christian ministry community and will take in a passing traveler. So take a look if you're too tired to make it to Tahsis."

The rain was intensifying and the thought of a proper shower being so close after three weeks was an overwhelming temptation. I landed on the pebble beach at Esperanza next to a pontoon and walked to the nearest building to find someone.

I knocked on the door and stepped on a creaky floorboard, easily announcing my presence, but the place seemed dark and deserted.

"Hello? Anybody home?" I said after flipping on the lights.

Nobody answered, but my eyes saw something that my bowels understood before I had time to react – the sign for the men's bathroom to which I dashed while pulling off the dry suit.

As I took care of business, I pulled out my phone to look at photographs and noticed something that surprised me – a signal bar. I opened the BBC website and the home page refreshed with the latest events happening in the world.

I scrolled down the page to see.

Street protests were happening in front of the Supreme Court, the stock market had been swinging wildly on the events of war in Europe and tensions with China, and even a former head of state had just been assassinated in the middle of a speech.

Oh, dear God! Shut that thing off, said a voice in my head. *Why fill your head with worries that don't concern you?*

To keep up on important things in the world.

But why? said the voice, *Your world is a small boat sailing through one of the thousands of fjords on a rainy day in the Pacific Northwest. The important things are the tide, the wind, and where you're crashing tonight. Oh, did you check if the stall had toilet paper?*

It did not, but thank goodness the adjacent stall did.

I started searching for a place to stay in Tahsis that would be close to the water so I would not have to carry my kayak very far. JF warned me that hotels and campsites would start filling up quickly as July to September is peak tourist season in British Columbia. Fortunately for me there was one place still available at the Tahsis marina market not far from the boat ramp. I called and made a reservation.

I checked the tide chart. The falling tide would continue for a couple more hours giving me just enough time to paddle into Nootka Sound with the help of the current. I would be arriving in the evening, but now that I knew for certain that I had a shower and a bed waiting for me, I felt extremely motivated to keep going.

Lastly, before taking off, I called Mom who was overjoyed to hear from me.

Arriving with an hour of daylight left, I set up the kayak cart, tossed the gear into the cockpit, and portaged to the marina which was on a floating dock.

On the floating platform was the fish market where there was a washing station used by fishermen to clean their day's catch. A local fisherman stood there in his bright orange suspender bibs while he gutted and cleaned a sockeye salmon. He displayed a refined muscle memory over the entire process, and deboned the 20-pound fish with his filet knife like a samurai wielding a sword. I watched him ply his trade for a while before he paused and looked up at me.

"Wow, you work fast," I said.

"It's like playing a musical instrument, eh. You feel your way through the fish like your fingers reaching for the keys on a piano. You do it enough times, it becomes second nature."

"Except with the piano, if you hit the wrong key it just sounds bad. If you cut the fish wrong, you might lose a finger."

"Ah, yes, you don't want to do that. That's what the chainmail glove is for." He showed me a gray stainless-steel glove made of thousands of tiny woven rings as small as the eye of a needle which he used on his free hand.

"Can you do one slowly for me to see how it's done?"

"Ah sure, why not, eh." He seemed delighted to have someone interested in his craft. He then grabbed another sockeye from his wheelbarrow and slammed it on the skinning board.

"First you gut and gill the fish. You put the knife beneath the gill plate and with one motion you slice toward the back of the head until you feel a knot. At that point you press a little harder and it comes free from the body." He demonstrated reaching into the gill and pulling out a bloody blob which he tossed on the water where fish swooshed around violently to grab it.

He turned the fish around and inserted the knife near the back fins.

"That's the fish's anus, yes, the fish has its anus on the same side as its belly. It makes sense if you're a fish."

He slid the knife into the body of the fish and in one single motion, opened the belly like a coat zipper.

"You can see all the guts. Now we find the heart and cut above it on each side. Then you put your middle finger in the stomach and give it a gentle pull and there, everything comes out together."

There was some blood left inside the body cavity which he scraped and washed. "Usually you do this while you're out on the water and you fill the body of the fish with ice so it won't spoil if you're out for more than a day.

"And that's it, more or less. Not too bad, eh? Got a few more to go."

I left him to his work and found my way to the marina gift shop which doubled as the lodge's reception. Here I found a blond teenager working the cash. I recognized from his French accent as the person I'd spoken with on the phone. As I later learned, it's common for teenagers from Quebec to get summer jobs in British Columbia.

"Ah oui! Saint ciboire! I tried to call you back three times! I am so terribly sorry. I got the dates wrong. We are fully booked tonight, but tomorrow we have a room for sure."

"Oh, come on, you've got to be joking. It's nearly dark. Where am I going to go at this hour?"

"I'm so sorry. But you can come back tomorrow morning for sure," he said unconcerned.

"Can I camp in the parking lot?" I asked.

At that moment, the Gods made another small intervention to solve the situation.

"Oh, good lord no, don't camp in the parking lot. The bears walk into town at night and they'll pay you a visit."

Jane was an elderly lady who owned a local fishing lodge with her husband.

"In summer, my clients come from all over Canada and the States. They usually stay for about a week or two and we take them out fishing nearly every day. Whatever they catch we take to the processing plant for vacuum packaging and they take it home."

"And do folks catch a lot?"

"My husband, William, who you were talking with just now, he'll be fileting today's catch for at least another hour. Folks catch enough fish in a week to last them through winter. Anyways, I was saying, don't sleep in the parking lot. The bears really do walk into town looking for food, especially at night. You come and stay with us tonight at the lodge and join us for dinner. I'm making beer-battered ling cod and chips for some clients we have this week."

I would have left my things at the marina, but Jane insisted we bring everything. "The bears will get it if we leave it. I'll get your things washed. Gosh, three weeks camping. Wow, and you started in Seattle! You need a shower!"

I broke up the kayak and tossed it in the back of her pickup with all the gear and we took a five-minute drive up a winding road along the mountainside looking over the low clouds on the water. Soon we arrived at a Swiss-style wooden chalet with floor-to-ceiling windows which, on a sunny day, would let you see far down the length of Nootka Sound. I thanked Jane for her generosity – and even more so after eating her beer-battered fish and chips.

"Oh my! This is the definition of fish and chips! The Brits should come do some classes with you to see how it's done."

Her guests were an interesting bunch. There were four unrelated men who'd come from different parts of Canada for the week to go fishing. As it was explained to me, the fish lodges sell week or two-week package deals. Guests pay five-thousand Canadian which includes the lodge, boat, captain, meals, and catch processing.

"It's a pretty good deal when you think about it," said one man whose sunburned arms were the colors of the Polish flag. "The fish gets overnighted when you catch your flight home and you pick it up on your door. Plus, they'll give you all the beer you can drink."

"M'name is Thor! Yes. Like the Norse God of Thunder. My family is Icelandic and we are descendants of Leif Erikson."

"Sure you are," said one of the guests. "And so is everyone else in Iceland. Isn't everyone there a third cousin? And why's your namesake from Marvel so much prettier?"

There was general laughter. The man who'd spoken wore a mustache with upward tails and had a large-barreled chest. He spoke with an unmistakable British accent that sounded like he was giving the BBC nightly news. Nigel had been living in Canada for the past 15 years and worked in Montreal for the Molson-Coors beer company.

"The Quebecois are a touchy bunch when it comes to the French language. When I talk to them in English they answer me in French. If I talk in French, they laugh at my effort like a bunch of Parisians. *Hey guys, I'm trying* ... At least they have good beer. We have some cold Molson if you want one. With all the paddling you're doing it will help you grow big muscles like these!" he said, comically flexing his arms.

"I think he is more impressed by the Molson muscle hanging over your belt!" Thor shot back.

After several more rounds of fish and chips irrigated with beer, William the master fish carver decided to tell us a story about two local Native groups who'd been at war for many years until they decided to settle their differences with a song contest.

"Like an indigenous rap battle?" someone asked.

"Well sort of, but with drums. And Chief Maquinna himself knew this song. I know it too and I can beat it on the table. You guys want to hear it?"

The crowd enthusiastically voted to hear it, but Jane immediately vetoed the proposition saying it would wake up the other guests. "The beer makes you mumble the words like a baby," she snapped.

The talk then came around to my story and what I had seen thus far. I told them about the big halibut one of the folks with me had nearly caught, but they seemed unimpressed.

"I landed a two-hundred-and-fifty pound halibut two days ago," the Molson man said and then showed me the photograph on his phone. It was a big fish for sure, almost as long as he was tall.

"And almost as wide as your big belly, too," someone interrupted, filling the room with contagious laughter. "The camera always adds at least fifty pounds to the fish. And it's not that long; you are barely five feet tall. You only look tall 'cuz you're sitting on the high stool."

When asked where I was going next I said that I'd be paddling around the Hesquiat Peninsula about 30 miles south and would then make my way to Tofino in a few days. Things got a little quiet. William broke the silence with some stern advice as though he suddenly sobered up.

"Pick your day when you go around Estevan Point at the end of the Peninsula. It's very shallow there; and it gets very rough with a strong northwest wind."

We got back to more chatting and drinking until Jane finally put everyone in their place.

"Alright, it's eleven, time you men head to bed. You're all off to go fishing at five. Felipe is the only one allowed to sleep in."

July 11 and 12 – Day 43 and 44 – Tahsis and Around

The lodge was empty when I woke up. It must take serious dedication to be up early to go fishing, especially after a night of drinking and six hours of sleep.

While I loaded the gear into the kayak, I came across the Mickey Mouse bath toy inside one of my dry-suit pockets. I placed him on the window ledge overlooking the sound.

"Quite a journey you've been on," I said to him before closing the door behind me.

Tahsis is nestled deep in the far recesses of Nootka Sound more than 20 miles from the Pacific Ocean. It straddles both sides of the Tahsis River mouth for about 300 yards on the only patch of flat land rimmed by the steep forest slopes. When I looked at it on a map, it became evident why the Nuu-Chah-Nulth on Nootka Island made this their home during the winter months. The valley is well sheltered from the storms that regularly engulf Yuquot and can barely be felt this far inland. The Nuu-Chah-Nulth's seasonal move also coincided with the chum salmon run which peaks in October and November on both the Tahsis and nearby Leiner rivers.

I left the lodge pulling my kayak behind on the cart and headed down to the marina to make sure I grabbed the one available room before somebody else had the chance. From there I walked my way to the main part of town by the river. When I crossed the bridge to the east bank I was surprised for the second time on this journey to find a package wastewater treatment plant, the aeration tank having been carefully hidden behind a row of trees. For a town this small (barely 2,000 residents), the investment in a wastewater treatment plant must mean they're anticipating considerable population growth in the coming years, and making sure that as few houses as possible remain on septic tanks so both the rivers and the bay remain free from nutrient runoff and contamination.

Might be a good place to invest in some land, build a townhouse or two, and set up a few Airbnbs, I thought, but soon discovered that I wasn't the first to have this idea. The north road leading out of town along the Tahsis River had several blocks of houses recently constructed, with demarcations for several more.

At the town center I stumbled on the local supermarket and gas station. A sign on the door indicated that they were closed for the day but would open tomorrow between midday and 6 p.m. Behind the gas station was the Tahsis Recreation Center which despite its shabby outward appearance, had an indoor swimming pool, a four-lane bowling alley, and a movie theater. Due to the pandemic, however, there had not been any showings in the past two years, but a paper sign noted that the grand reopening would be taking place on Halloween night. Bingo nights, however, were still happening through Zoom calls.

Further along the bay road I found myself beyond the town limits, and entered a dense woodland where the sun only occasionally shone through. A short side trail from the road boasted of a waterfall on the Leiner River, but after walking down the path I was disappointed to find only some very minor rapids.

On the way back, however, I found something much more upsetting. In the middle of the trail was an enormous excrement pile enough to fill a supermarket bag. I was certain it had not been there 10 minutes earlier.

Mystery solved I suppose. Bears do indeed shit in the woods.

Heading back I stopped at the town museum. At the entrance it had a large dugout canoe though it looked nothing like the ornately decorated and bright-colored vessels made by the west coast tribes who used to ply the open Pacific waters. This canoe was of crude craftsmanship with nearly every mallet blow of the chisel clearly visible and seemed barely seaworthy. Next to the canoe was the local school's 1957 softball uniform, "the Shamrocks," whose gold and purple-red colors reminded me of the Gryffindor Quidditch team in Harry Potter.

What really caught my attention was a dusty book of photographs from the 1940s laid open on an inclined table. It showed a large lumber mill at the waterfront and the hillsides almost completely denuded of trees, which surprised me as I had just walked past that location next to the fish processing plant. The mill was gone, the once sprawling industrial site was an empty 22-acre field, and the forests on the hillsides had grown back. I later checked the historical aerial photos on Google Earth and as recently as 1984, most of the surrounding land was still bare and brown. From its founding in 1940, Tahsis was a company town centered around the lumber industry and subject to the boom-and-bust cycles tied to commodity markets. In 1982, a glut in inventory forced the Tahsis mill to lay off 450 workers out of a total town population of just over 2,500. The mill finally shut down for good in 2001.

The next day I had the all-important appointment with the Tahsis supermarket and I arrived promptly five minutes before opening. My shopping list consisted of the usual items I consumed on the kayak: canned pasta, canned fish, grated cheese, power bars, and anything else that might look appetizing. While I perused the aisles looking for things, I noticed a strange sign that read, "We are out of candied salmon."

Intrigued, I asked the shopkeeper, a short bald man with a thick dark centipede-like mustache, what it was.

"Oh, it's a Pacific Northwest delicacy. It's sort of like beef jerky but made from smoked salmon. Quite good I must say, when marinated with maple syrup and black pepper. We sell out quickly when we have it, but you'll find it in Tofino. If you're hungry, we serve a late breakfast."

"What do you have?"

"Pancakes and maple syrup."

I couldn't say no and ordered a tower of blackberry pancakes. I was surprised by the blood-red hue of the maple syrup and the rich smoky flavor I had never experienced. I mentioned it to the shopkeeper who let out a laugh.

"Ah, you probably only had American maple syrup or the stuff sold at the airport in the fancy maple-shaped bottles. That's a low-quality sham pushed on tourists. If you look at the nutrition label on the back of the bottle, I bet you it will say 'sugar added' somewhere. That means it's mostly corn syrup. We try to keep the real Canadian maple syrup in Canada, for Canadians."

July 13 – Day 45

The forecast showed good weather but with strong northwesterly gusts by afternoon. That suited me just fine as the 23-mile paddle to Yuquot was sheltered on both sides by high mountains which allowed me a late morning start. When I pulled into the bay at the southern end of the island facing back toward Nootka Sound, large swells were curling around the headland hinting at the commotion in the sea just on the other side.

I made the short walk to the lighthouse after pulling my kayak above the driftwood to judge what the next 15 miles of open ocean to the Hesquiat Peninsula would be like. There were two patches in the sea where the wind shaved off the tops of the swells and the water was covered in a persistent foam pile. Not a single ship was in sight.

"Tomorrow morning it will be much calmer, but you should still be careful when you get to Estevan Point. It's very shallow there and the waves will definitely be breaking close to shore." The person talking to me was an elderly lady with short blond hair.

"You're Felipe, right?"

"I am," I said, a little surprised.

"Ah, Justine mentioned you would be passing by in a few days. 'Look for a tall guy in a yellow kayak and a green dry suit. He'll stop there for sure,' she said."

"You must then be Donna the lighthouse keeper," I said with a laugh. "Justine said you bake really good cookies."

"Did she? Unfortunately, I don't have any right now. I'm on a diet."

"She means she has put me on a diet," said the man who appeared beside her and extended out his hand. "Hi, I'm Doug."

"We have to get a picture of us three. I promised Justine I'd send it to her."

We took a photograph in front of the lighthouse building. Doug showed me the access way to the top of it. It was one of the steepest staircases I had ever seen.

"Sorry but I can't let anyone walk up there. At least not without a safety harness. We've recently added a new LED lamp. It's only thirty-five watts but the mirrors focus the light beam for up to eighteen miles. On a day like today, the Yuquot lighthouse makes for a fitting end to the Nootka Trail for hikers. On a bad day, however, you'd barely be able to see the James Cook Cairn in front of us."

On his third voyage in search of the Northwest Passage, Captain James Cook sailed through Friendly Cove and very likely anchored in the same bay where I landed my kayak. He first came to Yuquot in March 1778 with two ships, the HMS *Resolution* and HMS *Discovery*, which would later be captained by George Vancouver. He then spent over a month re-provisioning his ships before heading north to Alaska. He named the bay Friendly Cove after peacefully exchanging brass tools for sea otter pelts with the Nuu-Chah-Nulth people. The peaceful interactions between Cook and subsequent European explorers that passed through Friendly Cover were in no small part due to the diplomatic skills of Chief Maquinna of the Nuu-Chah-Nulth that controlled the region. He was said to be a skilled negotiator, spoke both English and Spanish, and had a distinct look; he was over six feet tall, very broad shouldered, and graced with a high-bridged nose like someone of Roman ancestry, whose imposing presence commanded deference from Natives in neighboring tribes and Europeans who traveled to meet with him. Today, almost every town in British Columbia has a street or school named after him.

The cairn was a solid pyramid of uncut stones about 11 feet tall with two bronze plaques written in Spanish and English noting the European history of the settlement. It also referenced the Nootka controversy of 1790 when the Spanish captured several British ships in the sound and nearly started a war if not for the negotiations and friendship between Vancouver and Quadra. No mention, however, is made of Chief Maquinna who no doubt would have hosted and met both parties.

"You should go and see the church," Doug suggested. "It's the only building left from the old town. Well, that and Williams's carving shop."

"There's no settlement here?"

"Nope, not since the 1960s. Kind of sad that a place inhabited for almost 4,300 years was eventually abandoned. The BC government offered everyone a buyout to move to Gold River on the mainland where there's road access and it was easier to provide services. The only people left is the Williams family. Their son, Sanford Williams, comes for a few weeks in summer to work in the carving shop. In fact, he's there now. Pay him a visit and he might show you what he's working on."

It was still early afternoon so I took Doug up on his suggestions and went for a walk.

Adjacent to the lighthouse was the grass field with the Friendly Cove church. From the outside it was unremarkable, inexpressive, and desperately in need of a fresh coat of paint. The steps were overgrown with slippery moss and the front door was precariously hanging on to its hinges. Inside, however, the site was quite extraordinary. As I walked on the creaky floorboards to the altar, I was flanked by two delicately carved and colorfully painted totem poles with two perching eagles and a fierce blue Native warrior with his tongue stuck out. In the center overhang above the entrance was an eagle carving with wings outstretched, although a little chubbier than its two perched brothers. Above him were two snakes with limbs holding up the sun and moon. It was a rather odd feature that the snakes had limbs; perhaps they were from before the time of Adam and Eve.

I next dropped by the carving shop. The front door was open and sunlight was radiating through a large glass window illuminating the wood dust in the air.

From the entrance stretched a long table with hand-carved plaques, boxes, sticks, paddles, and rattles. On the wall a photograph of a black, blood-red ceremonial mask of a hybrid human-animal deity caught my eye. Its head had a sprouting dorsal fin, its fish mouth had rounded teeth like an orca, and its pupils were in the shape of human faces. The caption read "Chieftain transitions from human form into killer whale." It was at once artistically beautiful and frightening.

At the back wall of the shop behind a table sat a Native man who, although advanced in age from the look of his many wrinkles, had a full head of dark-black hair. He was broad shouldered and wore a black sleeveless shirt which exposed his big biceps like those of a bodybuilder.

His attention was focused on a wooden plaque which he was busy carving with a delicate knife under a bright lamp like a dentist delving into the mouth of a patient with his drilling tools.

"Good afternoon. Doug the lighthouse keeper said I should pay the shop a visit. Are you Sanford Williams?"

"I am," he said in a deep voice. "Make yourself at home."

Williams was from the Mowachaht First Nation. He had been carving for almost 40 years and his work is displayed in galleries and government buildings throughout Canada.

I saw that he had several plaque carvings in the works. One depicted a flying eagle. It was ready for the dye colors with every polygon labeled red and black. A war club called a cheetolth was another fascinating cedar carving in the shop. It had a long handle in the shape of a diving eagle with outstretched wings and talons. Back in the tribal warfare days, something like this must have smashed a lot of skulls.

Mr. Williams went back to focusing on his work. I took one photograph of a totem pole propped against the wall, but then felt somewhat embarrassed about taking more as I was not planning on buying anything. I noticed a wooden Greenland-style paddle carefully engraved from end to end with the imagery of a quivering flock of bizarrely shaped ravens. Thinking back on it now, I wish I had bought it. It would have been the conversation starter for a hundred different stories.

After looking through the totem poles in the shop, I walked back to the open grass field below the church overhanging the black sand beach facing the Pacific. I sat cross-legged beneath the wood carving of a Native deity stoically gazing at the barreling waves and ate a canned pasta dinner, hoping for fair weather on the open crossing.

July 14 – Day 46

As Donna had foretold, the northwest wind lightened in the early morning. The swells were slow and gentle as though the sea was still asleep. The words from William, the fisherman from Tahsis, echoed in my head. "Pick your day."

Today is the day, don't beat around the bush, said a voice in my head while I was brushing my teeth. *Get going before the sea knows what you're up to.*

The light breeze meant I felt confident to put up the sail and ride down the face of the swells at great speed.

This tranquility, however, was fleeting and I was soon reminded of the image of the sleeping giant of the sea tossing about in his sleep. Conditions progressively deteriorated and the swells grew larger. After I buried the bow on a few wave troughs even while throwing my body weight backward, I took that as an unequivocal sign that the seas were about to wake up and immediately put away the sail. It wasn't long

[ABOVE] Tahsis Harbor. [BELOW LEFT] Walking trail through regrowth forest, Nootka Sound. [BELOW RIGHT] Fresh catch at the Tahsis market.

[ABOVE], The Author with the lighthouse Keepers at Friendly Cove.
[BELOW] Friendly Cove Lighthouse, entrance to Nootka Sound.

Historic Yuquot Church, Friendly Cove.

[ABOVE] Yuquot Church, Friendly Cove. The motifs are a mixture of native and European influences. [BELOW LEFT] Totem of Watchman welcomes visitors to Friendly Cove. [BELOW RIGHT] Large swells near Esteban Point obscure the mountains ahead.

[ABOVE] Calm waters in Little Esperanza Sound.
[BELOW] A congregation of millions of jellyfish, Hesquiat Bay.

before the swells rolling past me were tall enough to obscure even the headland and lighthouse at Estevan Point, whose foaming breakers forced me to give them their due distance.

I felt a mixed sense of comfort while the waves rose and fell around me. On one hand, a lapse in concentration would be all that was needed for a breaker to sneak up and toss me like a toothpick; on the other, I was hyper-attentive to the danger, and paradoxically, the chance of a serious incident was probably lower than average.

Accidents happen for dumb reasons when you least expect it. I vividly remember five years earlier when out on a paddle I dislocated my shoulder. It had been a day like so many others. I was paddling home, having gone as far as Miami Beach when I passed a sandbar that I had been to many times before. Nothing seemed out of the ordinary; I wasn't tired, it wasn't windy, and the sea wasn't particularly rough. And yet, a small three-foot wave caught me unaware and I capsized. While I was turned upside down holding tightly to the paddle, I felt a muscle spasm on the right shoulder. I pulled open the spray skirt instead of trying to roll back up and when I jumped on the stern to re-enter the cockpit, the sudden lack of buoyancy to support my weight multiplied the pain tenfold. I screamed in agony and fell back in the water.

I felt around the pain point on the shoulder where I discovered a lump and realized it was no muscle spasm. My arm had come out of the shoulder socket.

There was no one around to turn to for help and I was about a half mile from shore, but in the water the pain was bearable and the onshore breeze was pushing me toward the beach. I started kick swimming and pushing the kayak with my good arm. *Sooner or later I'll get there*, I thought.

After an hour, the depth became shallow enough to stand and I crawled out of the water in front of the Key Biscayne Kiteboarding School barracks. "Can you get my phone out of the kayak hatch?" I asked the first person who walked by.

"You need me to call an ambulance?" the person asked.

"No. Ambulances are super expensive, and I have a high deductible healthcare plan." The thought of spending over ten thousand for a ten-minute ride was a stronger painkiller than any opioid. "If you can dial 'Mom' from the contacts and hold the phone next to my head, that would be super helpful. She'll take me to the Urgent Care center."

But out here on the Pacific, there would be no magic Mom-come-save-me button. Keeping my wits about me, I rounded Estevan Point and as I got into Hesquiat Bay behind the wind shadow of the peninsula, the swells loosened their unsettling grip.

I continued farther into the bay where I had read about a place called the Cougar Annie Garden, the historical homestead of a crazy woman who coerced men into living with her in the wild and produced a multitude of children before she died at age 97. *Perhaps there might be something interesting to see,* I wondered. The garden, according to the guidebook, was a grassy field with a shack that made for a good campsite, but unfortunately, I hadn't marked it in the GPS and was relying on the guidebook's hand sketches to find it. I paddled around in the furthest reaches of the bay looking for it and stopped at several promising coves, but unfortunately, found nothing. No shack, garden, or tombstone of the cougar lady.

July 15 – Day 47

Finding a decent camping spot in Hesquiat Bay was difficult. The beaches were steep and the high tide mark showed the water reaching almost all the way to the driftwood logs. Not wanting to take any chances, I climbed up the escarpment above the beach and after finding a reasonably flat spot free from tree roots and branches, carried up the gear and the kayak.

The next morning I found a set of tracks on the wet sand. At first I thought they were wolf paw prints, but after a closer look I noticed that they didn't have the claw marks immediately in front of the toes, which could only mean they belonged to a mountain lion. Judging from their distance above the waterline, the prints could barely have been an hour old, and I wondered if the animal they belonged to might be observing me from the bush.

Better get going before I find out if Cougar Annie is looking for me.

It was the first close wildlife encounter of the day. Fifty yards off the beach in waist-deep water I found myself paddling through a creamy pink smudge that I thought was a shallow sandbar but turned out to be a mass of jellyfish. Thousands, perhaps millions of moon-shaped flying saucers the size of dessert plates were puffing about in all directions like little galaxies. How these creatures that can only drift where the currents take them came to aggregate together in this bay was a mystery to me.

After 10 miles I reached the entrance to Hot Springs Cove at the north side of Clayoquot Sound. I started hearing the deep gasps of humpback whale spouts. They were far enough away that the mist had dissipated before the sound reached my ears, but I soon heard them again, the second time much louder and closer. Then a minute later I saw three misty clouds break above the water with rhythmic puffs one after another. They were moving in my direction.

In total I counted six different spouts until some were so close that I could see the blow hole break above the water, followed by the animal's dorsal arch and tail fluke.

How incredible that a creature bigger than a bus can sneak up on you, I thought.

The light refraction from the water to the air makes it so that unless the whale is almost directly beneath the kayak, it will remain completely invisible.

I concluded that like the manatees in South Florida, humpback whales also enjoy the tranquil warm waters and bubbling steam plumes from hot springs above the seafloor (though in South Florida, the hot bubbly water comes from the cooling ponds of the nuclear power plant). It must make them feel like they are relaxing in a jacuzzi.

Justine had mentioned that due to the pandemic, the hot springs were closed to the general public. "Oh, but you should just go for it," she said. "There's a way to get to the springs from the water. If you look around there's a small landing you can put-out at and climb up the rocks to get to the pools."

On the cliffs above the shore I saw several steam clouds emanating from between the rocks and trees. The hot springs here form from a fault in the crust some three miles deep through which the rainwater percolates until it is heated into pressurized steam and forced up through fractures in the rocks above. I was eagerly hopeful to share in the whale's apparent laziness and bathe in a warm steam pool overlooking the ocean. I looked at every crevice and hole to find the elusive landing Justine had mentioned, but everywhere the waves rumbled right up to the cliffs, and as much as I could imagine myself relaxing in the baths, I could also clearly see how my kayak would be crumpled up against the rocks. Perhaps with a party of two or more and an empty kayak it might have been possible to get out quickly and scramble up the slippery rocks with the boats, but alone, the springs would have to stay tantalizingly out of reach.

I continued around the backside of Flores Island. With the incoming flood tide I made it to the narrow channel on the north of the island that separates it from Obstruction Island at the time of the turn, and then caught a ride with the ebbing flow toward Tofino. Nonetheless, it was a tortuous path that made for a total of 44 miles, the most to date, and I was sufficiently exhausted and out of energy snacks in the last 15 miles. It was time to partake of the powers of one of my few caffeinated energy flasks. I call these tiny 60-milliliter bottles filled with a syrupy yet bitter pink liquid the He-Man potion. I held my nose and chugged the bottle in one go like the Drink Me potion from *Alice in Wonderland*. After five minutes I became possessed with a kind of reverse inebriation and the chest-thumping vigor of a silverback gorilla. The paddle strokes felt like feathers and even my vision seemed sharper. I have used these magic potions a few times before, once in Puerto Rico in a do-or-die rounding of a headland against powerful gusting headwinds and swells, and another occasion during the Florida circumnavigation when crossing a 50-mile stretch of mangrove swamps. They are a lifeline to get you out of a bind, but they have a dark side; when the effect wears off, the hangover is akin to your spirit abandoning your body and you better hope that you've arrived at where you intended to go.

The low tide exposed a labyrinth of shallow sandbanks and gray mudflats just beyond the harbor on the east side of Tofino which dashed my hopes of arriving with any daylight. Three times I climbed off the kayak to waddle through the knee-deep boot-sucking mud. Sweat-soaked and mud splattered from the effort, when my feet finally touched the firmness of the harbor boat ramp, I felt compelled to get on my knees and say a prayer to Cementious, god of concrete and hard surfaces, for ending the ordeal.

After getting the boat on the cart, I stripped down to the long-sleeve underwear, tossed the offending garments into the cockpit, and started portaging into town. Having been relegated to near total isolation since leaving Port Hardy, I felt unaccustomed to the sudden influx of sound, colors, and people in Tofino. The twilight on Main Street was mingled with a kaleidoscope of street lamps, the pub banter was a tenacious chatter of drums and guitars, and so many people were walking about in between the pickups trucks with racked surfboards stuck in traffic, that it felt as though I had just entered a human anthill. It all seemed hazy like I was half dreaming, though that may have been the buzz of the He-Man potion wearing off.

My unusual half naked outfit got a few looks from some bystanders at a cafe, but I was too exhausted to care. As I walked with my kayak behind me I found a pizzeria with a neon sign that said they'd be closing in 10 minutes. I stopped for a moment, and in order to keep a bare minimum of decency, put on my soaked shirt before walking inside and noticing the last two slices of cheese pizza under an orange heat lamp.

"I'll take these two and that last chocolate cookie you got in the glass display."

The waitress, who was probably a university student working a summer job, looked at me with a mixture of confusion and dread, uncertain what to make of my request. I thought she was contemplating calling the manager to have me shooed away.

"Oh, you have a bottle of sparkling water as well; I'll take that too," I said. "I've been paddling all day. I'll pay with a credit card." That was my way of saying that I wasn't some crazy hobo.

"From where?" Her French accent gave away that she was from Quebec.

"Yesterday I was at Friendly Cove," I answered in French. "Lots of folks from Quebec working in BC, eh?"

"Yeah, lots of us get jobs in BC over the summer break. It's a great way to see another part of the country and to practice some English too. I can tell you're not from Canada. You're American and you know French? What a rarity. Thank you for speaking French!"

"We are about to close. You want the last chocolate croissant? They're very good and you look like you're hungry!"

SOOKE
CANADA
UNITED STATES
SHERINGHAM POINT
NANAIMO
JORDAN RIVER
JUAN DE FUCA STRAIT
VANCOUVER ISLAND
PORT RENFREW
OLYMPIC PENINSULA
NEAH BAY
PACIFIC RIM NATIONAL PARK
SEA LION ROCKS
CARMANAH POINT
CAPE FLATTERY
PORT ALBERNI
TSUSIAT FALLS
BAMFIELD
PACHENA POINT
VALENCIA 1906
CAPE BEALE
THE BROKEN GROUP
PACIFIC OCEAN
UCLUELET
AMPHITRITE POINT
PACIFIC RIM NATIONAL PARK
FLORENCIA BEACH
OLD GROWTH SPRUCES
LONG BEACH
MEARES Is.
TOFINO
N

PART 7 - TOFINO TO SOOKE

July 16 – Day 48 – Tofino and Around

I slept until late. After camping with a thin mattress, you really appreciate how great it is to have a bed to sleep on.

The hotel receptionist was extremely accommodating with my kayak and let me keep it behind the bar on the outdoor patio. "No one will see it here and it will be safe. You have to keep an eye on things in this town. Bicycles and surfboards left out unattended have a tendency to grow legs and wander off never to be seen again."

Surfing is a popular sport in Tofino with the beaches facing the Pacific Ocean said to have the perfect bathymetry to generate waves for every skill level. The main street downtown has almost as many surf shops as pubs, the town hosts surfing competitions and festivals throughout the year, and gets nearly a million tourists. The receptionist seemed to know what she was talking about. Every surfboard for rent or on display was tied with a steel cable and lock. Tofino, like almost every urban center in British Columbia, also has a sizable and very visible homeless population.

My morning priority was to find a laundromat. All my clothes were in desperate need of a wash. By weight, there was now more salt and sweat than fabric, and I held my breath as I tossed them into the washer.

Now to find some breakfast while these clothes get disinfected.

There was a homely coffee shop a block away with a line spilling out the front door.

This must be a good place.

When it was my turn I ordered a hot chocolate, a kitchen-sink cookie, and a four-egg omelet with cheese and bacon.

"Oh, I'm sorry, we don't take credit cards," said the cashier when I went to pay

"Really? Is your machine broken?"

"No, we just don't accept credit cards. We're a cash business. The bank is next door, so we just deposit the money at the end of the day. It saves us from having to pay credit-card fees."

"I don't have enough cash on me. Can you make an exception?"

"Nope, sorry. You can use the ATM."

I went to the ATM at the bank. It charged me a 5 percent currency conversion fee which got me a little mad. Not with the bank, but with the coffee shop, which I would venture to guess doesn't pay all their taxes (what cash-only business wouldn't?).

When I paid my bill, I made it a point to hand them a $100 bill.

"Sorry. That's all the ATM gave me," I lied. "Oh, and by the way, would you mind giving me 20 loonies? They're for the laundromat. I have a lot to wash."

The cashier opened the register and I made off with almost all his change.

I made a short excursion on my kayak to Meares Island where my guidebook said was a stunning grove of ancient spruce trees. Getting there was challenging. The low tide exposed the quagmire of mudflats and sandbanks I had swamped through the night before, and I was forced again to walk though sinking down to my knees. When I arrived at the island dock, it was at the trough of the low tide with no place seemingly safe to leave the kayak.

"Don't leave your boat so close to the water. Put it on top of the dock. The water rises fast, and it will be floating before long."

The voice was from a kayaker who had just appeared from around the channel bend and had spotted me walking on the tidal beach uncertain about what to do. He was a guide leading five other paddlers.

"I was wondering about that. The dock is a little too high to lift the kayak on my own."

"I'll help you get it up there."

His words could not have been more prescient. I walked three miles down the boardwalk trail from the dock to see the giant spruce trees. When I returned, the entire sandbank was covered in knee-deep water.

After returning to Tofino, I strolled down to the docks where I came across a curious billboard: "The Smoked Fish Store" it read, and under the main sign was the catchy slogan, "Follow your nose."

Indeed, the air on the docks was saturated with a delicious scent of smoked salmon and I reeled through the walkway to the shop's front door like a fish on a hook.

"I hope there's a strong padlock on your door. This is where the town bears must hang out at night," I said to the shopkeeper who let out a laugh.

"The bears keep the drifters away," he said. "What would you like?"

"You have candied salmon?"

"Of every kind."

I looked through the glass case which had colorful sticks of salmon lined side by side like ice-cream flavors in a gelato shop. Some ruby red, and others with deep pink hues. One was chopped into cubes encrusted with a glossy layer of brown sugar, and another was flakey and dusted in black spices.

I chose a cut of cherry-red sockeye smoked in maple syrup and a pink salmon with teriyaki sauce and black pepper. The flavors of each were such that merely thinking about them was enough to feel the taste on your tongue.

"This is fantastically good! I wish I could take some home with me, but I don't want this food with me in the tent and have to share it with a bear."

"Since the pandemic we've been delivering everywhere in North America. It's vacuum sealed and guaranteed to arrive fresh on your door. If you want next-day delivery, we do that too." He handed me a business card and I stashed it in my wallet for safekeeping.

July 17 – Day 49

In the middle of the night I had a case of Chief Maquinna's Revenge and was nearly turned inside out. A warning, I suppose, to never again mix candied salmon with Nutella. If the hotel wasn't fully booked, I would have stayed another night to let the storm in my bowels calm down.

I paddled out of Tofino through the narrow gap between Wickaninnish Island and the mainland. This stretch of coastline from Tofino to Ucluelet was exposed to the southwest swells that roll in from the Pacific. Although the weather was calm, the sea was undulated with long rolling swells that originated far out at sea and hurled toward the beaches in perfect barrels that a skilled surfer would be able to ride nearly the whole length of the shore.

The most popular of these surf beaches is Long Beach which shares a name with its more famous cousin in California. It had a dedicated campsite but unfortunately it was completely booked for the entire summer.

"You could try going to the next beach at Florencia Bay," my friend Lee texted while I was on the water. "But don't get caught camping there. The park police will kick you out."

His warning reminded me of the time in my journey around Florida. I had pitched my tent on an extremely inviting public beach only to have the park rangers show up at sunset and tell me to get back in the ocean.

I paddled past the southern headland on Long Beach and squeezed my way into Florencia Bay, riding the swells between the headland and a small rocky islet that protected the north shore. The waves built progressively southward along the beach toward the south and were rolling in slowly but with a steep face forming before breaking gently over a shallow sandbank some distance from the shore.

Perfect conditions for some kayak surfing, I thought. I had been wanting to get in some surfing practice and this seemed like the perfect location.

Unfortunately, every surfer in Tofino and Ucluelet thought that as well, and they were so thick on the water with their black neoprene wetsuits that from a distance I mistook them for a raft of sea lions.

I found a quiet spot where I could land and walked to the section of beach where the sand was covered with a forest of sunshades and beachgoers observing the surfers floating on top of their boards, patiently waiting their turn on the wave. When you surf with a kayak, the paddle gives the power to accelerate faster and catch the wave much earlier; the greater length of the kayak also allows for a much longer run on the wave but also requires a much greater clear space. The last time I went kayak surfing with my friend Lee we were in a group of eight, and we all had to agree which areas were for surfing and which were for paddling back out. If we did not do that someone would eventually ram their bow into an unsuspecting victim.

People are going to be really mad if I kill a surfer or two with my kayak.

Kayak surfing, it seemed, wouldn't be happening. Instead I walked down the shore and struck up a conversation with a man from Ucluelet on the beach with his kids getting some afternoon sun. His daughter, a little girl of about six, happily occupied herself with making sand cakes for us, while his son built a castle with wet sand-drip spires. The conversation turned to my journey and where I'd be staying for the night. I asked him if the park rangers really come and check if anyone is camping on the beach?

"Yes, they do. Every day they come and they're strict about it. They will almost certainly catch you, but I heard that they normally don't go to Halfmoon Bay on the south side. You can try camping there."

He pointed at a short strip of sand hugging the south headland of the beach only visible during the troughs between swells.

"It's separated from the main beach by a cliff and you can only get there through a very steep trail; almost no one goes there, so I doubt the rangers would want to walk all the way there late in the day and have to come back in the dark."

I thanked him for the advice, got back on my kayak, and paddled across the bay where I squeezed between two rocks to disembark on the strip of sand he'd pointed to. I dragged my kayak behind some large driftwood where the shiny yellow deck would not be as visible from the main beach and waited until 9 p.m. when it was nearly dark to pitch the tent.

July 18 – Day 50

At 5 a.m. I thought I heard a boat engine which jolted me awake. I peeked my head out the tent to see what was going on but there wasn't a soul in sight, the weather was calm, and the swells had died down somewhat. I ate, packed up, and was on my way.

Ucluelet was only 10 miles farther south. The harbor entrance was rugged and narrow with jagged rocks and towering cliffs. On the mainland side was a plumpy-looking lighthouse painted shiny white that marked the tight turn into the harbor. It was known as Amphitrite Point, named after one of Poseidon's wives. The name must have been given in part to appease the sea god's fury who, during winter storms, hurls 50-foot waves at the cliffs which have sent many ships to their doom. The lighthouse looked down on an archipelago of rocky islets where even fair-weather swells kick up puffs of white spray. Some 200 feet from the base of the cliff bobbed a sounding buoy that made a low humming noise when it rose and fell with the swell. The buoy marks the safe route into the harbor, not too close to either the cliffs or the islets which in a fog you would struggle to see, but you would be able to hear which side of the buoy your ship was at, and find the deeper water where the swells would not be breaking.

Today, however, the sea was calm and sleepy like someone reluctantly waking up early on a weekend morning. The buoy sounded more like a yawn, and I paddled gently into the harbor with the push of the swells past towering kelp beds swaying gently in the translucent water.

I made a quick stop on a beach outside town and made a call to JF. He appeared 10 minutes later with the air mattress I ordered on Amazon.

"You look so different in normal clothing. I'd begun to think that the red dry suit was your natural skin," I quipped.

"I'm sure you'd look much fresher after a bath as well. You need laundry done?"

"My gosh, it's only been two days since I slept on a bed. Has my cleanness worn off so quickly? Perhaps … Laundry not so much. Got that done in Tofino, but thanks."

I was really hoping he'd offer a shower and a bed, but I felt embarrassed to ask for such a big favor. He said he had to get back to work planning for the next group of clients he'd be taking on, and we were soon headed our separate ways.

After finding a hotel on the backside of town, I walked to the lighthouse and the cliff I had observed from the water a few hours earlier.

It is a little strange to see the same landmark from both the water and the land. From the land the vast expanse of the ocean looks ominous. Even the fishing boats in the distance are barely more than specks that disappear in the folds of the swells that roll as far as the horizon. Having my feet on dry land gave a comforting sense of security from the thought of not being out there. And yet, when I am out there, tucked inside the cockpit of my kayak, I don't feel dread or lost in the vast expanse. If you can see the land from the sea, you feel safe because you know where you are, but if you're on land looking out, you see just how big and overwhelming a place the sea can be. If, however, you're at sea and you lose sight of land, then maybe you might feel the dread of knowing you're lost.

July 19 – Day 51

South of Ucluelet is a wide bay with hundreds of islands called the Broken Group and the northern end of the Pacific Rim National Park that stretches for the next 60 miles of coast. On a map the islands resemble the shards of a shattered green wine glass and are a maze of narrow passages, tidal flows, and hidden beaches. Many families of sea otters live among the islands staking their territorial claim on every bed of kelp, and sea lions populate the rocky islets sticking out from the sea in their hundreds, and are constantly yelling at one another like a rowdy crowd at a football match.

Occasionally, a pod of orcas patrols the sea lion colonies looking for easy pickings. The most vulnerable sea lions are the gluttonous ones who go out hunting for herring and eat more than they should. They get bloated and struggle to keep up with the herd when they head back. Although sea lions are very acrobatic in the water and can turn and twist on a dime, they are no competition for the speed and agility of the orca which can whack the 300-pound animals into the air with their tails just like a tennis ball.

Alas, if any of these trials of life were happening today, they were hidden in a veil of dense fog which I paddled through feeling the way like a blind man with a cane.

I saw only one boat pass by me earlier in the day. It had a quiver of a dozen kayaks on its back deck, and some hours later at the western edge of the Broken Group I ran into the flock of paddlers they belonged to.

"Wow, you're here already. That was fast. We saw you from the boat this morning."

They were a group of 10 friends from Ontario on a five-day kayak/camping trip in Pacific Rim National Park and had booked this trip six months earlier.

"You can't pick the weather, but you must pick the dates. All the campsites in the park get booked months in advance this time of year."

"Oh really, will I find anywhere to camp?"

"Almost certainly not, especially along the West Coast Trail from Bamfield to Port Renfrew. People plan on hiking that stretch of the park sometimes years in advance. Maybe there's a no-show if you're really lucky, but you won't know until you're there."

That got me worried. It would be at least 60 miles to paddle from Bamfield to Port Renfrew which even in ideal conditions would be a stretch to complete in a single day. JF and Justine had warned me that camping illegally in the park could result in much more than just being berated by some angry park ranger. The previous summer a group of six paddleboarders traveling the length of the park were caught on a beach, fined $3,500 each, and had all their equipment seized. *That would be a rather unfortunate and embarrassing way to end my journey*, I thought. *I suppose I can paddle through the night if I must.*

After leaving the Broken Group archipelago, the bay widened into a four-mile crossing exposed to the Pacific Ocean. The ocean breeze picked up, cleared the fog, and large swells began rolling in. Each wave period must have been about a minute; they rolled gently and carried me farther up the bay until I was lined up with the narrow harbor entrance into Bamfield on the north end of the West Coast Trail. The harbor bisected the town down the middle with no bridge to connect the west to the east side which seemed to be only accessible to pedestrian traffic along a winding boardwalk.

I coasted down the harbor looking for somewhere to stay. The rustic looking Harborside Lodge Marina seemed inviting. I called the reservation number on their billboard.

"Hello, good afternoon, would you have a bed for one person tonight?"

"We do, when are you arriving?"

"I am the yellow kayak floating by the dock. Are you the lady on the porch with the cell phone?"

"I am," she said laughing. "Pull up on the beach and you can get settled in."

[ABOVE] Old growth spruces are some of the largest trees in British Columbia.
[MIDDLE] Waves break at the entrance to Ucluelet Harbor. [BOTTOM] Weary sea lions
observe the Author from a cautious distance, Port Renfrew.

[ABOVE] Bull kelp beds, colloquially know as the Kraken's tentacles because they wrap around the kayak, Florencia Beach. [BELOW] Port Renfrew Campsite, the barrel sheds are surprisingly comfortable sleeping quarters.

Boardwalk in Bamfied

When I undressed from my dry suit, I noticed that my right arm was soaked but my left arm was dry. That could only mean one thing.

"God damn it! This bloody dry suit is leaking," I shouted, feeling very mad with Kokatat, the makers of the dry suit. The entire journey I had been extra careful to make sure this wouldn't happen, treating my dry suit like it was the King's robes. I washed it in freshwater at every chance, I waxed the zippers and sprayed the wrist and neck gaskets with silicone, and beat off any grain of sand I found in it. How the arm sections sprung a leak was beyond comprehension. Perhaps my arm movements while paddling were causing parts of the suit to rub against each other, but that should be what the suit was designed to do.

They better hope I am in a better mood when I'm back because I am going to have a word with them. How can they charge twice the price of their competition and deliver such mediocrity?

I went for a walk on the boardwalk in the afternoon to put my mind on something else. I found a mini market which had my favorite food – ice-cream. I asked for three scoops of chocolate fudge on the waffle cone, and then had a second three-scoop serving of mango.

"I guess I should add more ice-cream to my diet," the owner of the mini mart said laughing. "How can you not be fat and eat so much ice-cream?"

"I'm living life to the fullest right now," I laughed.

"With six scoops, I'd be surprised if anyone said they weren't."

July 20 – Day 52

I paddled out into a morning fog so dense that even the bow of the kayak was hard to see. After rounding the Cape Beale Lighthouse on the southern edge of the Broken Group Islands, I lost sight of land. Just like at Cape Scott, the only indication that told me that cliffs might be close were in the sounds of breaking waves.

When the fog cleared at midday, I was greeted by the sight of Tsusiat Falls, a broad waterfall that plunges from a 50-foot cliff into a pool immediately behind a beach covered with driftwood logs. From the sea it was an unusual sight. The forest along the shoreline was a solid green horizon except for this single notch of white foam. It seems very likely that these falls were also created in the same manner as the other mighty waterfall I had seen with the Skils group. The river used to flow directly into the ocean until an earthquake uplifted the entire shore. The layered rocks of sediment deposition that made up cliffs above the beach seemed to suggest that would have been the case.

I considered landing by the falls, and maybe even camping there, but the sight of several hikers stopping for pictures was enough to dissuade me. If the rangers were to be on the lookout for illegal campers, this would be a good spot to check.

South of the falls I stumbled onto a slanted rocky islet a thousand feet from the shore that hosted a huge colony of sea lions. There must have been at least 200 of them. From a distance they looked like piles of raw sausages in the glass display of a grocery store.

This must be the sea lion sandwich deli for orcas, I thought. It wouldn't have surprised me to see a pod there.

The sea lions were very much aware of the danger and kept a close eye on me from their perch, turning their heads to follow me with dead seriousness. Some individual on the rock must have given a warning call to friends on the water; no sooner had I passed their rock, a raft of them started following me with their heads poking out of the water.

Well, it kind of looks like an orca, one sea lion seemed to say to another, *even if the yellow color isn't quite right. Seabiscuit, what do you think?*

I don't know Chunky, why don't you go closer and confirm? I'll let the others know what happened to you.

July 21 – Day 53

I didn't make it all the way to Port Renfrew. After 45 miles I felt exhausted and once I had located a beach that seemed out of the way of prying eyes, it was hard to resist not putting out.

A slight headwind had also picked up and the sea was starting to get rough and choppy. I had to do the first true surf landing of the journey and I think a kayaking instructor would have graded me with a 10 out of 10. I surfed on top of a three-foot green swell until just before the shore; when it was about to break, I made two back strokes to let go of the wave which thundered with a barrel onto the steep sand on the tip of my bow while I coasted gently over the foam pile. I then quickly climbed out and pulled up the kayak with the help of the next wave.

Launching the next morning, however, was quite a bit tougher. The swells were dumping and I opted to set up above the reach of the waves. That meant I had to do a gorilla-style crawl, pushing myself and the kayak down the sand with my hand knuckles to get picked up by a receding wave. Unfortunately, that hardly ever happens perfectly.

On the first attempt, the rushing wave had me spun sideways. Once that happened, it was almost impossible to realign in time for the next wave, which spun me even more and I had to climb out and start again. I was luckier on the second attempt; I held my position perpendicular to the wave as it rushed up the beach and as the rip was pulled back down, it carried me into the deeper water as straight as an arrow.

However, the launch happened together with the start of a challenging set of breakers. The first wave I overpowered with two strong strokes over the crest and I thumped the bow on the back of the backside like an icebreaker. The second wave was bigger and crashed in front of me. The foam wall pushed me back almost all the way to the sand. After it dissipated I pointed the kayak out to the open sea again. This time, when the wave was about to break on top of me, I duck rolled and let it wash over, though it still shook me with violence and carried me back some distance before releasing its grip. When I rolled back up, I was broadside to the next wave but mercifully it did not break and rolled gently underneath me, and I had enough time to paddle beyond the break zone and catch my breath.

The morning fog was not quite as dense as the day before and it clung mostly away from shore where it began to dissipate in the late morning sun. Once I reached the mouth of Port Renfrew Bay, I suddenly caught the magnificent if somewhat bittersweet sight of the Olympic Peninsula in Washington across the Juan de Fuca Strait.

It's almost over, I thought.

Over 50 days had gone by. This rhythm of waking up every morning, climbing into the kayak, and setting off into the sea now felt like the natural state of affairs. If somebody were to ask me, "What do you do?" I would be tempted to answer that I paddle a kayak. *It's not my living, but it would be the way I would like to live.*

I turned into the bay in between the mainland and a rocky islet called Owen Island from where I caught sight of a group of hikers carrying heavy backpacks as they scrambled over the tidal pools below the trees. I must have been an interesting sight as they soon stopped when one of them pointed at me. I gave them a wave; they waved back and snapped a photograph, but they were too far from earshot when I shouted out to them to text me a photo.

The mist thinned quickly the closer I got to the back of the bay and soon the sun was bathing the landscape in a light so bright I had to squint even with sunglasses.

I continued to the back of the bay along the north shore past a series of boulders and sea caves until I reached the mouth of the Gordon River where a small group of backpackers were awaiting the barge for the West Coast Trail. In November, the southwest winds funnel large swells into the bay that thunder onto the beach for days making the approach into the river a hazardous ordeal in low tide. But today, in the middle of summer, the same wind had the sea looking like a deep blue mountain lake.

The wind was, however, carrying a delicious smell of fried fish.

I followed my nose along the beach before crossing the bridge over the San Juan River on the opposite end of the bay, past a small hamlet of houses, and arrived at the Bridgeman's West Coast Eatery.

It must have been the only open restaurant in town. It was packed with a line spilling out the door and I waited an hour to get seated.

"What is Caddy Lager?" I asked the waiter, pointing at the drinks on the menu.

"Oh, that is our local craft beer. Named for the Cadborosaurus, the great sea serpent that lives in the Juan de Fuca Strait. Caddy is its nickname."

"Oh, so you folks have a version of the Loch Ness Monster?"

"Except ours is real. Fishermen see it all the time. Though sometimes they say it's a type of Basilosaurus or some kind of ancient whale. There's not enough fish to sustain a sea monster in a freshwater lake in Scotland, but there's plenty of prey in the ocean."

Since I had never heard of the drink, he offered me a free shot to try. After sipping the drink I concluded that the mythical Cadborosaurus must definitely be real.

"Seems kind of like Bud Light, " I said.

"I don't think so. Canadian beer is way less watery than the American stuff. Bud Light tastes like the sea snake's pee."

July 22 – Day 54

The longest day yet, 49 miles!

I was carried by a strong afternoon northwest wind and averaged a speed of five miles per hour. In the morning I had the rising tide with me, but when it turned and was flowing against the wind, the currents created immense boils and standing waves at the headlands that were dotted with lighthouses. This forced me to take a somewhat tortuous route; I hugged closely to the shore along the bays taking advantage of the back eddies before conjuring up a burst of energy to pass the headland into the next bay. By the time I arrived at the entrance to Sooke Bay, 20 miles from Victoria, I was spent. The fog never really lifted and the Olympic Peninsula remained hidden the entire day. On three occasions I heard the loud horn of a large tanker as if it was announcing my return to the urbanized world, but the ship remained invisible in the fog. The thought of invisible tanker ships had me concerned for the eventual crossing back to the United States.

The mouth of Sooke Bay was nearly sealed off by a long sandy spit covered with driftwood. The water at low tide was so shallow that I had to walk over mudflats on several sections before I could paddle the last mile of the day to reach the campground up the Sooke River. I was so worn out I barely seemed to know what I was doing and was having some mental difficulty clipping the tent poles together and figuring out how to align them with the tent fabric. I barely remember a conversation with a man at the camp who came to look at my kayak and mentioned that he too had paddled around Vancouver Island 20 years earlier.

"It's the kind of thing you do when you have a youthful vitality. I wish I could be you right now. Enjoy the rest of the adventure. You're almost done."

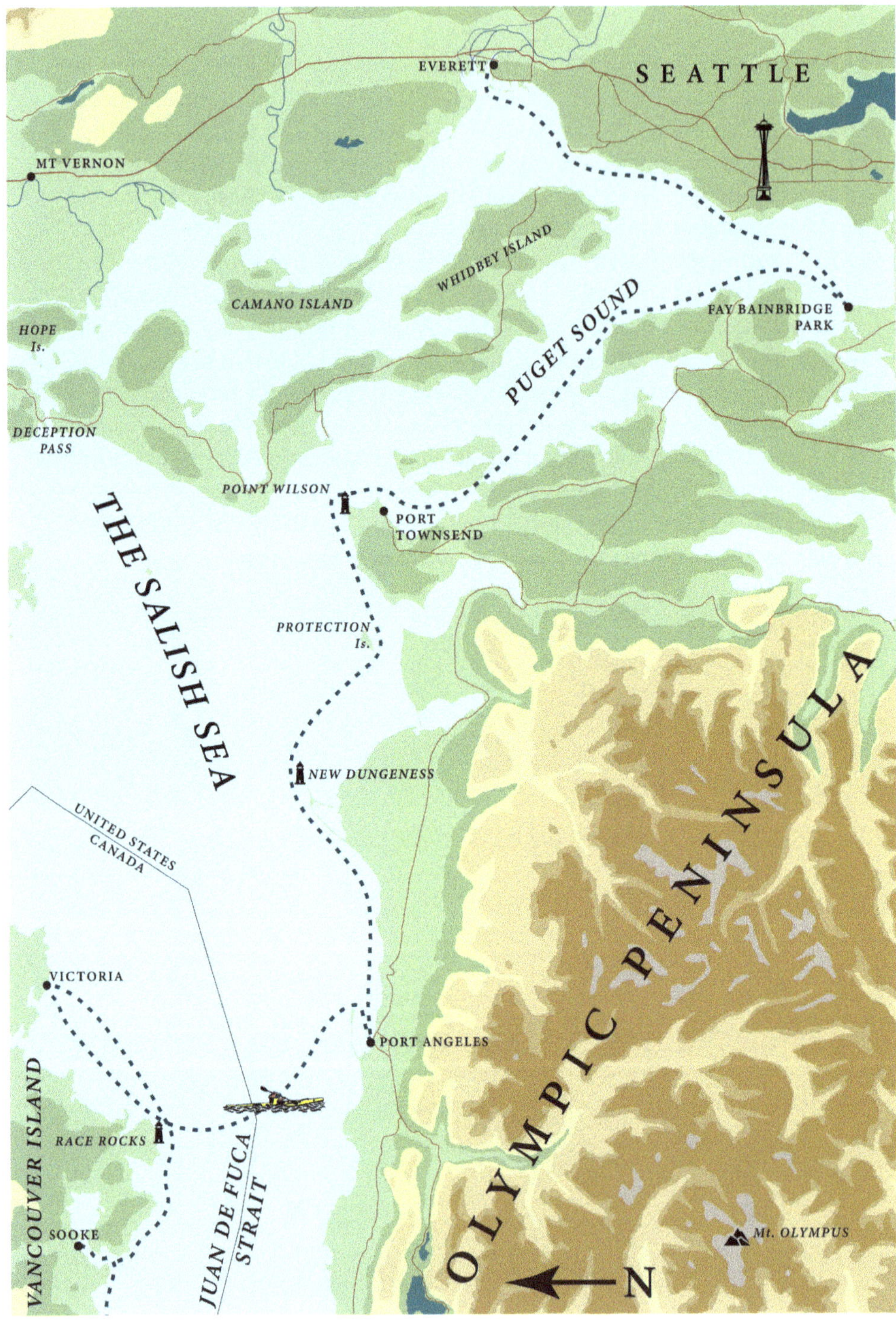

SEATTLE
EVERETT
MT VERNON
WHIDBEY ISLAND
CAMANO ISLAND
PUGET SOUND
FAY BAINBRIDGE PARK
HOPE Is.
DECEPTION PASS
POINT WILSON
PORT TOWNSEND
THE SALISH SEA
PROTECTION Is.
NEW DUNGENESS
UNITED STATES
CANADA
OLYMPIC PENINSULA
VICTORIA
VANCOUVER ISLAND
PORT ANGELES
RACE ROCKS
JUAN DE FUCA STRAIT
SOOKE
Mt. OLYMPUS
N

PART 8 - CLOSING THE CIRCLE - SOOKE TO SEATTLE

July 23 – Day 55

When I switched on my phone that morning I had a message from Lee.

"Hey, before you get to Victoria, go explore the Race Rocks. You'll be going right by it."

"What's there to do there?" I texted back.

"Lots of cool stuff. There's an underwater shelf where the current has to change direction, you get all kinds of fun whirlpools and standing waves to play in," he said. "There's also puffins, sea lions, sea otters, and if you're lucky, you might even spot an elephant seal. Though probably not this time of year. This is as far north as they come in the Pacific coast. If there's one there you won't miss it, they are huge! Even the sea lions look small compared to them."

Race Rocks is a small group of six rocky islets 10 miles south of Victoria. The largest, which is barely more than 600 feet across, has a black-and-white striped lighthouse to warn passing ships on their way to Victoria to make a wide turn and avoid the dangerous reefs. It is also an ecological reserve and hosts a large colony of sea lions.

"Can you land there?" I asked

"Oh no ... not unless you're in serious trouble. If you tell the caretakers at the lighthouse that you had to stop to take a leak, they will be really pissed at you. Have a bottle handy."

I paddled down the Sooke River and the bay back to the Juan de Fuca Strait. The sun burned away the morning fog very early, and by 9 a.m. the snow-covered mountains of Olympic Peninsula in Washington were towering over the straits. They looked so close that the 12 miles it would take to cross the channel seemed like a little hop.

Gauging distances in the sea with the naked eye, especially from the kayak, is incredibly deceiving. When paddling, the eye is barely four feet above the water and objects start to disappear below the horizon after just three miles. It plays with your depth perception. Massive cruise ships look like toy boats and towering lighthouses become Lego bricks held just an arm's length away. If you see an object along the horizon, you need to have a good feel for its size if you want to know how far away it is.

My father sometimes tells a story about the time he and my mother decided to swim out to an island just off the shore of Sahy Beach near Santos in Brazil. In good weather, the islands look so invitingly close that you'd think you could hit a baseball there. They set out, but after swimming for an hour decided it wasn't worth the remaining effort and turned back. With Google Earth I measured the distance, and from beach to beach it was almost one-and-a-half miles! About half the distance you'd swim in an Ironman triathlon.

When I saw the first cargo ship leaving the straits almost the entire hull was beneath the horizon and the only part of it I could see was the bridge. That meant it was at least a good nine to ten miles away and given that it would be sailing some distance from the shore, the opposite bank of the Olympic Peninsula was really much farther than it looked.

Covering the 14 miles to Race Rocks took considerable early effort. The tide was falling for most of the morning and I hugged my way close to the shore, taking advantage of eddies in the current wherever I could.

The ebbing tide slacked about an hour before I reached the islands, but the change in the flow direction went extremely quickly and I was soon putting in effort to not be carried away and had to hide in eddies behind the islets.

The archipelago had an ominous look; all the islands were barren and gray without even a patch of plant life. In the water, the bull kelp strung their long tentacles like messy green ponytails anchored to the islets. These kelp beds were also the ideal place to rest from the current.

I paddled down the channel between the lighthouse and the islet to its west with the current at nearly eight miles an hour, but came to a complete stop when I veered onto the floating bulbs of bull kelp like a truck coming to a halt on the runaway ramp of a highway. I also wasn't the only one there.

"Oh! Hi there!" I said to a harbor seal that popped its head through the reeds to see the unexpected commotion. But he wasn't the curious type and soon dove down before popping back up at a safer distance.

After some rest and a few photographs, I turned north with the current and headed toward Victoria, still 10 miles away, where I could already see the capital's skyscrapers in the clear weather. The closer I got, the more it seemed I was crossing into a different world. Everywhere power boats rumbled in and out of Victoria Harbor like cars at a busy intersection. A cruise ship was docked in the harbor behind the breakwater lighthouse and commercial planes flew low on their way to Victoria International. Like the constant background crunching of swells washing onshore, the sounds of the urban environment filled the air and felt omnipresent. Here, "dead quiet" had a different meaning.

I was at a loss as where to land. I obviously could not camp, but to find an accommodation that was close to a boat ramp, reasonably priced, with vacancy, and not kick up a fuss about a kayak - this was going to be a tall order.

For a moment I thought I had it. On the GPS I located a boat ramp west of the harbor entrance near Saxe Point Park. There was a hostel less than four blocks away but when I called, there was only a prerecorded message: "Hi there, we are so sorry to inform you that the hostel is closed until the first of August. We are on vacation in the Bahamas! If you wish to make a reservation, leave us your number and we will call you when we're back, eh."

"Hi there, hope you are having fun in the tropical sun! Sadly, I'm only here tonight and tomorrow. Sorry I missed you. Maybe see you next time!"

I paddled into the main harbor where I found another boat ramp behind the cruise ship docks closer to the center of town. I started dialing every hotel. Everyone was fully booked, but on the fifth attempt I had my breakthrough.

"Yes, we have one room left for two nights. Breakfast is included, $300 a night," said the lady at Huntington Manor.

It was as good as I was going to get, so I booked it over the phone. At the check-in I had my usual friendly talk with the receptionist before popping the question.

"So, I have a big kayak with me. Do you guys have a place I can keep it?"

The receptionist, a young girl who I judged from her matter-of-fact expression must have had other guests with strange requests, climbed down from her desk, walked out the front door, and espied my boat parked on the entranceway.

"You can put it in the underground garage. I'll give you a card to open the gate. Go all the way down and put it in the space behind the white delivery van and the wall. No one is driving the van this week, so management won't see it there. Keep quiet about it, eh."

"You got it! Thank you!"

July 24 – Day 56 – Victoria and Around

The harbor is the heart of Victoria. When seen on a map, it is very evident why the location was chosen for the settlement. After the 1846 Oregon Treaty that ceded the lands below the 49th parallel to the United States, Puget Sound, the largest and deepest natural harbor in the Juan de Fuca Strait, became part of the Washington Territory, along with the trading post of Fort Vancouver on the Columbia River where James Douglas (one of the protagonists of the Pig War) was chief factor of the Hudson's Bay Company. He was tasked with setting up a new trading post on Vancouver Island.

On the southern extremity of Vancouver Island there were two bays creating

Race Rock Lighthouse. The kelp beds provide a welcome rest stop from tidal currents.

[ABOVE] Victoria Parliament Building.
[BELOW] The Author (right) with Lee Richardson, Victoria harbor.

The crossing of the Juan de Fuca Strait. The mountains of the Olympic Peninsula on the horizon are 6,000 ft high, and more than 25 miles away.

[ABOVE] Container ship on the Juan de Fuca Strait. The ship is longer than a football field. [BELOW] The end of the Expedition. The public water fountain was extremely convenient to wash all the equipment before packing up for shipment to Miami.

a peninsula about two miles long and three miles wide that provided a good defensive position and deep waters for safe anchoring. The location also had other benefits; being on the rain shadow of the mountains along the coast, the weather was much milder than at Nootka, and with warm summers and temperate winters with minimal snowfall; the surrounding country was also the flattest stretch of land in Vancouver Island, well-suited for cultivation and raising cattle and sheep. The local First Nations people, the Songhees and the Esquimalt, were also friendly and happy to engage in the fur trade with Europeans.

As I walked along the southern shore of the harbor, I arrived at the Fisherman's Wharf, a colorful collection of floating houses, shops, and restaurants where you were allowed to toss the scraps from your fish and chips to the eagerly awaiting sea lions on the dock. Interestingly, one of the floating buildings on the wharf was a floating bed and breakfast with a boat ladder for any guests that chose to arrive on a Zodiac or dinghy. It would have been the perfect accommodation for someone with a kayak.

As I continued along the water I stumbled upon a little green field next to the Seattle ferry boat ramp called Quadra Park where, hidden beneath the canopy of overhanging trees, was a bronze statue of Spanish navigator Juan Francisco de la Bodega y Quadra. It had been dedicated by King Jan Carlos of Spain. I wondered if it was the same statue the receptionist at the Heriot Bay Inn had mentioned. The plaque under the statue inscribed that it was, "In honor of their meeting and the ensuing friendly association, Captain George Vancouver named this land Quadra and Vancouver's Island."

Two blocks further down was Victoria's most imposing structure: the Parliament Buildings of British Columbia. The main façade was 500 feet wide with a mixture of baroque features sprinkled with a neoclassical look and made entirely of a fine-grained andesite stone with varying shades of gray.

The building had a large main central copper dome with a golden statue of a man on top, but I did not know who it was. The dome was flanked by 12 other copper domes all of which had developed the telltale evergreen rust from exposure to the weather. The color gave it an elegant pairing with the green fields that stretched from the steps to the boulevard on the marina.

"That's Captain Vancouver up there," said a passerby who noticed me gazing at the statue.

"Is that so?"

"Yeah, though some folks don't like it. You know, colonialism and indigenous right's stuff. They don't like the Queen Victoria statue down here either," he said, pointing down the park. "It got sprayed some years ago by vandals."

Such statues honoring historical figures regularly spark controversy. The ruling classes get to decide who is worthy of honor and no revolution would be taken seriously without a good old-fashioned tear-down of once-beloved statues. In fairness to British Columbia, I did find hidden in one of the recessed walls of the Parliament the sculpture of an Indigenous man with muscular arms, a bridged nose, and dressed in a sea otter robe whom I would venture to guess was Chief Maquinna. Maybe it's time the authorities promoted him to the front lawn.

Lee swung by with his wife and young daughter for a visit and we made an afternoon trip to Beacon Hill Park which looks across the Juan de Fuca Strait to Washington. There wasn't a cloud in the sky and the snow-capped summits of the Olympic Peninsula were as clear as if someone had traced their outlines on a canvas with a thick black pen to separate the mountains from the sky. They seemed so close, but the opposite shore was almost 30 miles away. I sat on a bench near the parking lot at the top of the hill, while Lee's wife watched over their daughter and a few other kids that had clambered up the branches of a weeping willow tree.

"It's a big deal to paddle around Vancouver Island. How do you feel now that you're almost done?" Lee asked.

"I don't know," I said. "There will be nobody waiting there for me when I get to the finish line. Maybe it would be better if it didn't end."

"All good things, and bad things, eventually end. Otherwise, how would you tell what's good from what's not?" Lee asked rhetorically. "People take vacation from work, not work from vacation."

"You get to paddle for work." I said with some jealousy.

"It's still work. Especially when someone has to fetch you out of the murky water," he said, reminding me of our time at the Shubie River tidal bore in Nova Scotia. I gave an embarrassed laugh.

I thought back on the day I finished the journey around Puerto Rico and the subsequent days after, but only one word came to mind: loneliness.

"When you get back home," Lee said, "you can start to plan another adventure. An adventure wouldn't be an adventure if it didn't end with some sort of return to normality. Otherwise everything would just be ordinary. And you're not done yet; those little boats you see way down there in the middle of the straits are container ships three hundred meters long. Watch out for them when you're crossing tomorrow."

I was going to respond with something when Lee's daughter came running across the grass.

"Can we go see the ponies at the petting zoo?"

And so, we went.

July 25 – Day 57 – Crossing the Juan de Fuca Strait

I tried to extract as much value from the free hotel breakfast as I could gulp down. So much so that the waitress was compelled to point out that I was on my third serving of pancakes with maple syrup.

"I'm paddling to the United States," I said. "Got to top off the tank."

We talked for a while and after telling her that I was a wastewater engineer, she noted that Victoria had recently finished a new wastewater treatment plant built on the mouth of the harbor on McLoughlin Point. "You'll definitely see it on your way out. Can't miss it. It's perched right on the cliff."

The McLoughlin Point Wastewater Treatment Plant was commissioned by the BC government at a cost of nearly a billion dollars to provide the greater Victoria region with tertiary wastewater treatment (which includes settling, biological nutrient removal, and disinfection). I was surprised to learn that until 2020, the municipal authorities only carried out simple screening and relied on the goodwill of the currents to flush out the rest to the Pacific Ocean. Hardly any flow was ever chlorinated, which would have given me serious misgivings about paddling into the harbor without knowing where the effluent plume was at. The capacity of the plant is 28 million gallons per day which based on the current population of the Victoria metro area of about 400,000, is about the right size with a little extra capacity for a couple of decades of growth.

I paddled out through the mouth of the harbor on my kayak where I saw the wastewater plant perched on a rocky headland defended by sharp angled seawalls made to seamlessly match the appearance of the cliffs. On top of the flat roofed buildings were planted several saplings which in time would grow to be fully fledged trees. The land plot was tiny, only a little over three acres, and I admired how the engineers put all the equipment and structures together like a jigsaw, though I struggled to pick out the secondary settling tank, which you need to remove the bacterial growth from the biological treatment process. *The engineers must have opted for some kind of static precipitator combined with coagulation to save on space*, I thought.

I was left feeling some jealousy that Victoria had a shiny new wastewater treatment plant that was both functional and beautiful, made to look like a science museum. My work colleagues certainly chastise me for saying out loud what we all know; the wastewater plants in Miami are horrendously ugly. The dry wells of the two master pump stations that feed the Central District Plant in Virginia Key would make such an ominous dungeon setting for a horror movie, that even the Greek Titans would beg to stay locked in Tartarus than spend a day there.

The first 10 miles of the crossing consisted of backtracking to Race Rocks. I hugged my way along the coast but I was soon caught in the rising tide bending northward around the headland. This forced me to point toward Race Rocks and I did my best to keep the islands to my east but was soon overpowered. Although my compass heading was due south, my movement was roughly southeast. Fortunately, Port Angeles was far enough to the east of Victoria that I didn't need to compensate for the drift, and the current weakened in the middle of the straits.

It wasn't a particularly busy shipping day. I only saw two container ships during the crossing. They sailed close enough for an interesting photograph but not so close to be a hazard. Once again, like many parts of this journey, reality turned out to be much less stressful than I expected.

I arrived in Port Angeles on the south shore of the straits late afternoon on a shingle beach with a walkway rimmed with vertical wind turbines. Compared to Victoria, Port Angeles felt like a backwater town as I portaged the kayak down a main street with hardly any cars.

Well, back in America, I thought. This was the strangest arrival in the United States I've ever had. Usually, it's a hassle to arrive on an international flight, and in Miami the winding customs lines take the better part of an hour to navigate. The customs office here was an inconspicuous prefabricated metal box on the ferry terminal with only a paper notice taped to a glass door to indicate its purpose. After ringing the front-desk bell, I had a hard time explaining to the officer on duty that I wanted to be processed into the country.

"What's your boat registration?" he asked

"I don't have one. It's a kayak. The Canadian customs just used my name and the word kayak when I crossed from San Juan to Sidney."

"I guess we can do that."

He asked a series of questions about what I was bringing with me. I was surprised he never asked if I had any alcohol; he must have forgotten. The previous night I had swung by a liquor store in downtown Victoria and purchased two bottles of Canadian maple rum. One for me to take home and eat with pancakes and ice-cream, and another for David in Everett who was holding on to my kayak bags.

July 26 – Day 58

I didn't realize how tired I was until I laid on the hotel bed for a quick rest before dinner only to wake up at 3 a.m. and then decided to sleep for another three hours.

It was one of the calmest days I've ever experienced on the water. The blazing sun and sky seemed ready to fall on top of the flat water and the only thing that kept it from doing so was the shimmering vapor-soaked air pushing up against it.

"Good God! It's so hot," I shouted. Rolling in the water to cool off worked but only for a few minutes. The temperature had to be at least 90°F, if not more, and being dressed in a dry suit felt like an act of voluntary torture. I had only two clean shirts left which was all the motivation I needed to be done in the next two days, no matter what.

I reached a large island that was almost two miles across just beyond the entrance into Puget Sound. It was called Protection Island and most of it was a plateau covered in low grasses and surrounded by vertical cliffs of loose sandstone, except for the south shore where a spit of sand had some 200 seals lounged in the afternoon sun. Even though I was a fair distance away, one must have sighted my unusual looks, sounded the alarm, and set his friends into a stampede for the water.

"Come on guys, I think you're being a little dramatic. I don't even look like an orca, and if I did, would you really want to run for the water where I would catch you?" They kept swimming after me, keeping their heads above the water like dozens of periscopes.

On the east side of the island was a small bay butted against the cliffs where hundreds of seabirds flew around in circles. Some were puffins with oddly expressive black eyes, white faces, and ringed red beaks looking like they were dressed in tuxedos and ready for a masquerade party. I had not seen puffins the entire journey.

I camped on the mainland a little beyond Protection Island at the base of a sand cliff with a narrow beach. The cliff was a glacial moraine; the sediment was so loose that little pebbles rolled down without warning making thumping sounds when they hit the water. The very top was a layer of dark topsoil from which the roots of trees dangled like little feet in the air, high above their fallen comrades on the beach.

You like to tempt fate, don't you? said the voice in my head.

It won't happen tonight, not on this spot at least, I thought with more hope than certainty. A few more pebbles rolled down the hill at night with little crackling thumps but none hit the tent.

July 27 – Day 59

The hottest day yet. I could not believe it, but the forecast called for a high of 101°F though with the humidity, the heat index would be closer to 115°F. *Even in the Florida summer it doesn't get that hot,* I thought. The local public radio station announced that the Pacific Northwest would likely be experiencing their worst ever heat wave for the next five days. A high-pressure system had moved in from the Pacific Ocean, blocked itself against the Cascade Mountains, and was now sitting almost directly on top of the entrance to Puget Sound. There was no low-pressure trough on the way to dislodge it which meant bright blue sunny days with few to no clouds for the foreseeable future.

If it's anything close to how bad things were last year, it's going to be a tough few days for the sea lions and the seals, I thought. The kelp beds and the barnacles would also be suffering. By the end of the heat wave, I could only imagine how unbearable the smell of plant decomposition and rotting shellfish along the shores and beaches would become. I had to roll the kayak every 15 minutes to avoid overheating. For the first time in the journey I wished I had brought a wetsuit. I was soaked in sweat and my whole body was encrusted with salt.

I rounded Point Wilson where a small lighthouse marked the entrance into Puget Sound and Vancouver Island faded away from view.

"Until we see each other again. Who knows when that will be. You gave me safe passage. Thank you," I said aloud as if the island could hear me.

It felt like saying goodbye to a close friend. So many hazards could have been hurled at me. I could have been left waiting for days to round any of the capes and headlands and run out of food. I could have misjudged the days of mild weather and the calm waters only to be caught in a deadly storm. The odd rock at the wrong place with the wrong wave could have ended the journey early, or the bear in Cape Scott could have been having a bad day. None of those things happened. The island took good care of me.

July 28 – Day 60 – The Last Day!

As far as kayaking went, the day was peaceful and uneventful. I left early in the morning from the shingle beach on Fay Bainbridge Park, across from downtown Seattle with the morning silhouette of Mount Rainier and the Space Needle behind me. As is my custom for the last day of a long expedition, I ate all the remaining food to eliminate as much dead weight as possible. No more canned fish, no more canned pasta, and no more Nutella jars to lug around.

The boat ramp at Everett looked exactly the same as it did 60 days ago; the tide was low and the water looked murky. I paddled until the boat's nose touched the concrete, then pulled up the spray skirt and stood on dry land. It took only about a minute before Mom and Dad started calling.

"I'm done!" I said.

You should play it up. It's a big deal. The world's forty-third largest island. No small feat, said the voice in my head as I started to empty the hatches. I found the bear bangers which didn't get used the entire journey. *Might as well,* I thought. *I can't take these home with me.*

I pointed one to the sky over the water and fired a blast which was loud like a rifle and reverberated through the air. It even startled the passengers on the boat moored two ramps over. Five minutes later the police showed up asking if someone had fired a gun.

"Sorry. It was just a bear banger I was getting rid of," I said flushed with embarrassment. I showed them the empty bear flare while holding one of the maple rum bottles. It was not the look of innocence. Fortunately, they just let me off with a warning. It would have been awkward to have finished the journey with a stint in a Seattle jail.

This one tense moment aside, closing this circle was like parking a car in the garage and shutting off the engine after a long drive. For the first time in 60 days, there was nowhere else to paddle. No headland to go around, no swell to climb over, no wave to duck under. The rhythmic motion of putting one arm in front of the other for hours on end was over.

I was, however, missing something important: that sense of fulfillment, the relief you feel when you are finally back to the world of familiarity after a long ordeal. Everywhere I looked people just went about their ordinary lives. Whether I had just finished paddling 1,000 miles or returned from a quick paddle around the marina, that meant nothing to anyone but me. That was my business.

I pulled the kayak behind me up from the ramp with the cart wheels squeaking over the tarmac, and was now invisible.

Beach Landing the Rockpool Taran, Florida Circumnavigation

An exceptionally calm day near St Augustine Florida, Florida Circumnavigation

EPILOGUE

July 29 and 30 – Days 61 and 62.

My arrival in Everett may have been the end of the journey, but not the end of the work.

After washing my kayak and gear on the local fountain next to the Indigo Hotel at the Everett waterfront, I called up the moving company to schedule a pickup. They said they could come by in the morning the following day. I managed to complete the journey a few days before my budgeted time, which meant I had to reschedule my flight home, let David know I would be swinging by his warehouse to pick up the kayak bags, and inform my colleagues at work of my updated arrival date.

In the midst of the rush, I got a call from a local coworker who'd been following my journey from my social posts. For the six years I have been at my current job, I had only known Tim through his company profile picture and the sound of his voice on the phone.

"Welcome back," he said. "If you're not too busy, I'll take you out for lunch and we can swing by the office."

Our company had an office in downtown Seattle inside a large retail complex that included a hotel and restaurant on the ground floor. I noticed that many of the stores in the complex and along the downtown street were empty or shuttered with several seeming like they had recently gone out of business.

We took the elevator to the 13th floor and Tim unlocked a door from a small hallway. The office was an open floor plan with a cubicle farm and several meeting rooms along the windows. It was a space that could have hosted over a hundred employees, but on this Thursday it was dead quiet for a workday without even the humming air conditioning to be heard. Along one of the corridors, a wall on one side was covered with photographs of projects under construction. We walked past several empty cubicles, some of which had been converted into storage areas for extra filing cabinets, desks, and boxes. Some of the names on the cubicles I recognized as colleagues I had worked with.

"Nearly everyone works from home these days," Tim explained. "We're getting rid of most of the space when the lease comes up for renewal."

On the way out we walked past the only occupied cubicle hidden behind a pile of empty cardboard boxes. If it weren't for the jingle of the computer turning off we would have missed it.

"Hi guys. I'm just here to make a few large prints for a set of plans. Will be heading out soon. I'll turn off the lights when I'm out."

Tim dropped me off at a park near the Space Needle. "I'll talk to you when you're back in Miami. Great to see you finally! It's a rare chance to meet any colleagues these days."

He drove off and disappeared around the right turn on the next traffic light.

It was a really hot afternoon, probably over 100°F. I walked the two miles to the waterfront where the breeze over the sea cooled things down a little and I could find a place to sit and kill time before heading for the airport.

I thought back to an animated comedy series I watched as a kid. The main character (whose name I have long since forgotten) was a mutant from the future who lived unhappily with the state of his world and existence. He found a way to travel back to our time where he believed he could alter the events that would change his future. After thinking that he had succeeded, he went back to his time but was disappointed to discover that nothing had changed.

I don't remember how the series ended. I think the character went back to the past for a few more rounds. I empathize with him; the ordinary world is full of people but it feels lonely. Being in the kayak on the water may be solitary, but life is filled with the thrill of adventure.

When do I fill the hatches and leave again?

Whenever you feel like it, said the voice in my head. *No one is making you stay.*

Departure from Boca Chita Key, heading towards Miami, Last day of the Florida Circumnavigation

Selected Bibliography

Books:

Alderson, Doug (2004), Around Vancouver Island. Rocky Mountain Books

Barnett, James K.(2017), Captain George Vancouver in Alaska and the North Pacific. Alaska Print Brokers

Coleman, E.C. (2018), The Pig War. The History Press

Grant, Peter (2019), Vancouver Island Book of Everything. MacintyrePurcell Publishing

Lillard, C. (1986). Seven Shillings a Year. Horsdal & Schubart.

Jewitt, John R. (2000), White Slaves of Maquinna. Heritage House Publishing Company

Taylor, Jeanette (2010) The Quadra Story. Harbour Publishing

Vancouver, George (1798), A voyage of Discovery to the North Pacific Ocean and Around the World. Andesite Press

Websites:

Aecom (n.d.) McLoughlin Point Wastewater Treatment Plant, Retrieved on July 2023 from https://acecbcawards.com/2022-awards/2022-municipal-civil-infrastructure/mcloughlin-point-wastewater-treatment-plant/

CBC (12/04/2020), Johnson, Lisa, Kelp is disappearing from parts of the West Coast. These scientists are trying to save it. Retrieved on July, 2023 from https://www.cbc.ca/news/climate/kelp-rescue-marine-heatwaves-1.6671796

Daily Hive. (12/17/2020). $775-million solution: Victoria's raw sewage is no longer flowing into BC waters. Retrieved August 2023, from https://dailyhive.com/

vancouver/mcloughlin-point-wastewater-treatment-plant-victoria

Lighthouse Friends. (n.d.). British Columbia Lighthouses. Retrieved August, 2023 from https://lighthousefriends.com/pull-state.asp?state=BC&Submit=Go

Mirror (May 4, 2023) Horror Injuries of Seaworld Trainer Killed by Orca, Retrieved on July, 2023 from https://www.mirror.co.uk/news/us-news/horror-injuries-seaworld-trainer-killed-29851202

Montreal Gazette. (2/21/1974) Horton's World. Retrieved August, 2023 from Death Shocks Hockey https://news.google.com/ newspapers?id=UXowAAAAIBAJ&pg=1014%2C1700712

Nauticapedia (2020), John McFarlane, The Mysterious Area Whiskey Golf. Retrieved on August, 2023 from https://www.nauticapedia.ca/Gallery/Winchelsea.php

North Island Gazette (May 18, 2027) Grand Opening of Kwa'lilas Hotel, Retrieved on July, 2023 from https://www.northislandgazette.com/home2/grand-opening-of-kwalilas-hotel-1377348

Pacific Sands (n.d.) Vancouver Island Shipwrecks. Retrieved on August, 2023 from https://www.pacificsands.com/2019/11/27/if-our-west-coast-waters-could-talk-historic-vancouver-island-shipwrecks/

Skills (n.d.) SKILS, Canada's premiere outdoor skills and leadership development company
Retrieved on August 2023 from https://skils.ca/

The Hockey Writers. (8/25/2023) Tim Horton, A Legacy of Hockey, Donuts , & Coffee. Retrieved September, 2023 from https://thehockeywriters.com/tim-horton-legacy-hockey-donuts-coffee/

Tlatlaskwala First Nation (n.d.), Tlatlaskwala First Nation. Retrieved on July, 2023 from http://www.tlatlasikwala.com/

About the Author

Felipe Behrens began a passion for sea kayaking for a rather mundane reason. It was a way to avoid the traffic when he would go visit his mother in Miami Beach on the weekends. "If you have to sit around for a few hours, better it be on a kayak paddling under the causeways, than in the bumper to bumper traffic on top of them."

His exploits, combined with a childhood propensity to find himself in unexpected adventures, have taken him on multi month journeys to circumnavigate the Florida Peninsula, Puerto Rico, and Vancouver Island in British Columbia. When not out on his kayak circling the islands in Biscayne Bay, practicing rolls, or trying to catch some waves, he works as a wastewater treatment engineer in Miami Florida, and writes about his travels. You can read more about his adventures at www.aroundonmykayak.com

Buy one item and get the second item Free for any combination of products seen here.

Scan the QR Code, select your Items and use the Coupon YAYCANADA! at the check out!

GREAT ADVENTURERS USE GREAT GEAR!